ROGER BACON AND HIS SEARCH FOR A UNIVERSAL SCIENCE

ROGER BACON AND HIS SEARCH FOR A UNIVERSAL SCIENCE

A Reconsideration of the Life and Work of Roger Bacon in the Light of His Own Stated Purposes

STEWART C. EASTON

GREENWOOD PRESS, PUBLISHERS
WESTPORT, CONNECTICUT

Reprinted by permission
of Columbia University Press

First Greenwood Reprinting 1970

Library of Congress Catalogue Card Number 70-100159

SBN 8371-3399-8

PRINTED IN UNITED STATES OF AMERICA

AUTHOR'S NOTE

IT was unfortunate that what is perhaps the most useful new account of the life and works of Roger Bacon from the pen of Father Theodore Crowley, O.F.M. (*Roger Bacon: The Problem of the Soul in his Philosophical Commentaries*, Louvain and Dublin, 1950), appeared too late for detailed criticism in this book. It is gratifying to find that on so many points we are in substantial agreement after studying the same material—on far more than either of us agree with earlier writers on the subject. A few footnotes have been added while the book was in the press to indicate areas of agreement and disagreement. But no attempt has been made to alter any of the text in consideration of Father Crowley's findings, which need far more careful attention than I have been able to give them at this stage, especially in the matter of the authenticity of the *Liber de retardatione accidentium senectutis*, and the much disputed matter of Bacon's imprisonment. I think he does less than justice to Father Mandonnet's real arguments against the traditional order of the famous *Opera* to the Pope. But his opinion of the importance of an understanding of Bacon's character if we are to explain his relations with the Franciscan Order coincides with mine, though we come to different conclusions.

I wish to acknowledge here the invaluable assistance received from Professor Thorndike of Columbia University throughout the whole preparation of the book, and also from Professors Evans and Bigongiari in several important details. I am also indebted to Miss Madeleine Edelstein for her patient hearing and rehearing of the complex arguments in Chapter VIII until the various parts fell into place. Full responsibility for the conclusions, of course, rests altogether with me.

STEWART C. EASTON

City College of New York

LIST OF ABBREVIATIONS

N.B. All titles of books and articles are given throughout in abbreviated form. For the full titles and dates, see the formal bibliography, pp. 236 ff.

The following abbreviations are not self-explanatory.

Archiv . . . *Archiv für Litteratur und Kirchengeschichte des Mittelalters.*
Brewer, *Op. Tert.* J. S. Brewer, ed., *Opus tertium.*
Charles. E. Charles, *Roger Bacon, sa vie, ses ouvrages, et ses doctrines.*
Chartularium. *Chartularium Universitatis Parisiensis.*
CSP. J. S. Brewer, ed., *Compendium studii philosophiae.*
CST. H. Rashdall, ed., *Compendium studii theologiae.*
Gasquet. F. A. Gasquet, 'An Unpublished Fragment of a Work by Roger Bacon'.
Little, *Op. Tert.* A. G. Little, ed., *Part of the Opus Tertium of Roger Bacon.*
Opus Majus. J. H. Bridges, ed., *The Opus Majus of Roger Bacon*, 3 vols.[1]
Opus Minus. J. S. Brewer, ed., *Opus Minus.*
Steele, Fasc. — *Opera hactenus inedita Fr. Rogeri Baconis*, Oxford, 1905 (?)—41. All the works in this series are not edited by Steele, but the series is always cited as Steele, Fasc. I, etc.

[1] Since this is the only edition of the *Opus Majus* used, the reference *Opus Majus* always refers to the three volumes of Bridges' work, whether it is concerned with Bridges' personal introduction or notes, or with Bacon's text, edited by him.

TABLE OF CONTENTS

ROGER BACON AND HIS SEARCH FOR A UNIVERSAL SCIENCE

CHAPTER I

INTRODUCTION

WHEN Voltaire wrote his *Siècle de Louis XIV* he made it clear that he regarded the eighteenth century as the greatest age so far known by mankind. While he retained some admiration for the Greeks and Romans, the Middle Ages was for him a period of unrelieved barbarism.

In the twentieth century we are hesitant to call any people barbarian, or any period of history barbaric. Relativism in philosophy, whatever its effects on philosophy itself, has led to an interesting new approach to history, and a new sin has entered the catalogue. As far as we can, we should cease to examine the past in the light of current assumptions; in particular we should cease to judge past thought by the criterion of a present-day scheme of values. We must rather regard it in the light of *its own* system, and *its own* assumptions; or we shall be guilty of the sin of present-mindedness. We must not expect, moreover, to find any individual thinker suddenly transcend the whole scheme of beliefs by which his contemporaries lived. If we find that in some particulars he appears to have transcended it we must make the assumption that we are liable to have misunderstood his contribution. Many others in his time were probably thinking in the same way; probably a 'progressive' movement existed of which we were unaware. It is then only our own ignorance that made us believe in his uniqueness, and our task is clear. We must set out to dispel this ignorance by studying his contemporaries and looking at him from a new angle.

Moreover, philosophical relativism has had one other remarkable result. We have become more charitable to the past. In our twentieth century we have come to doubt whether there are any absolute values at all; whether it is ever legitimate to say that an action, or even a thought, is good or bad, true or false. For more than two thousand years Euclidean geometry was accepted as 'true'. When in the nineteenth century it became clear that this was not the only possible geometry, a few blithe disciples of progress said that Euclid was wrong, as a few physicists to their shame in our own age claimed, after the experimental demonstration of the Einsteinian theory of relativity, that Newton had been wrong. Then came the calmer pragmatists who declared, with great charity as well as scientific good sense, that Euclidean geometry merely defines the properties of a certain kind of space; while Newton's mechanics and physics are 'true' for the world of ordinary sense experience, but insufficient for the realm of the atom and electron.

This general attitude has now affected the study of the Middle Ages. St. Thomas Aquinas' physics has been declared to be 'ethics',[1] not wrong or mistaken as Voltaire or a nineteenth-century materialist would have maintained, but justifiable within his thirteenth-century framework of ideas. The Franciscans, when they instituted a censorship of writings in 1260, were acting in a manner to be expected of them in thirteenth-century society, since 'freedom of speech' could never have been a thirteenth-century ideal. Medieval and Moslem thinkers 'were convinced Aristotelians because of the factual evidence from mathematics, physics, biology, astronomy, and psychology, and because of the capacity of the Aristotelian science to account for all this evidence'.[2]

In considering the life-work of Roger Bacon, therefore, I have tried to keep free from any bias either for or against him. Since the revival of interest in his work, stimulated so effectively by the researches of Cousin, Brewer, and Charles nearly a century ago, he has remained an extremely controversial figure. I am not specially interested in his apparent anticipations of modern knowledge and the 'modern' viewpoint, nor his supposed originality and uniqueness. I have worked on the assumption that he cannot have been unique, and that his originality, as, indeed, all human originality, has rested on his treatment of materials familiar to large numbers of people in his time. As a thinker he may have been original, but he was only unique in the sense that all thinkers are unique; he laid the impress of his own mind upon his material by selecting what he considered relevant to his purpose and interpreting this in accordance with his own subjective scheme. This scheme I have believed it to be the proper task of the historian to try to discover from Bacon's own life

[1] 'Modern science is physics, while medieval science was something at once less potent and more important—ethics.' J. H. Randall, *The Making of the Modern Mind* (Boston, 1940), p. 100.

[2] F. S. C. Northrop, *The Meeting of East and West* (New York, 1946), p. 263.

and writings, and I have tried to give some indications of the limitations of the material that he used. The only judgment I feel able to pronounce is on the completeness and relevance of his scheme for his own thirteenth-century world.

The scheme was not born in an instant in his mind. Throughout a long life it developed. As Bacon grew older it must be presumed that his interests widened; increasing quantities of material became available to him, all of which he attempted to synthesize into a working philosophy of life which satisfied him and he believed had value for others. As his mental powers declined in his old age, I believe there was a contraction of his interests, as there were probably fewer means at hand to satisfy them. This is the generalized picture of human life as we usually know it, even in our own day; and I believe it can be traced in the life of this thirteenth-century friar, if we read all the works known to be by him, and take full advantage of those writings which can be dated with certainty.

This means that in studying his output it is essential to examine at the same time what we know and can reasonably conjecture of his life. The writings cannot be regarded as the work of a disembodied spirit and treated *in vacuo* without doing grave violence to his whole system of thought. An exclusive study of the early *Quaestiones* given at the University of Paris, more than twenty years before the famous *Opera* written for Pope Clement IV, will tell us much about the curriculum of the Faculty of Arts in Paris about the year 1245, and about Bacon himself as he was at that time. But they cannot be supposed to embody his final philosophical views. On the other hand, a study of the works only of his full maturity may give us a better picture of the culmination of his thought, but it neglects the elements that are historically important in the development of his mind. Moreover, it overlooks the special circumstances which prompted the work for the Pope, and its hortatory nature. In Bacon's own term these works were *persuasiones*, composed with the expressed intention of persuading Clement to a definite course of action. Such work requires a very careful selection of what is likely to promote the objectives, and an emphasis on certain parts which is not necessary for a philosopher engaged in expressing the best thought of which he is capable. The student of Bacon must in every case make allowance for the purpose of the writer, in the *Quaestiones*, the *Opera*, and the *Communia Naturalium* alike. And this can only be done if the conditions in his life at the time are closely correlated with the material produced.

This has presented a peculiarly difficult task when there is so little reliable information available on his actual life, and no convincing chronology has been established, or can probably ever be established, for his writings. I have been forced to rely on Bacon's own statements, meagre internal evidence, and to a much lesser degree later unreliable tradition. I have had to fill this out with much conjecture, the enlarging of brief and sometimes enigmatic hints, together with my best estimate of the probabilities, based on what Bacon reveals of his own character. If, especially in the later part of this study, the conservative reader may think the hypothetical reconstruction exceeds those decent limits the historian should observe, the writer can only apologize to him and say that he is not personally attached to these hypotheses, and will welcome any informed attempt to destroy them.

If this study takes the form of a biography it is because at every stage of the inquiry Bacon's personal history is important for the understanding of his work. On the other hand, as this cannot be understood except by considering the environment in which he was working, much space will inevitably be given to the intellectual atmosphere of the thirteenth century in both England and France, and especially the enormous influence of the recent translations of Aristotle and the 'Arabs'. This necessary information will be brought into the story when it is required. But I have tried to keep it within bounds, and to refer the reader to the extraordinarily valuable bibliography of the whole movement to be found in Professor van Steenberghen's study of Siger of Brabant.[1] As far as I am aware, this selected bibliography has been nowhere surpassed, and it is of sufficiently recent date (1942) to be of considerable use to the student of the intellectual history of the thirteenth century as it has been revealed by recent research.

But primarily the biographical form has been chosen because of the lack of a full biography of Bacon which takes modern research into account. While not underestimating the immense labours required for Emil Charles's pioneer biography, and his many valuable insights, I cannot doubt that his work,[2] for our day, is at least partly spoiled by his general estimate of Bacon as an outstanding modernist, and a 'martyr of science', which colours his whole interpretation. Moreover, he was extremely unfortunate in that the Amiens library

[1] F. van Steenberghen, *Siger de Brabant* . . . pp. 7 34–46. (For this and all other abbreviations, see the complete bibliography.)

[2] E. Charles, *Roger Bacon, sa vie* . . . (cited as Charles).

would not permit him an extended use of its unique MS. of the *Quaestiones*, which has since been published in full.[1] And ninety years of criticism and innumerable monographs have contributed immeasurably to our knowledge both of Bacon and of his contemporaries. Yet this work remains the only full-length study of Bacon's life and works to this day.

J. H. Bridges, the editor of the *Opus Majus* and other works of Bacon, wrote in 1897 a valuable introduction which was later expanded into a book and published separately.[2] But the book is very short, and even of this, the life occupies only a small part. For the seventh centenary of the presumed date of Bacon's birth, A. G. Little edited an invaluable collection of essays, the first of which is devoted to his life, and the last to the fullest bibliography of his works that has yet appeared.[3] Little also enlarged a few of his ideas on Bacon in a lecture delivered to the British Academy in 1928.[4]

In 1916 Professor Lynn Thorndike wrote two important articles in the *American Historical Review* which were based not only upon Bacon's own work, but upon the work of Bacon's contemporaries, which was largely unknown to earlier biographers.[5] Thorndike's work laid the foundation for all later studies of Bacon, who had previously been considered too much in isolation. Some of his many useful suggestions have been followed up and examined more closely in this study.

In 1921 Robert Steele wrote up his views on Bacon's life and work,[6] and was one of the first to take account of the Amiens MS. which he had already begun to edit. Many of Steele's opinions on the development of Bacon's thought and his attempts to correlate them with his life were, I think, over-hasty; but his knowledge at least of Bacon's corpus of writings was probably second to none at that time.

In 1928 appeared one of the most useful and critical studies of certain disputed facts in Bacon's life, hidden away in an account of his philology. In fact, more pages are devoted to his life than to his philology. While I do not agree with some of Vanderwalle's conclusions, I have found his work most valuable and suggestive.[7]

[1] Charles, p. 66, note 3.
[2] J. H. Bridges, *The Life and Work* . . . (1914).
[3] A. G. Little, *Essays* . . . (1914).
[4] Little, 'Roger Bacon. Annual Lecture . . .' (1928).
[5] L. Thorndike, 'The True Roger Bacon . . .' (1916). These articles were later incorporated into his *History of Magic* . . . (1923), II, 616–91.
[6] R. Steele, 'Roger Bacon and the State of Science . . .' (1921).
[7] C. B. Vanderwalle, *Roger Bacon dans l'histoire* . . . (1929).

Since 1929 other works have appeared, but they have added very little to our knowledge, and none seems to have been based on any profound study of the sources.[1] Various monographs on special aspects of Bacon's work have appeared continually during the century. The most important of these are included in the bibliography.

The other great American historian of science, George Sarton, was excluded by the scope of his undertaking[2] from an extended study of Bacon's life and work. But everything that he wrote about him was clearly based upon a profound understanding of his work and his place in the history of science, and it was clear that he could have written a fine study of him if he had been able to devote the time to it. From the few sentences he gives to Bacon I draw the following, with which, after the completion of my study, I confess myself in full agreement:

> He had a strong belief in the unity of knowledge, but that unity was accounted for as a subordination of all knowledge to theology . . . this mixture of mysticism and scientific positivism was Bacon's main characteristic: each ingredient would explain his growing impatience with metaphysical discussion: the combination of both was overpowering. Bacon was not a philosopher, but he was one of the greatest thinkers of all ages.[3]

A few words are necessary on the use of certain modern English terms which do not exactly correspond to the Latin words used by Bacon. The most important and ubiquitous of these words is 'science' itself.

Webster gives several meanings in current use in English. His first is 'the knowledge of principles or facts'. This is the most common meaning of the Latin word *scientia* in Bacon's writings. In the great medieval question: 'Is theology a science?' which is discussed in Appendix B of this study, the word science has this meaning, and is to be especially distinguished from faith. Do we know that God exists, or do we only believe it? St. Thomas claims that we know this truth, and would know it even if there were no inspired book in which we believe. The context will show whether this is the meaning required in each instance.

Webster's second meaning is more specific: 'Accumulated and accepted knowledge which has been systematized and formulated

[1] A special critical bibliography of Baconian biographies is given below, pp. 237–40.
[2] G. Sarton, *Introduction to the History* . . . (1931), II, 952–67.
[3] Sarton, *Introduction* . . . II, 960.

with reference to the discovery of general truths or the operation of general laws'. The medievals may have been struggling towards this conception, but the use of the word science with this meaning will be avoided in this study.

Webster's third and fourth meanings were known in the Middle Ages and they are used by Bacon. 'Systematic knowledge relating to the physical world and its philosophy, called also natural science', and 'any branch or department of systematized knowledge considered as a distinct field of investigation or object of study'. Wherever possible the third meaning will be called 'natural science', and the fourth, wherever it occurs, will be self-explanatory. However, the special sciences dealt with by Bacon would not to-day in every case be considered as branches of science at all, and in only a few cases does the science cover the same material as in our time. For Bacon, 'mathematics' covers astronomy and astrology, music, arithmetic, and geometry. The science of weights is considered as a part of alchemy. Most of these distinctions, when relevant, will appear in the text.

I am translating Bacon's *scientia experimentalis* as the 'science of experience' rather than as experimental science. To us it is not a special science at all, but an integral part of the scientific method. Bacon distinguishes it from knowledge which is deduced from prior knowledge or from self-evident principles and axioms, and he distinguishes it from the data of revelation. One of its uses is to confirm this deductive material to enable the mind to rest in the assurance of certitude, although it can also provide new and useful natural knowledge, whether or not it fits into any theoretical system.

Experiments are anything which has been experienced. They may be planned to serve as confirmation of deductive material or to add to existing knowledge, as in our modern usage; or they may be merely empirical data noticed in ordinary life. When Bacon says that the scholastics do not make experiments, he does not mean that they have no experience of life, but only that they do not subject their theories to the test of experience. They treat their theories as autonomous—superior knowledge to their daily experience. It is contended in this study that Bacon himself made few planned experiments, but that he did give much thought to the meaning of experiments carried out by others, and considered seriously the place of ordinary life-experience within a theoretical scheme of universal science. He does not emphasize, in the manner of modern science, the new knowledge that can be gained from planned experiment.

Bacon, in short, is not an inductive scientist, nor does he support the point of view of his later namesake that it is the purpose of the experimental scientist to discover laws of nature by inductive means. Since this subject, however, is dealt with at length in Chapter X below, nothing further need be said here.

CHAPTER II

EARLY LIFE AND EDUCATION

TRADITION assigns the birth of Roger Bacon to Ilchester in Somerset. This tradition is no older than the middle of the fifteenth century, and stems from the Warwickshire antiquary, John Rous, though he speaks of Ilchester as in the county of Dorset.[1] Little points out that Ilchester is only five miles from the boundary of Dorset. Another tradition gives the honour of his birth to Bisley in Gloucestershire.

Much effort has been made to discover his family; but again the evidence is inconclusive. Charles Jourdain even tried to assign him to France, pointing out the numerous Bacon families, especially in Normandy. After amusing himself for a while with this idea, he then contents himself with the incontrovertible statement that a large part of Bacon's life was spent in France. He studied and lectured at Paris, and may have taken his degree there, while it is not certain that he ever lectured at Oxford.[2]

There is now no doubt at all that Bacon was born in England. He states this directly in one passage discovered since Jourdain's day, and implies it in several others.[3] His family seems to have had enough money to be able to give him some financial support, at least until its ruin in the civil wars of Henry III. Moreover, as he claims to have spent, presumably in the days before he became a friar, more than two thousand pounds on books and experiments, it is clear that its position was substantial.[4] He also speaks of one brother who was rich enough to be able to ransom himself several times after being taken prisoner. In the same place he speaks of his mother and family as if there were several other members.[5] Another brother was a scholar.[6] This scholar has sometimes been confused with a famous Dominican doctor, Friar Robert Bacon, who died, however, in 1245.

[1] Little, *Essays* . . . pp. 1–2.

[2] C. Jourdain, *Excursions historiques* . . . (1888), pp. 132–37.

[3] 'My parents and friends who supported the lord King of England were ruined . . . I sent to England for money, but I have had no reply to this day because exiles and enemies of the King have occupied the land of my birth.' F. A. Gasquet, 'An Unpublished Fragment . . .' (1897), p. 500. (Cited as Gasquet.)

[4] Brewer, *Op. Tert.*, p. 59.

[5] *Ibid.*, p. 16.

[6] 'If I had been able to communicate freely I should have composed many things for my brother, a scholar, and for other dear friends of mine'. Brewer, *Op. Tert.*, p. 13.

As Roger writes in 1267 that he would have composed tracts for him if he had been free, this can hardly be the scholar in question.[1]

This is really all we know about his private circumstances. There is a well-known story in Matthew Paris[2] concerning a Roger Bacon who exercised his wit at the King's court in 1233. As Jourdain, Little, and others have shown how common the name was, and the incident does not seem in keeping with what we know of Roger's character, it may be disregarded. If it is true, it is still of no importance.

The date of Bacon's birth as 1214 has been generally accepted, simply because there is no reason for the adoption of any other. There is no reliable information on the matter at all.

Charles is responsible for the calculations which place it in 1214. He pointed out[3] that Bacon himself had said in 1267 that it was now forty years since he had learned 'the alphabet', and for all but two of these years he had been 'in studio'. Charles thought that 'in studio' meant in the university, which it can certainly mean. Since in the Middle Ages one entered the university about the age of thirteen, and forty years had elapsed since Bacon's entry, he would be fifty-three years old in 1267, and thus was born in 1214.

But Charles and his followers neglected to consider that he had also apparently learned his alphabet forty years previously. And a family rich enough to be able to give one member two thousand pounds to buy MSS. and make experiments, and to ransom another who had been taken prisoner in a civil war, would surely not have waited till Roger was thirteen before teaching him the alphabet. And one did not, in any case, so far as we know, learn the alphabet at a university.

So either the translation of 'alphabetum' in its literal sense as alphabet, or 'in studio' as at the university, must be abandoned. I am inclined to think that fewer difficulties will be created by allowing 'alphabetum' as a figurative term for the rudiments of knowledge, or, as we should call it, the ABC. This is supported by a use of the word elsewhere in Bacon's work in a similar sense—alphabetum philosophiae.[4]

While it may not be strictly true that Bacon spent his entire life in universities, nevertheless, I have found no period prior to 1267 when he was not at least in touch with either Oxford or Paris, and able to attend lectures, even though he was at the same time teaching pupils privately and carrying out his duties as a friar. Even as late as 1292, when he was writing his last work, he speaks of his difficulties in

[1] Little, *Essays* . . . p. 2.
[2] Matthew Paris, *Chronica* . . . III, 244–5.
[3] Charles, pp. 4–5.
[4] Brewer, *Op. Tert.*, p. 66.

gaining enough knowledge for his present purpose merely by reading and listening,[1] so that study was probably, as he says, a lifelong habit.

The period of forty years cannot be taken quite literally, as Bacon is fond of giving periods of time in multiples of ten.[2] But in the absence of any more exact information we are entitled to take it literally, and make the assumption that he went to the university about 1227, and was born about 1214, without danger of going too far astray. On the other hand, the possibility must not be altogether ignored that he only learned the alphabet and started to study, though not at a university, about 1227, in which case his birth must be placed around 1220. The former date, however, as we shall see, fits in better with the other events of his life.

We have established, then, that Bacon was born in England in the first quarter of the thirteenth century of a fairly rich, and possibly noble, family. And this is really all we know about him until his work as a *magister regens* in the Faculty of Arts at Paris in the fifth decade of the century, except what can be gleaned from a few casual remarks written in later years. We know how much, for instance, he admired Robert Grosseteste, Bishop of Lincoln, and Brother Adam Marsh; and how much Grosseteste, at least, influenced his own work. But, as will be shown later, there is no evidence that he knew either of them in his first period at Oxford.

Only in his last work, when his mind may have been wandering back to the scenes of his youth, does he make any direct references to specific masters who taught at Oxford. He tells us that the blessed Edmund, Archbishop of Canterbury, was the first to lecture at Oxford on the book of the *Elenchi* 'temporibus meis', and Master Hugo lectured first on the *Posteriores*.[3] He does not, however, claim to have heard St. Edmund, though he had seen Master Hugo.

Nothing further is known of this Master Hugo, in spite of much recent research on the masters of the period,[4] but it is confirmed from other sources that St. Edmund of Abingdon taught logic in the new schools at Oxford. This, however, seems to have been before 1214, and from about 1202 to 1208. And when he again began to lecture in the 1220's it was on theology.[5] In his old age Bacon may not actually have remembered that Edmund had given up the teaching of logic some time earlier, and would only recall that he had lectured

[1] *CST*, p. 26.
[2] E.g. Brewer, *Op. Tert.*, pp. 38, 59, 65; *CSP*, pp. 425, 428, 429, 469; *CST*, pp. 34, 53.
[3] *CST*, p. 34.
[4] D. A. Callus, 'Aristotelian Learning . . .' (1943), p. 239.
[5] *Ibid.*, p. 240.

in his time at Oxford. It is, in any case, extremely unlikely that Bacon studied with him, as he is seldom hesitant in mentioning masters he has heard, and he would be too young to be studying either advanced logic or theology in the 1220's.

The other reference is to the teaching of Richard of Cornwall in 1250,[1] so that, if Bacon heard Richard at all, it was after his return from Paris, and not in the period we are studying.

Bacon's education at Oxford will have to be inferred from our knowledge of the curriculum that was offered at the time. As he claims to have always been studious, and several times in his later work he emphasizes the value of academic education, and is severe in his criticism of those who have not attended lectures, we may assume that he fulfilled faithfully the requirements of the time.[2] Moreover, the students were in any case expected to be present regularly at lectures. This is shown by the earliest known statutes of the university, issued in all probability during the very time Bacon was studying there.[3]

Since Bacon's education is of the utmost importance for understanding his later attitude to contemporary authorities in the schools and his strictures upon theologians who presumed to lecture without ever having studied properly,[4] an attempt will be made to reconstruct this period of his life and discover the extent of his own formal studies. It will be our contention that much of his anger against the authorities in the schools and the mendicant Orders stems from his pride in his own status as a fully educated Master of Arts, while his opponents had entered an Order in their youth and never received a degree in arts.

Moreover, Bacon certainly idealized this period of his youth. In my time, he says, in the days of Robert Grosseteste people were properly educated; there were good mathematicians then, and theology was taught on the basis of the biblical text and not of commentaries. But in the last thirty or forty years education has declined.[5] Whatever strange things posterity has attributed to Bacon, it cannot be shown that he was against the education of the schools in general.[6]

Education in the thirteenth century was based on the *trivium* and

[1] *CST*, p. 53. [2] *CSP*, p. 486. Steele, Fasc. II, 10.
[3] *Statuta antiqua* . . . (1931), p. 107. [4] *CSP*, pp. 425–8.
[5] Especially due, in Bacon's opinion, to the excessive use of the *Book of Sentences*. *Opus Minus*, p. 329.
[6] 'Pulchritudo tamen et utilitas et magnificentia specialiter in quinque relucent: videlicet prout ventilatur in studio, occupationibus studii doctoralis utilibus et magnificis, in omni facultate legendo et disputando, et caeteris exercitiis scholasticae disciplinae.' *CSP*, p. 395.

quadrivium (grammar, rhetoric and logic; arithmetic, music, geometry, astronomy), as it had been for centuries. But such an education could be rudimentary or profound according to the conceptions of the time, the manner of teaching, and above all, the text-books in use and the teachers who expounded them. Almost anything that it was desired to teach could be squeezed into the framework.[1]

In Bacon's time the leading university of Europe was undoubtedly Paris, though for specialized subjects such as law and medicine others might be preferred. Paris was under the special protection of the Papacy, as is shown by the extraordinary efforts made by Pope Gregory IX to reopen it after it had been closed down in 1229.[2] The strength of the Parisian curriculum lay especially in the arts (the various branches of philosophy) and theology.

Though it has not yet been established that Oxford was originally founded as a university (*studium generale*) by an exodus from Paris, as Rashdall claims,[3] it was certainly in its early years greatly influenced by Paris, offered similar courses, and was probably the second most renowned university after Paris in the fields of philosophy and theology. And those Englishmen who most distinguished themselves at Oxford could look forward to a professorial position at Paris as the crown of their academic career, if they first completed their education with a few years of more advanced study at Paris.

But in the 1230's Oxford seems to have had one great advantage over Paris, an advantage so great at that time that it may well have laid the foundation for her subsequent success and reputation. Aristotle had fallen under a cloud at the University of Paris, and the study of his *libri naturales* and *Metaphysics* had been formally banned, pending possible expurgation. Public lectures on these works could no longer be held.[4] Though there were no doubt occasional infringements of this ban, and Aristotle could still be read privately, it was a serious blow to the prestige of the university; and we have glimpses of a number of efforts made in the Faculty of Arts to edge Aristotle into the curriculum again. But public lecturing on Aristotle may not have been restored even *de facto* fully until there was an interregnum

[1] When the University of Paris wished to offer courses in Aristotle's *Ethics* in the Faculty of Arts this subject was classed as rhetoric for no better reason than that rhetoric was a required subject. H. Rashdall, *The Universities of Europe* ... (1936), III, 140–53.

[2] *Chartularium* ... I, 125–8.

[3] Rashdall, *The Universities of Europe* ... III, pp. 29 ff., and notes.

[4] See especially G. Thery, 'Autour du decret ...' (1925–26). The ban dated from 1210, when a number of professors had been condemned by the local archbishop. Recent research has shown that materialistic philosophies had been derived at that time from various Aristotelian teachings, especially by David of Dinant.

in the Papacy and the Parisian doctors regained some degree of autonomy. This subject will be dealt with later in connection with Bacon's own lectures on Aristotle at Paris in the 1240's.[1]

Though the two-year closing down of the whole university from 1229 to 1231 was not directly connected with the banning of Aristotle, we know that it was in the minds of the scattered professors. A remarkable letter is still extant, one of the first examples of the 'advertising circular' to come from the Middle Ages, in which the University of Toulouse, newly founded after the Albigensian Crusade, offers as one of its attractions lectures on the *libri naturales* 'which have been prohibited at Paris'.[2] Henry III of England also invited the dispossessed scholars to England. We do not know, however, whether Aristotle was one of the attractions offered. The only promise recorded of Henry is that their persons will be safer.[3]

But although documentary evidence is lacking, one fact is certain. The most influential churchman in England, Robert Grosseteste, Bishop of Lincoln from 1235 to 1253, had already been *magister scholarum* at Oxford from 1214, from which position he retired to continue teaching elsewhere, this time to the newly arrived Franciscan friars in their Oxford convent.[4] And Grosseteste, in spite of an extremely independent mind, could not have been described as anti-Aristotelian.[5]

Now Grosseteste, as we know from several passages in Matthew Paris, put up with no dictation from either king or prelate; and it is in the highest degree unlikely that any ban on Aristotle could have been enforced during his period as *magister scholarum*, or later as the bishop of the diocese in which Oxford was situated.[6] The study of

[1] Amongst the considerable recent monographic literature on the subject perhaps the two most complete accounts are M. Grabmann, *I Divieti ecclesiastici* . . . (1941), and F. van Steenberghen, *Siger de Brabant* . . . (1942), especially pp. 389–446, both of which works are fully documented and take into account all previous research.

[2] 'Libros naturales qui fuerunt Parisius prohibiti poterunt illic audire qui volunt naturae sinum medullitus perscrutari.' Johannes de Garlandia, *De triumphis* . . . p. 97.

[3] *Chartularium* . . . I, 119.

[4] Thomas de Eccleston, *De adventu* . . . (ed. Little), p. 60. A. G. Little, 'The Franciscan School . . .' (1926), pp. 807 ff.

[5] Though in many places in his work Grosseteste seems to favour Plato as against Aristotle, an examination of the particular passages suggests that he criticized Aristotle for his philosophical conclusions rather than for his scientific material. The depth of his quotation from the *libri naturales* of Aristotle is considerable, and his whole work uses Aristotelian terminology, especially such conceptions as *potentia* and *actus* which derive from Aristotle's *Metaphysics*, and the communication of motion from the *Physics*. Though as a Platonist Grosseteste prefers St. Augustine, it is impossible to think that he would have used his great influence against his other master. When Bacon says that he 'altogether neglected the works of Aristotle . . . and preferred to use his own experience and other authorities' (*CSP*, p. 469), this is to be taken with the grain of salt that we must usually use in accepting his more controversial remarks. See *infra*, pp. 89–90.

[6] Matthew Paris, *Chronica* . . . V, 395, 407.

Aristotle, therefore, at the university was probably only limited by the general requirements of the curriculum and the works and teachers available.[1]

No record of the curriculum at Oxford in the Faculty of Arts during the 1230's is known. The first extant list of works used is dated 1268.[2] On the other hand, we have a partial curriculum from the University of Paris for 1215, several modifications are known during the following decades, and a fairly complete list is available for 1255, when Aristotle was officially reintroduced as a required course of study.[3] There is also known an extremely valuable *vade-mecum* of some professor who was teaching at Paris between 1230 and 1240. This contains information about the contents of the books then in use, with a systematic classification of subjects.[4]

Taking into account the way in which Oxford is known to have imitated Paris, and making allowance for books and translations not yet available in the 1230's, the following list will probably not be far wrong:

TRIVIUM.	Grammar:	Grammatical works of Donatus and Priscian.
	Rhetoric:	*Barbarismus* of Donatus, and part of *Topics* of Boethius except Book IV. (Not yet the *Rhetoric* of Aristotle, as Bacon himself tells us.)[5]
	Logic:	*Logica antiqua* or *Ars vetus* (Aristotle's *Categories* and *De interpretatione*; Porphyry's *Isagoge*).[6]
		Logica nova or *Ars nova* (Aristotle's *Prior Analytics, Topics, Sophistici elenchi, Posterior Analytics*).[7]

[1] A recent study on the introduction of Aristotle to Oxford shows that the *libri naturales* were taught by John Blund at Oxford certainly by the 1220's and almost certainly before 1209, these dates coinciding with the introduction of the same books into Paris (Callus, 'Aristotelian Learning . . . (1943), pp. 241–44). Callus finds that Blund's 'approach to the problems is uncertain, rather from the dialectical than the metaphysical angle', and is heavily dependent upon the Arabs, especially Avicenna. It was not until the middle of the century with the work of Adam of Buckfield that Aristotle became really assimilated in the minds of the Oxford masters.

[2] *Statuta* . . . pp. lxxxviii ff., 25–27. Rashdall, *The Universities of Europe* . . . III, 153 ff.

[3] Rashdall, *The Universities of Europe* . . . I, 440 ff.

[4] Archivo de la Corona de Aragon (Barcelona) MS. Ripoll. 109. Described by M. Grabmann, *I Divieti* . . . pp. 113–27, and elsewhere, and evaluated by Van Steenberghen, *Siger de Brabant* . . . pp. 415–18. It seems clear from this still unpublished document that the ban on Aristotle was at least partly observed; for though the *libri naturales* and the *Metaphysics* are enumerated, the professor thinks it only worth while to devote a few lines to each, in comparison with the considerable number given to the works of logic which were still in favour. See also pp. 41–43, below.

[5] In Bacon's opinion rhetoric should be a part of logic. *Opus Majus*, Brewer, *Op. Tert.*, p. 307. The *Topics* of Boethius, to a modern reader, might appear more suitable as a logical text, but it was used in Middle Ages as text also for rhetoric. Rashdall, *The Universities of Europe* . . . I, 441; *Chartularium* . . . I, 78.

[6] The *Logica antiqua* had been available for centuries in the translations of Boethius.

[7] These had only been available in translation since the twelfth century, and so were relatively new.

Obviously this programme is heavily weighted on the side of formal mental training. The student learnt from it primarily the principles of disputing and the tools available for it. Bacon criticizes especially the grammar, and makes many suggestions for its improvement as well as urging the use of other languages than Latin, since Latin cannot be understood by itself, and innumerable errors will be made.[1] As he considers logic to be an innate faculty, formal education in the subject is not so important for him as knowing thoroughly the subjects on which it is to be exercised.[2] On the other hand he believes, or pretends to believe, that only a small part of the corpus of Aristotelian logic was available; as this is one of his complaints we must assume that he still hoped for more and better logic to develop the innate faculty into an even more subtle weapon than it was.[3]

Quadrivium

The *quadrivium*, the second half of the academic curriculum, was far more elastic than the *trivium*. Traditionally it was composed of four subjects: arithmetic, geometry, astronomy, and music. With the right texts and the right instruction it could be made into both a liberal and a scientific education. But until the rediscovery of Aristotle, and no doubt for a long time afterwards, in most *studia* these subjects were taught in a very strange manner indeed. Boethius was the authority for both arithmetic and music. Euclid was the authority in geometry, which for this reason probably was better taught than the rest of the *quadrivium*, even though Bacon has many complaints to make of the time wasted in unnecessary proofs.[4] We can see the fruits of Bacon's education in music when he quotes Boethius as saying how valuable it was for the Church, for theology, and even for medicine.[5] Too often arithmetic had been valued for the understanding of perfect and imperfect numbers in the Pythagorean manner, rather than for the performing of mundane calculations. The Bible and the commentaries of the Fathers were the best aids to astronomy.

But all this had probably changed some years before Bacon's time, and the change must have been accentuated during the rule of Robert Grosseteste. It is impossible to over-estimate the importance of the rediscovery of Aristotle, who provided Western man with his first scientific philosophy and a tremendous body of empirically acquired

[1] See especially Part III of the *Opus Majus*, I, 66 ff.
[2] Brewer, *Op. Tert.*, p. 104.
[3] *Ibid.*, pp. 197–98.
[4] Steele, Fasc. XVI, 118, 121 (*Communia Mathematica*).
[5] Brewer, *Op. Tert.*, p. 299.

knowledge. Further information had been added by the people we call the Arabs (though only a small minority was actually Arabic by descent), especially in the field of astronomy and medicine. All the known works of Aristotle had also been commented on by Arabic philosophers. Since the middle of the twelfth century the fruits of Arabic learning had gradually become available to the West, but we do not know for certain how much had percolated through to the curriculum of the University of Oxford by Bacon's day. A respectable body of the *libri naturales* was certainly studied regularly by 1268, and may have been thirty years earlier. The list includes the *Physics*, *Metaphysics*, *De anima*, *De generatione*, *De coelo et mundo*, and the *Meteorologica* of Aristotle.

The *Physics* and the last three named would make the courses in astronomy respectable, and the *Metaphysics* would add depth to all the studies, even though it cannot be fitted clearly into a definite place in the *quadrivium*.

Grosseteste himself was extremely interested in *perspectiva*, or what we should call optics. The great authority in this field for all the Latins, including Bacon, was Al Hazen, a Moslem scientist whose work was translated by Gerard of Cremona in the twelfth century. Grosseteste's own work may have been used in his own lectures, and he, no doubt, used Al Hazen. The Aristotelian works were available in twelfth-century translations from the Greek, and some from the Toledan school of which Gerard was a member, from the Arabic. In Bacon's time new translations from the Arabic appeared, which, according to him, had a great success. Bacon, however, tells us that the translations were execrable, and the supposed translators either did not know their material, did not know the language, or, as in the case of Michael Scot, did not even make the translations but merely lent their names to them.[1] Probably the success was due more to the new and interesting commentaries of Averroes which accompanied them, than to any exceptional merit in the translations. It is interesting to note that Bacon himself preferred the *Antiqua Translatio* of the *Physics*, from the Greek, to the new translation from the Arabic which he refused to use for his courses.[2] Ptolemy's *Almagest*, which was later to become a standard text-book, though translated in the twelfth century, was not yet itself in the regular university curriculum,[3] though manuals based on it were in general use. And nothing

[1] *CSP*, p. 472, and many places elsewhere. It is one of Bacon's favourite complaints.
[2] Steele, Fasc. VIII, x.
[3] Van Steenberghen, *Siger de Brabant* . . . p. 417.

new seems to have been added to the departments of music and arithmetic.[1]

So on the whole the *quadrivium*, though many of the old and outdated authorities were still in use, was gradually being improved by the addition of new works. In this respect Oxford may have been in advance of Paris, through the influence of Grosseteste. But undoubtedly the greatest of these new works were the new and exciting books of Aristotle, as many as the students could persuade their teachers to offer and as many as the ruling faculty in its wisdom allowed them.[2]

This, then, was Bacon's first education. Like other students of his time, he probably received his Baccalaureat in six years—though not if he really had to start with the alphabet!—and became a Master of Arts after two further years of the same kind of study including the explanation of philosophical texts.[3] After practising disputation he would then be permitted to teach in the Faculty of Arts.

Such an education would leave him a secular master only. If he wanted to become fully qualified in the sacred Faculty of Theology, eight more years of study for a baccalaureat in theology, and a further eight for the doctorate, awaited him.[4] It was necessary for him to decide.

At this period he may have been any age from, say, twenty-one to twenty-six, and the time was probably the second half of the fourth decade of the century.

[1] For the latest and most authoritative work on the Aristotelian translations see E. Franceschini, 'Aristotele nel medioevo,' *Atti del IX congresso nazionale di filosofia* (Padua, September 20–23, 1934); A. Birkenmajer, 'Le rôle joué par les médecins et les naturalistes dans la réception d'Aristote au XII et XIII siècles,' *La Pologne au VI congrès international des sciences historiques* (Oslo, 1928; Warsaw, 1930); S. D. Wingate, *The Medieval Latin Versions of the Aristotelian Scientific Corpus* (London, 1931); G. Lacombe, *Aristoteles Latinus* (Rome, 1939), Vol. I. This last work, which was intended to cover the whole field authoritatively, does not yet, in its one published volume, contain enough for use by itself, and so does not replace the earlier titles. If the project is ever completed now that its chief editor is dead, it will no doubt include all the material from the separate monographs.

[2] The popularity of Aristotle among the Parisian students is sufficiently attested by the numerous sermons against their excessive attention to philosophical studies instead of to pious exercises which would benefit their souls. M. M. Davy, *Les Sermons universitaires* . . . pp. 85–87.

[3] F. Ueberweg (ed. Geyer), *Grundriss der Geschichte* . . . (1928), pp. 353–54.

[4] *Ibid.*, p. 354.

CHAPTER III

EARLY MANHOOD

THE whole period prior to Bacon's appointment as *magister regens* at Paris is entirely undocumented. We simply do not *know* what Bacon did at this time. Yet it must have been of supreme importance for his whole career. He had to make his decision as to what his life's work was to be. I shall therefore in this chapter try to indicate the choices before him, show what he *could not* have done, and finally by the process of elimination suggest what he probably did. This should be found consistent with what we do know of his later life, and to some degree account for it.

After *inceptio* in the Faculty of Arts at Oxford, did he go on to theology, and become a master in this also? Did he remain at Oxford and teach in the Faculty of Arts as a secular master? Did he go on to Paris to complete his education in the Faculty of Arts there; or with his Oxford degree go to Paris to study theology? Or were his interests now aroused by the natural sciences, diverting him to this field? Or in languages in which he certainly became interested later? Or, finally, did he become a friar already at this early stage, and to some extent retire from the world? These are the chief possibilities. Some may be dismissed at once on sufficient evidence; others require more consideration and cannot, perhaps, be discarded altogether on the basis of our present knowledge.

In this study it will be taken as proved that Bacon never became a master or doctor of theology. I am aware that this was still regarded as an open question by Vanderwalle, who devotes a special appendix to it,[1] and by Glorieux, who follows Vanderwalle in his brief biographical account, and has unnecessarily included Bacon for this reason in his published list of Parisian masters of theology.[2]

Later chroniclers are divided upon whether or not to give him the title, as recorded by Little,[3] who thinks, however, that Bartholomew of Pisa is the most reliable on such matters, and therefore accepts his testimony. Vanderwalle points out that Bartholomew also called Bacon 'omni facultate doctissimus', although he did not grant him

[1] C. B. Vanderwalle, *Roger Bacon dans l'histoire* . . . (1929), pp. 156–59.
[2] P. Glorieux, *Répertoire des maîtres* . . . (1934), II, 60.
[3] Little, *Essays* . . . p. 6, note 1.

the official title of doctor of theology.[1] But such an expression is a loose one, and in any case Bacon cannot have held a degree in every faculty.

The question is one on which no later chroniclers should, in my view, be taken as sufficient authority. They may not have known for certain, and in view of Bacon's obvious interest in theology may have assumed his competence and his degree. More important is the absence of Bacon's name from any list of doctors either in Oxford or Paris, though this again is not conclusive, as our lists for the thirteenth century are not complete. But I consider conclusive two factors not fully considered hitherto, though Charles was aware of the problem, and had to do some sharp manœuvring of dates which cannot be accepted in the light of later research, in order to show that Bacon did gain his doctorate.[2]

The first is that Roger had no time to do the necessary theological study, in view of the other interests which can be dated with greater certainty. The second is his really abysmal ignorance of the material studied in the faculties of theology in his day, and his sharp disagreement with and prejudices against their methods. It is certainly untrue to say, as Vanderwalle does, that Bacon was familiar with the writings of Peter Lombard, Alexander of Hales, Albertus Magnus, and Thomas Aquinas. A close examination of his references to these men shows precisely the opposite. He knew what was going on in the faculties in a general way, but only as an outsider would know it. Anyone who has studied a subject intensively for fourteen years must have been influenced to some degree by the study, and can hardly have been so completely unwilling as Bacon to accept any of its premises. Bacon's attitude to theology was extremely old-fashioned, and quite at variance with the advanced opinion of his day. He had no idea at all of the long process that went on all through the thirteenth century of trying to make theology a science, culminating in the considerable success attained by St. Thomas Aquinas. Bacon wanted theological studies to consist primarily of scriptural exegesis, which had been the practice before the rise of advanced logical studies and natural philosophy. His method was that of the twelfth century, and was still the method of Grosseteste, though probably with modifications.

Bacon is not only out of sympathy with this modern viewpoint, but he shows no signs of knowing anything about it, not even enough to attack it intelligently. His attitude is the typical one of the outsider,

[1] Vanderwalle, *Roger Bacon dans l'histoire* . . . p. 157.

[2] Charles, pp. 9–11.

a combination of prejudice and ignorance, and it is to me quite unthinkable that he could possibly have been familiar with the method from many years' study from the inside. A further point serves to confirm this. There are no known works on theology from the pen of Bacon except general criticisms of theologians, and his final attempt to create a special kind of theology through the use of natural science. Every student of theology at Paris and Oxford had to learn to comment on the *Sentences* of Peter Lombard, as part of his training; and if we have nothing else of a master's works, we usually have, or know of, a commentary on the *Sentences*. These are, indeed, in medieval studies, extremely valuable as showing the early thought of a master, e.g. Albertus Magnus, Thomas Aquinas, or Bonaventura. No such writing is known in the case of Bacon, nor does he once quote from the *Sentences*.[1]

Bacon was profoundly interested in theology, and he certainly regarded it as the highest form of knowledge, as we shall show. The *Opus Majus* is one long plea to the Pope to promote the study of the special sciences so that they may throw light on theology. It cannot, in my view, be regarded as only an attempt to interest the Pope because of his suggestions for theology, while his heart lay with the study of the sciences in themselves. Neither Bacon's own psychology nor the special objectives of his other work can be understood unless this real obsession with theology is appreciated. If it be asked why, if he were so vitally interested in theology, he did not study it formally, the answer that will be proposed here is that at a time in his life when he could have chosen this path he failed, for understandable psychological reasons, to make the choice, and thereafter he never had the opportunity again. He was no longer able to spare from his other interests the long time necessary to qualify himself in theology. A discussion of this hypothesis will be postponed until the other choices available to him at the age of twenty-one have been considered.

It can be said almost with certainty that he was not a friar at the time of his Parisian lectures. From his remarks about the boys who enter the Orders at an early age[2] it would look as if he, in fact, had been a man of more mature years when he entered himself. The *Quaestiones* given at Paris are purely philosophical, of the kind that would be given in the Faculty of Arts by a secular master, and

[1] For the position of these commentaries on the *Sentences* see the very valuable little book, M-D. Chénu, *La Théologie comme science . . .* (1943), esp. Chap. II.

[2] *CSP*, p. 426. *Opus Minus*, p. 327. Steele, Fasc. II, 11.

utterly different from the work of any known friars who have written after being subjected to the devotions and religious instructions of their Order. Finally we know that as a friar he was pledged to poverty. Yet at a much later date Bacon dwells on the expenditure of his own funds for experiments, and this could only have been done when he was *in alio statu*.[1] Indeed, in my view the best way to determine the approximate date of his entry into the Franciscan Order will be to ascertain as far as possible the years of his early scientific studies and the expenditure of his private fortune, and fix the entry itself towards the end of this period. But probably the most conclusive evidence is from his own lips in the Gasquet fragment. 'When I was *in alio statu*', he says,[2] 'I composed many things for the elementary instruction of youths', which must refer to his *Quaestiones* which, as will be shown later, take the form of class discussions and include at least some definite questions asked by the students and answered by Bacon as professor.

I do not believe that during or at the conclusion of his studies in the Oxford Faculty of Arts, Bacon became interested in the scientific pursuits which later occupied his life. From the early part of the twelfth century there had been a considerable interest in scientific matters amongst the English scholars. Many English names pass through the pages of Thorndike's monumental history of magic and experimental science—Adelard of Bath, Alexander Neckam, Daniel of Morley, Roger of Hereford, Bartholomew of England, and Michael the Scot. But none of these ever seems to have taught in England. They went abroad looking for Arabic treatises and Greek scientific work. If they came home, as did Daniel of Morley, it was only to become dissatisfied with the state of English studies.[3] Two of the greatest translators of the period, who also wrote scientific works, Alfredus Anglicus and Michael Scotus, spent most of their lives abroad. Pope Honorius III and Pope Gregory IX both tried to persuade the Archbishop of Canterbury, Stephen Langton, to give Michael a benefice because 'they who sincerely seek the incomparable treasure of science are deservedly to be supported with free livings'.[4] But Michael refused an archbishopric in poor Ireland, which was the best offer he received, and went to the Emperor Frederic II in Sicily instead!

So, though there was no lack of native talent, it is improbable that there was much opportunity for studying the natural sciences in

[1] Brewer, *Op. Tert.*, p. 59.
[2] Gasquet, p. 500.
[3] L. Thorndike, *History of Magic* . . . II, 174.
[4] *Chartularium* . . . I, 105, 110.

England before the time of Robert Grosseteste, and certainly not at the young University of Oxford. Indeed, it may have been the new stimulus from the arrival of the mendicant Orders in England that really set this study going, as was so eloquently argued by the anonymous writer of one of the first articles on Bacon to appear in any English periodical.[1]

Robert Grosseteste, as we know, was persuaded to resign his Oxford appointment about the year 1229 and lecture to the Franciscans. He remained in this post until his elevation to the see of Lincoln in 1235. It used to be assumed without question that Bacon studied with him in these years, since his works are so full of praise for the great bishop's scientific attainments.[2] But the date of Bacon's studies would make it more probable that he was just too late to attend this series of lectures.[3] As Grosseteste lived till 1253, there was plenty of time later for Bacon to become acquainted with him and his work.

But there is no evidence to show that Bacon's scientific interests were at all awakened at this time. Indeed, all the evidence points in the opposite direction. A group of lectures that he gave in Paris several years later is very revealing on this point. The lectures are a general commentary on the pseudo-Aristotelian work, *De plantis*, and will be dealt with in more detail later.[4] From these it is quite clear that Roger has a considerable, if quite casual, knowledge of the agricultural practices of his time, such as grafting and budding. But they are certainly not looked upon with the eyes of a scientist, but rather as apposite examples for doctrines on the nature of the vegetative soul. They equally lack the professional attention given to botanical studies by Albertus Magnus.[5] Bacon was not interested in plants except as a philosopher, though in later life he recognized the importance of 'Agriculture' as one of the special sciences. But it seems that he had no great competence in it, as he does not appear to have ever attempted to compose a work on it, in spite of his desire to write a 'complete and perfect' science.

If he were already interested in medicine it is surprising that throughout the *Quaestiones* there is no sign of any of the medical

[1] *Westminster Review*, 1864, pp. 14–16.

[2] E.g. Charles and his followers (Charles, pp. 4–5). Charles names Richard Fishacre and Edmund Rich of Abingdon as having influenced Bacon; but neither of these can be called a scientist, and, as we have seen (pp. 11-12 above), he was probably too late for Edmund.

[3] And in any case there is no definite proof of, and much probability against, the theory that Grosseteste's lectures were on scientific subjects. See Appendix A below.

[4] Steele, Fasc. XI, 173–252.

[5] Thorndike, *History of Magic* . . . II, 539.

knowledge he later acquired, no quotations even from Pliny. In his later philosophical works these quotations are everywhere. He quotes Avicenna, but not very frequently, and then only as a philosopher. Bacon is evidently entirely ignorant of alchemy, and, in fact, seems to deny its validity altogether and, like a true scholastic of the kind he criticizes later, he seems to disapprove of it on the *a priori* grounds that it is impossible.[1]

But, most extraordinary of all if he had already started to study science, there is no mention of the fundamental book—the book that I shall try to show was the most influential in his whole life, the book which perhaps more than anything else turned him from his life of philosophy to a study of natural science—the pseudo-Aristotelian *Secret of Secrets*. Anyone who reads the greater works of Bacon's maturity, his considerable corpus of medical opuscula, and, of course, his own annotated edition of the *Secret of Secrets* itself, cannot fail to appreciate this omission. And the reason for the omission was simply that he had not yet read it.

It is for this reason that I must also reject the *Liber de retardatione accidentium senectutis* as belonging to these years, in spite of the opinion of its editors.[2] It is mentioned specifically in the *Opus Majus*,[3] and although Bacon does not say there that he wrote it himself, it is similar enough to his other medical works for us not to doubt its authenticity and the usual attribution to him in the MSS.[4]

[1] Alchemists know, he says, that metals cannot be transmuted *per speciem*. Then he proceeds to quote 'Aristotle' on the *Meteors*, but the book he chooses for quotation is the one added by Avicenna. Aristotle, he says further, meant that nature can transmute species, but not art. It cannot be transmuted 'secundum speciem, et non negat quod non possit per naturam. In essentia et differentia specifica non potest transmutari, sicut dicit Aristoteles de metallis'. Steele, Fasc. XI, p. 252.

[2] Steele, Fasc. IX, xxi–xxv.

[3] *Opus Majus*, II, 209.

[4] The evidence for the early date of 1236 suggested by Little rests on Bacon's statement in one of the two extant versions that the book was begun 'ad suasionem duorum sapientum, scilicet Johannis Castellionati et Philippi cancellarii Parisiensis', while the other version says merely 'ad suasionem duorum sapientum Par . . .' and breaks off. The very form of the scilicet parenthesis suggests a gloss. There are several indications that it was written to a pope, while others would suggest a secular prince (carissime princeps). It is possible that he sent one copy to Innocent IV as one colophon suggests; the date of this Pope's old age seems consonant with Bacon's new interests in the early 1250's and the real immaturity mingled with enthusiasm that is discovered in the book. But that it was sent at the request of Philip the Chancellor who died in 1236 I feel bound to reject on the grounds of inherent improbability (Bacon would have been only in his early twenties, and why should Philip, an important Parisian dignitary, entrust the task of advising him or the Pope in his old age to a youth who was probably not even in Paris and could not yet have made his reputation?). Little says (*Essays* . . . p. 6) that the *Liber de retardatione* shows that Bacon did not yet know Greek, and so was an early production. I only find that he did not know the Greek medical writers yet at first hand. If this proves anything it is only that the work was one of his earlier scientific writings, but not necessarily prior to his work on philosophy. Crowley, however, in his recent work would reject the *Liber de retardatione* altogether for reasons of some considerable weight. *Roger Bacon* . . . pp. 24–25.

Miss Sharp, from a similar study of the sources, comes to the same conclusion that Bacon's scientific and philological interests appeared late, and only after he had become a Franciscan.[1] I think, however, that she goes to the other extreme and puts them too late, since Bacon must have spent his 2,000 pounds before he became a friar.

If, then, he was not yet interested in natural science, and was *in studio* all his life except for two years' vacation 'so that I could study better later',[2] he must have been teaching in the Faculty of Arts, studying in the Faculty of Theology, or studying something else on his own. Could this have been the languages that he professed to know so well later?

We know from one of his letters that Robert Grosseteste early in his episcopate was already studying and reading Greek for relaxation, although he had not yet brought over his translators.[3] This would be in the years after Bacon had graduated from the Faculty of Arts at Oxford. He *could* have been studying at the same time, possibly even with Grosseteste, using the same facilities. But I do not think that at the time of the *Quaestiones* Bacon knew Greek. Throughout the whole series of lectures he never once suggests that Aristotle has been badly translated. Once he flatly states that Aristotle contradicts himself,[4] but for the most part he tries to reconcile him with revealed truth instead of blaming misunderstandings on bad translations as he does later. In the *Quaestiones* he does not go in for discussions of Greek words which he does so frequently later, even in his philosophic work when there is no special need for it to persuade anyone.[5]

He may also have learned Hebrew at this time, but it is still more doubtful. His Hebrew, such as it was, was primarily used for the examination of the scriptures in the original tongue; it seems therefore probable that he will have studied biblical exegesis first. And at the time we speak of he had not yet taken up the study of theology. I think in any case he must have studied Greek before Hebrew, first because of his better mastery of Greek, and it was more accessible to him; and secondly because he argues later that Greek is necessary for the proper comprehension of Latin. While he gives many words that

[1] Sharp, *Franciscan Philosophy*,. . . p. 119.

[2] 'Ut melius postea studerem.' Gasquet, p. 507

[3] Grosseteste, *Epistolae* . . . pp. 173 ff.

[4] 'Ad objectum dico quod .3 *Metaphysice* dicit quod tangit in linea; unde contradicit sibi et in primo *de anima*.' Steele, Fasc. XIII, 327.

[5] If, however, the commentary *De sensu et sensato* (Steele, Fasc. XIV, 1–134) is Bacon's, and was written towards the close of his Parisian career, as suggested in Appendix C below, then he knew some Greek before he left Paris, as in this work he shows some familiarity with it (*ibid.*, p. 71).

are derived from Hebrew, he says that Latin *grammar* is derived from Greek, and he quotes Priscian to this effect.[1]

We know from his own words that he did not know Arabic at the time of his Parisian lectures, as his Spanish students laughed at him for his ignorance, and as he learnt several words from them.[2] A well-qualified modern scholar who has made a careful study of Bacon's works, and who is himself an Arabist, proves, I think conclusively, that Bacon in fact never knew Arabic at all.[3]

Now, if he did not at this time study languages or natural science, and yet he was by 1267 the author already of many books on science and knew enough to be able to write his great works to the Pope, it is certain that he must have crammed a great deal of reading into the years between his departure from the Faculty of Arts in Paris and the writing of the *Opus Majus*, even if we do not take too seriously his stories of lack of opportunity for study, and ten years' sickness, of which he complains in the Gasquet fragment.[4] So on *a priori* grounds I should be inclined to put the Parisian teaching as early as seems compatible with the current state of affairs at the University of Paris. But there is also a good deal of more reliable evidence which seems to fit in best with an early date.

Modern scholarship on the whole has come to accept the date of 1245 as being the most probable for the beginning of the Parisian lectures, and in the extant collection of *Quaestiones* there seems to be enough work for several years. F. Delorme, the editor of the questions on the *Physics*, puts them between 1246 and 1256, but the latter date seems to me to be far too late.[5] Duhem thinks 1250,[6] Charles is unable to get his dates straight at all, since he tries to argue from the untenable premise that Bacon obtained his doctorate in theology from the University of Paris, and this he could not do before the age of thirty-five.[7] De Wulf gives the date as before 1245 to 1250–52.[8] Little reminds us that Bacon claims to have seen with his own eyes Alexander of Hales (died 1245), William of Auvergne (died 1248 or 1249), and John of Garland (died 1252).[9]

[1] 'Deinde Latini suam grammaticam Graecis vocabulis a Graecis trahunt, et ideo praecipue debemus sequi Graecos'. *CSP*, p. 465. See also *CSP*, p. 462.

[2] 'Quod sicut multa alia prius ab Hispanis scholaribus meis derisus cum non intelligebam quae legebam . . . tandem didici ab eisdem.' *Opus Majus*, III, 82. Possibly, as Steele suggests (Fasc. XI, xviii), the famous laughter of the Spanish students, which impressed Bacon so much that he mentions it three times, drove him to the study of the languages in which he was deficient.

[3] M. Bouyges, 'Roger Bacon, a-t-il lu . . .' (1930), pp. 311–15.

[4] Gasquet, p. 500.

[5] Steele, Fasc. VIII, vii.

[6] P. Duhem, *Système du monde* . . . III, 260.

[7] Charles, pp. 9–10.

[8] De Wulf, *Histoire de la philosophie* . . . II, 270.

[9] Little, *Essays* . . . pp. 4–5.

Bacon *could* have seen Alexander of Hales while on a visit, but since all the other probabilities point to an early date this suggestion seems gratuitous. The only reason for putting the lectures later than 1245 is the fact that in this year public lecturing on the *libri naturales* and the *Metaphysics* of Aristotle was still officially forbidden. This objection will be dealt with in the next chapter. Meanwhile it is enough to say that the time required for his study of natural science and languages *after* he left the Faculty of Arts in Paris demands the earliest date consistent with other known facts.

Since we have ruled out temporarily all the other possibilities we can now ask again: Did Bacon begin to study theology at Oxford? Or did he not even start to study theology but contented himself with being a secular master and teaching philosophy at Oxford in the Faculty of Arts? Or did he go at once to Paris?

Let us take the last suggestion first. We have seen that Bacon believes in the lecture method and is proud of his own education. If he had been an exceptionally good student in the Faculty of Arts he could have acquired the very considerable knowledge of all the works of Aristotle that is shown in his *Quaestiones*. But it is not likely. He would have had to continue his study for many years yet and gain practical experience in meeting class problems, disputing, and answering questions. He has become highly skilled in this art by the time of the Parisian lectures; and even though he may have polished up the arguments before they were published, there are many indications that the lectures were delivered in class and copied down much as he gave them, although the erudition displayed in some of these arguments would mean at least some editing and expansion by the professor. Bacon refers to familiar objects in the room,[1] and we know that he was teaching in Paris and not elsewhere, since on one occasion he says 'if my palm could touch the Seine'.[2]

Now if he had left Oxford in the late 1230's and gone to Paris to study theology, it is certain that by this time he would have become less familiar with the Aristotelian *Physics* and *Metaphysics* since these were very strictly forbidden in the Faculty of Theology.[3] At best he could have read Aristotle's works for himself, but he could never have disputed or taught publicly on them. His work would have been to study the *Sentences* and Scriptures—and there is no sign whatever of such a preoccupation in the *Quaestiones*. If he had gone

[1] 'Ab isto pariete ad illum parietem' is a typical example. Steele, Fasc. XIII, 264. Cf. also *ibid.*, p. 203.

[2] 'Si palma mea tangat Secanam.' Steele, Fasc. XIII, 226.

[3] *Chartularium* . . . I, 114 ff.

to study in the Parisian Faculty of Arts he could not have listened to, or lectured on, the *libri naturales* and the *Metaphysics* as these were not only formally forbidden, but actually not being publicly lectured upon in the 1230's.[1] His earlier knowledge of these works acquired at Oxford would have become rusty, and, as we have seen, Bacon liked and approved of lectures. Moreover, why should he have gone to Paris to the Faculty of Arts, where he would not be allowed to study Aristotle, when he could have stayed at Oxford, continued to study him, and lectured and disputed publicly on him as a secular master? So I think it more likely that he would have stayed at Oxford rather than have gone to Paris at this time.[2]

It may be mentioned that for his own advancement another field of study altogether might have been the most valuable—the study of civil law. The position of authority in the schools required the study of theology for at least fourteen years, culminating in the doctorate. Even Albert the Great, who had gained a considerable knowledge of theology from his own readings, and acquired a high reputation as a theologian and a founder of theological studies, nevertheless found it necessary in mature life to go to Paris for a more formal study and the winning of the degree which would regularize his position. But high office in the Church, though theologians could gain it, especially in England—where John Peckham and Robert Kilwardby, both doctors of theology, though not lawyers, became Archbishop of Canterbury in succession—went perhaps more frequently on the Continent to students of civil law. Many popes, from Innocent III and IV to Boniface VIII, had studied at Bologna, and others such as Gregory IX were skilled canonists. It is a commonplace for theologians and priests to attack the excessive study of the civil law in the thirteenth century.[3]

Bacon adds his quota of attack. It is doubtful if his temperament would ever have permitted him to study law, and his attacks on the encroachments made by the civil law sound more genuine and seriously felt, and less petulant, than his attacks on theologians. He objects to the way theology is studied, but not to the subject; he objects to the use of civil law at all as irreligious. He would have

[1] See above, p. 15, note 4.

[2] I am aware that such arguments, based on the probability of an intelligent action, are far from conclusive, since we are by no means always ruled by what is best for us. There may have been some valid personal reason, of which we know nothing, for leaving England and going to Paris; and this was really the determining factor. The rational action in the circumstances has been sketched here more for the purpose of exploring the possibilities than for arriving at a decision as to what he actually did.

[3] See Davy, *Les Sermons universitaires* . . . pp. 88–90, for clerical fulminations against the study of civil law in 1230–31.

preferred to throw it out altogether and revert to the moral law as embodied, in Bacon's belief, in the ecclesiastical code. This is a part of his deep faith in a moral society, which I think was one of the determining factors in his later decision to become a friar, even though such a step was against his apparent interests.

There remains the question whether he studied theology at Oxford. I imagine he had some difficulty in making up his mind; but that he finally decided against the study of theology at this time. Later he realized more and more his deficiency in this respect. So he attacks violently the existing system, and especially contemporary theologians, for whom he never has a good word. It is clear that in his own mind he is confident that *his* qualifications are better, even for the teaching of theology. I think that his decision was influenced by the greater interest Aristotle had for him than the book of *Sentences*; by the fact that he could study Aristotle freely, and his admired masters were Aristotelians or had studied Aristotle intensively; and the knowledge was new and exciting. There were commentaries to be read, Avicenna above all and Averroes to a lesser degree—and we know these have been read by the time of the Parisian lectures, though perhaps not so thoroughly as later. They are not quoted so extensively as in the works of his maturity. I think that as a young man he voluntarily relinquished the advantages that he might have expected from following a career in theology, and chose instead to remain a secular master and teach, while at the same time continuing the studies of Aristotle and the commentators ever more deeply.

I think it probable that he regretted this choice in later life, especially when he was a friar. Friars who were masters of theology had risen to great heights. Alexander of Hales was welcomed into the Order with open arms and given the first chair of theology held by the Franciscans at the University of Paris. Robert Kilwardby and John Peckham became Archbishops of Canterbury, as we have seen, St. Bonaventura became general of the Franciscans at the age of thirty-six; Matthew of Acquasparta, Raymond of Gaufredi, later generals in the same century, all were doctors of theology. Thomas Aquinas later became the real authority that Bacon would so dearly have loved to be.

But Bacon, it will be contended, was neglected by his Order, and his knowledge of philosophy and later of science was not valued. And it was all his own fault because so early in his career he had opted for philosophy alone, when by swallowing the book of the *Sentences* he could have become a theologian and advanced to the heights.

But this knowledge did not make it any easier to bear. On the contrary . . .

It seems to me that the subconscious realization that he had made a wrong decision accounts for the whole of Bacon's later career and his peculiar psychological disposition in a remarkable manner. He chose to remain a secular master, and turned his back on the current studies of theology at the university because he did not appreciate the methods used and grudged the fourteen years' study necessary to reach the top. He proceeded, then, to teach philosophy and gain a limited success.

But after several years' teaching, what point had he reached? He was still a young man; but there was no future for him as an authority in the schools because he had not studied theology. And Bacon was ambitious to be an authority. He was furiously jealous of Alexander of Hales, who was 'an archdeacon and a master of theology of his day':[1] he called Richard of Cornwall 'the worst and most stupid author of those errors . . . the most renowned, who had the greatest reputation in that stupid crowd'.[2] And Richard, too, was a master of theology, lector to the Franciscans at Oxford from 1256.[3] But Bacon's greatest hatred was reserved for an unnamed man (whom I cannot think to be anyone but Albertus Magnus, however distorted Bacon's picture may be of him[4]), who had become an authority on theology without ever having had the necessary philosophical background, who had gained his position by entering the Dominican Order at an early age and having the full weight of its power behind him. Bacon sneers at the students at Paris who didn't think they knew anything unless they had listened to the 'boys of the two Orders'.[5] If he himself had done this there would have been no need to waste all his years of apprenticeship in philosophy. This unnamed man had cheated, and Bacon could not forgive him (or himself for not having been smart enough to do the same).

So, at the end of his Paris career, at the centre of his life, *nel mezzo del cammin di nostra vita*—he will have been about thirty-five—Bacon had to make his supreme decision. What was he to do with the rest of his life? He could not now turn back and eat his words, and set himself to study the book of the *Sentences* like any juvenile student of theology.

I think the pseudo-Aristotelian *Secret of Secrets*, which purports to be a letter sent by the philosopher Aristotle to Alexander the Great

[1] *Opus Minus*, p. 325. [2] *CST*, p. 52.
[3] Little, 'The Franciscan School . . .' (1926), p. 845.
[4] For a discussion of this problem see Appendix B below. [5] *CSP*, pp. 425–26.

(a mere thinker instructing the lord of the world), with its attractive mixture of mystical theology and science, showed him the answer. He could study and make himself master of science and thus become a theologian by the back door. His dislike of formal theology (his 'mistake' as he subconsciously felt) was now justified. It *was* a soul-destroying discipline. He will never change from this opinion all his days. As late as 1290, when he is well over seventy, he begins work at last on a compendium of theology. But it is still his own brand of theology, and the *Secret of Secrets* is still to the fore. And, even as he works, an old man with the fires of controversy now died down to a smoulder, he knows it is useless. Every now and then his hatred flares up briefly again—against Richard of Cornwall who had succeeded where he had failed,[1] against 'insane holders of theories',[2] against the 'never-ending multiplication of lies'.[3]

But the whole work is tired and feeble. The philosophic system had been better explained earlier. And, above all, the fourth cause of error, so conspicuous in his works to the Pope, the worst cause of all, is entirely omitted. Significantly, the 'conceit of ignorance', the fear of being thought ignorant of anything, has disappeared. Could it be that Bacon had repented—or only that life had taught him at last that it was safer to conceal one's private opinions of one's renowned contemporaries?

But first, long before this, came the fantastic effort to acquire knowledge of all the sciences and their use in the field of theology. From this time onwards his whole life is devoted to this study. Whatever he takes up can be, and must be, used for theology. Alchemy, optics, astrology, even Greek and Hebrew grammar, mathematics—all must be used. All these sciences are 'utilissima' for theology. And—most significant—these are the only disciplines that *are* valuable. He is right, and everyone else is wrong. Time and time again he attacks his contemporaries and puts his own views forward until he has at last the chance to present his case to the highest authority in Christendom.

The haste with which he works is shown by the surprising immaturity of so many of his scientific books, and an excessive credulity not shown by Albertus Magnus, whose studies were more Teutonic and thorough. The age, from our point of view, is superstitious, and the greater part of its scientific knowledge 'fallacious'. But sometimes Bacon is as bad as the least educated man of his day, though at other times he has thoroughly penetrated his subject, and what he

[1] *CST*, p. 52. [2] *Ibid.*, p. 55. [3] *Ibid.*, p. 58.

has to say is at least fully consistent, even if, from our point of view, mistaken. He rarely uses his painfully acquired logic and philosophy. No man *could* know personally all the fields he tries to study; so he is forced to rely upon 'authorities' without checking them, and often without the criticism of which he is quite capable, and without even selecting the best authorities. It is clear that he has read at great speed everything he can lay his hands on.

The two halves of his education were never thoroughly assimilated nor made consistent with each other. While he sees that the link between the theoretical and the practical is his *scientia experimentalis*, he rarely uses the knowledge, and his few serious efforts appear juvenile to us and hardly worth the trouble of relating.[1] All this has led historians of science such as Professor Thorndike with some justice to ascribe a higher place in the history of science to Albertus Magnus.

While this interpretation of the motives behind Bacon's work may explain the reasons for his antagonism to theologians and his devotion to science, it is not intended in any way to minimize the value of his science, which will be fully considered in due course. If we look through the pages of history we shall find hundreds of men of genius, artists of the highest rank, whose whole point of view was determined by an emotional drive, quite possibly even of a primitive nature. It has not vitiated their work; on the contrary, it may even be argued that no great work of art has ever been produced without it. It gives the work its slant, its personal bias, its special point of view; it gives the artist his particular vision of the truth. It is his own subjective reality; and this is communicated to the beholder as an experience, and from it he can learn.

Bacon, too, was a man of genius, an artist. His favourite adjective is 'pulcher' applied indiscriminately to all the branches of science. In four pages of the *Opus Minus* there are no fewer than nine uses of this word either as an adjective or a noun, in positive or superlative. Bacon has an aesthetic appreciation of the universe unmatched in his time and rare in any period. But he was not of the great company of discoverers, experimenters, men of science of whom Albert was the greatest in his own day. I do not believe he could have become a scientist of this kind while he was driven by such an overpowering desire to *persuade*. In his later life he was not a fair man, nor a just; we cannot imagine him examining evidence, weighing and rejecting

[1] As, for instance, his account of the attempt to break a diamond with goat's blood, which was an old tradition. Bacon tells us that diamonds can easily be broken when they are used to carve other gems; but not by goat's blood. *Opus Majus*, II, 168–69.

hypotheses, following the truth wherever it leads. In this he was behind Albert, and behind even Thomas Aquinas, who is too often regarded as the uncompromising exponent of a dogmatic position, where, in fact, his calm clarity and earnest pursuit of the truth put Bacon to shame. Bacon can give a masterpiece of brilliant exposition of a difficult theory, and then follow it elsewhere with absurd and puerile non-sequiturs;[1] he can produce a violent polemic and then ruin it with a piece of contradictory evidence which he does not see will vitiate the whole;[2] he shrinks from no purposeful and malicious innuendo and sly personal remarks, while at the same time attributing to himself the highest motives.[3] The one thing he can never be is generous.[4] But his greatest work still stands to-day with the hallmark

[1] As an example of brilliant exposition his statement of the case for astrology (*Opus Majus*, I, 396 ff.) would be difficult to surpass. Yet later in the same book (*ibid.*, II, 394–95), when considering the ethical value of the different religions known to him, he claims that Christianity is superior because Christ forgave sins. Surely he should have seen that this is an assertion, not an argument. How would the infidel whom he hopes to convince by the argument *know* that, in fact, the sins *were* forgiven? Mahomet could have *said* the same. To take another example from the same work (*ibid.*, III, 14), Aristotle, according to Bacon, 'did not know how to square the circle, a problem clearly understood in these days; his ignorance on this point indicates still further ignorance of more important matters' (translation by R. B. Burke). The same non-sequitur is used with regard to the famous unknown, 'si nescit minora, non potest scire majora' (*Opus Minus*, p. 327). This is not an argument; it is prejudice.

[2] He attacks Alexander of Hales and the unknown, saying that theologians 'accept infinite false and useless things about the sciences (*Opus Minus*, pp. 325–27). This, he says, is the result of the teachings of those two (istorum duorum). Yet these men have authority. Because the friars reverenced Alexander they ascribed to him a work which he did not write. This *Summa* contains numerous falsities and vanities. Alexander did not study Aristotle because in his day Aristotle was forbidden, and because he failed to study the physical works of Aristotle he could not understand his logic either. Because, 'as is clear to everyone who knows these sciences', the two go together. By this time Bacon has so worked himself up about this *Summa*, and is so anxious to say everything unfavourable he can about Alexander that he adds, 'cuius signum est quod nullus facit eam de caetero scribi. Immo exemplar apud fratres putrescit et jacet intactum et invisum hiis temporibus'. The proof of all this is that the work, which Alexander himself did not write, but others, is never copied, and lies rotting on the shelves of the Franciscan libraries! As Churchill would say, some authority!

[3] See Appendix B below for his attack on the unnamed master.

[4] Bacon's one known deed which might, in a trivial sense, be called generous, was his education of the boy John, whom he sent with his *Opus Majus* to the Pope. But as an act of generosity this is vitiated by the motives which inspired it. He wanted to have a young mind to work on, a boy whom he could instruct in all his knowledge, whom he could teach in a few months the whole of his painfully acquired wisdom. This boy, this Galatea, is to be made in his own image. With most fulsome and disproportionate praise, Bacon introduces John to the Pope as superior in every way to his elders who have not had the advantage of his tutoring, even though John is only twenty.

John cannot possibly have been such a paragon of wisdom and virtue—indeed, nothing is known of his subsequent career after he had acted as Roger's messenger—but it suited his mentor's purpose to think it. In the pages of Bacon's *Opera* John is only a projection of himself, one of his hopes of earthly immortality. It takes no great imagination to picture this youth as he really was, and his feelings towards the domineering master who was trying to cram all his knowledge down his throat in a few years, to say nothing of supervising his morals. It is not surprising that we have no record of any explanation of Roger's scientific system given to the Pope by John beyond late unreliable legend. The figure of the favourite pupil on whom so much had been staked fades out altogether from Bacon's later works, as if he had never been.

A further point that might show Bacon's generosity to the poor and neglected ones of this

of genius upon it; with all the faults of his brilliant and erratic nature impressed upon it for all to see: but still, without any doubt, a masterpiece.

Bacon may have started to study theology and given it up in impatience or disgust. But, if he did, then he soon returned to philosophy, and long before he had given up his freedom to become a friar. He started to teach, and while he was doing so, over the few years remaining to him at Oxford he deepened his knowledge of Aristotle and the commentators, and he perfected his technique of disputing. These he had at his disposal when he arrived in Paris.

I think it very possible that he attained a considerable reputation in the Faculty of Arts at Oxford—though such reputations were not to be compared with those of real masters of theology. And it seems very possible indeed that from this position at some time in the early 1240's he was invited to lecture in Paris when the Faculty of Arts in that university needed a man to teach Aristotle. They would not call upon any of their own professors, for these were not practised in the technique of expounding Aristotle because of the ban. With no one available, therefore, who had the necessary technique and experience, what more likely than that they should turn to Oxford? And here was a young and gifted master ready to hand, in the person of Roger Bacon.[1]

world may also be interpreted in another sense—his defence of Master Peter of 'Maharn-Curia' (usually called Peter de Maricourt). This man was not an authority either; in fact, he was unknown. 'He does not care for speeches and battles of words, but he pursues the works of wisdom and finds peace in them . . . nothing which can be known escapes him. . . . If he wished to stand before princes and kings, they would honour him and make him rich. . . . If he wished to demonstrate at Paris his knowledge of wisdom, the whole world would seek him out. But he cares nothing for honour and riches.' The strong, silent, incorruptible investigator, the idealized image of Bacon himself—and, above all, an unknown, a man who could never be a competitor or an authority, like those other safely dead figures of the past, his revered masters, Robert Grosseteste and Adam Marsh! (Brewer, *Op. Tert.*, pp. 46–47.)

[1] There is an interesting passage in Bacon's last work which may also throw some light on the time and circumstances of his entry into Paris. 'Some of the philosophy of Aristotle', he says, 'came late into use among the Latins because his natural philosophy and metaphysics and the commentaries of Averroes were only translated in our times; and they were excommunicated at Paris before the year 1237 on account of the eternity of the world and of time, and on account of the book concerning the divination of dreams which is the third book of the *De somno et vigilia*, and on account of many errors in translation.' (*CST*, p. 33.)

Now we have no reason other than this statement of Bacon to attribute any particular significance to the year 1237. The main prohibitions of Aristotle were in 1210 and 1215, followed by a renewal in 1231 until the works had been expurgated. Is it entirely gratuitous to suggest that this year was associated in Bacon's memory with a decision of his own in that year—that he would not go to Paris in that year because of the prohibition? This is one of the very few occasions when Bacon mentions an exact date instead of some round figure in a multiple of ten. The date of 1237 as the year when he finished his studies at Oxford and had to choose what career he was to follow, and whether to go to Paris or stay on at Oxford, would exactly fit our tentative reconstruction of his life.

CHAPTER IV

PROFESSOR AT PARIS

I

TO understand conditions at the University of Paris in the 1240's it is necessary to consider briefly certain significant events that had profoundly affected the whole academic life of the university.

In 1210, as we have seen, the works of one Amaury of Bènes and of David of Dinant had been condemned to be burned, and the metaphysical and natural scientific works of Aristotle had been prohibited in public lecture courses.[1] While it is improbable that Amaury's seriously heretical works had had much connection with Aristotle, the two monographs of G. Théry have shown convincingly that David of Dinant's philosophy was a kind of materialistic pantheism. It was drawn not so much from Aristotle himself as from a third-century commentator, Alexander of Aphrodisias, who had developed Aristotle's ideas in the direction of a greater materialism than his master.[2] Most of the later commentators had been influenced more by Neo-Platonism, especially the popular Avicenna; but Alexander's works were available in a twelfth-century Latin translation and had apparently obtained some currency.

Strictly speaking, David was not a metaphysician, but a logician. Nevertheless, his writings had had enough influence to attract the unfavourable attention of the Church in these early years of the century, and provided enough material for an incipient heresy by the time of Albertus Magnus forty years later. It is from Albert's attack on one Baldwin and his associates that Théry has been able to reconstruct the general ideas held by David and the use he made of them. He thinks Albert's anger against David and his followers was due to the illegitimate use of the master Aristotle, and that it is Albert's belief that Aristotle himself had been condemned because of the discredit this brought on him. Thomas Aquinas also finds it necessary to attack David's position, which he does with his usual lucidity.[3]

[1] *Chartularium* . . . I, 70; *supra*, p. 13 (note 4).

[2] Théry, 'Autour du decret . . .' (1926), Vol. VI.

[3] David of Dinant, says St. Thomas, believed that God and mind and matter were of the same genus, of which they are only the specific differences. While, in truth, in God, by hypothesis, all virtues exist in pre-eminent degree. His virtues transcend those of all creatures, and are not only different in kind. So David's philosophy is altogether built upon a confusion between diversity and difference. There is only an analogical resemblance between primal

We shall see that Bacon has no trouble with this conception, and that he is quite clear on the difference between mind, matter, and God.

In 1215 the decree against Aristotle and David and Amaury is made more definite and reaffirmed by Robert de Courson, the Cardinal-Legate of the Papacy.[1] Charles Dickson has studied the life of this cardinal, and thinks that the severe decree may have been made partly on his own initiative, as he was a fanatical and rather tactless theologian.[2] Nevertheless, he was a personal friend of Pope Innocent III, and would hardly have taken this action without his approval. The banned works, the *Metaphysics* and *libri naturales* (*Physics*, *De anima*, and other less important works), had evidently arrived in Paris a number of years before, perhaps from Salerno, where they had already been in use at the medical school for a considerable time,[3] and were by now well known in the Faculty of Arts. However, the theological works of the day do not have quotations from these books of Aristotle, which may be a sufficient indication that they were not yet studied in the Faculty of Theology at Paris. The decrees, therefore, may have affected only the Faculty of Arts.

We know, however, that in spite of the prohibition the philosophical work of Aristotle (though not necessarily the forbidden part) was being used in the Faculty of Theology, or at least by theologians. For in 1228 Pope Gregory IX addresses a letter to the Faculty of Theology in which he warns the theologians against trying to *confirm* theology by philosophy. He goes so far as to suggest that it is more meritorious in the eyes of God to believe without probability, much less proof, than to believe what can be *shown* to be true by philosophy.[4] He also tells the Dominican students who were permitted to attend the university that they must not study in the books of the 'Gentiles and philosophers', although they may inspect them briefly. They are not to learn secular sciences nor even the arts which are called liberal; they must only read theological works with which the Chapter must provide them.[5] This admonition, however, does not seem to have been particularly successful, since the same Pope, three

matter and the primal *function*. David simply did not understand the analogical arguments for the existence of God, that God was in no sense *univocally* the same as man (leading to anthropomorphism) or *equivocally* different (leading to agnosticism, as there can be no knowledge of a being altogether different). David, in brutally insisting on their univocal nature, showed himself to be a simpleton of a philosopher and a materialist. (Thomas Aquinas, *Comm. in Sent.*, II, xvii.)

[1] *Chartularium* . . . I, 78 ff.

[2] C. Dickson, 'La Vie du Cardinal Robert . . .' (1934), pp. 116–24.

[3] A. Birkenmajer, 'Le Rôle joué par les médecins . . .' (1928), pp. 1–15.

[4] *Chartularium* . . . I, 114.

[5] *Ibid.*, 112–13.

years later, after the university had dispersed and then reassembled, gave authority to the Prior of the Dominicans to absolve all masters and students who had violated the prohibition against lecturing on the *libri naturales*.[1] From which we may assume that some lectures were going on, if not in the university, at least among the Dominicans.

All this time there is no doubt that individual students were still reading Aristotle, since works written at the time show familiarity with him, especially those of William of Auvergne, who was Bishop of Paris at the time of the dispersal and retained his position until his death in 1248 or 1249. William, who would always have some supervision over the public lectures of the university, criticizes Aristotle for holding many false doctrines; but on the whole he has much more praise than blame for him, reserving his severer epithets for Avicenna, whom he often treats very unfairly, putting arguments in his mouth that he did not make, and then proceeding comfortably to demolish them.[2] The Chancellor of the University, Philip, is also in considerable debt to Aristotle.

In 1229, as has been said, the university was dispersed for two years, after a quarrel between the citizens of Paris and the students. Pope Gregory worked untiringly to reopen it, despatching letters all over Europe to kings, princes, and the higher clergy. When at last he was successful he marked the occasion by sending a letter to the university which has since been regarded as its charter of liberties. He had evidently realized that the study of Aristotle had gone too far to be completely checked, and that Paris was losing students to Oxford and Toulouse unnecessarily. So he told the Masters of Arts now that they might not use the *libri naturales* until they had been examined and purged from all suspicion. He conceded that the work of Aristotle in this field should not be condemned in its entirety, as there were things both 'useful and useless' in it. At the same time he warned the students that, though they could lecture in the Faculty of Arts as early as the age of twenty-one, no one could lecture in theology until he had attained the age of thirty-five; and the arts students must only lecture in their proper faculty, thus preserving the integrity of the theologians. He appointed a committee of three to perform the necessary expurgation.[3]

There is no record of the labours of the committee ever having been completed, perhaps because the leading member died in the same

[1] *Chartularium* . . . I, 143.
[2] An outstanding example of this is to be found in William of Auvergne, *Opera* .. . I, 687–93 (*De universo*).
[3] *Chartularium* . . . I, 138.

year. However, as Mandonnet pointed out, the whole method of Aristotle is, in a sense, anti-theological, and a method cannot be excised as easily as a few offending passages.[1] Theologians making use of a group of apparently harmless ideas might quickly find themselves making the same deductions from them as Aristotle, and thus be led into dangerous thoughts and heresies.

The increasing popularity of Aristotle, in spite of the prohibitions against public lecturing, is probably due, as was suggested in the last chapter, to the new translations from the Arabic and the commentaries of Averroes that accompanied them. All serious students of the Master cannot fail to have been interested at once in these commentaries. Aristotle himself had been available for many years; but at no time have his frequently cryptic words, with many thoughts only barely indicated and rarely fully worked out, been easy to understand. They cry out for running commentaries, explanations, examples, and the more complete working out of his seminal thoughts. The translation from the Arabic, which is a further remove from Aristotle than the old versions of Aristippus and his school from the Greek, could not be expected to be a great improvement. Bacon may not have been much of an authority on translation himself in spite of his pretensions; but Michael Scot, if we are to judge by his other work,[2] was a very turgid thinker and writer, and not at all likely to have fulfilled Bacon's demand that the subject-matter of a translation should be known by a translator as well as the language.[3]

But the Averroes commentaries are another matter, however barbaric the translation. Probably Averroes was already well known in the Latin world by reputation, and it was truly an event when his very full, and, on the whole, intelligent and faithful, explanations of the Master became known to the learned world.[4]

We have Bacon's own statement that 'from the time of Michael Scot, whose translations appeared in 1230 with authentic expositions, the philosophy of Aristotle has grown in importance among the Latins'.[5] The most recent and complete study of the entry of Averroes

[1] P. Mandonnet, *Siger de Brabant . . .* (1911), I, 21.

[2] Haskins gives one example, *Studies in Medieval Science*, pp. 266 ff. In fairness, however, it should be mentioned that the *Commentary on the Sphere*, attributed to him, though not with certainty, is considerably clearer and shows its author as a fairly good Aristotelian.

[3] Brewer, *Op. Tert.*, pp. 32–33. Bacon says elsewhere that Michael's supposed translations were done by a Jew named Andrew. *Ibid.*, p. 91.

[4] As valuable, say, as a commentary on *Ulysses* and *Finnegan's Wake* by a lifelong student of Joyce would be to graduates majoring in twentieth-century experimental English literature!

[5] *Opus Majus*, III, 66.

into the Latin world confirms Bacon's statement—note that in this case it is not a round figure but a date—and refutes convincingly the earlier opinion that Averroes was already widely read in the West by the second decade of the century. This opinion was due to a misunderstanding of the scope of the actual knowledge held by writers who spoke of him.[1]

De Vaux disposes effectively of all the supposed quotations of Averroes. The first two writers of importance who mention him have only a very casual knowledge of him, admire him greatly, and have found nothing offensive in his work.[2] William of Auvergne, as we have seen, attacks Avicenna rather than Averroes, and Avicenna can be much more easily reconciled with Christian faith than Averroes, as subsequent history was to show,[3] even though he may be more favourable to astrology, magic, and other practices not always approved by Christians. Philip the Chancellor has probably only dipped into the work of Averroes, and has not yet had a chance to read him thoroughly before he dies in 1236. Both these writers are probably making their brief quotations in the early 1230's, and their superficial knowledge is thus accounted for.

Though the entry of Averroes must have put pressure upon the university to include Aristotle in its curriculum and tempted the authorities to disregard the prohibition, can we say, with Thorndike, that 'the ban was tacitly lifted in 1231'?[4]

As it is of the utmost importance if we are to estimate correctly Bacon's position at the University of Paris when he gave his own lectures on Aristotle, a more extended discussion becomes necessary on whether the prohibition was indeed effective. Thorndike is here considering the commentary on the *Sphere* of Sacrobosco which is ascribed to Michael Scot. He has argued effectively for an early date for the *Sphere* itself, which a late thirteenth-century writer claims to have been composed by John of Sacrobosco at the University of Paris, and he believes that already by the 1230's the book had been in use long enough for a commentary to have been required. The first of

[1] R. de Vaux, 'La première entrée . . .' (1933), pp. 193–245.

[2] *Ibid.*, p. 242.

[3] See also De Vaux, 'Notes et textes . . .' (1934).

[4] L. Thorndike, *The Sphere of Sacrobosco* . . . (1949), p. 22. Presumably Thorndike is also relying on the opinion earlier expressed by B. Hauréau, *Histoire de la philosophie* . . . (1872–80), II, 117, and Mandonnet, *Siger de Brabant* . . . (1911), I, 22 (though cf. p. 23), and, of course, on the letter to the Dominican Prior referred to earlier. No one would question that there were infractions of the ban; the question at issue is whether these amounted to a 'tacit lifting'. Professor Thorndike has suggested to me also that even if the Commentary attributed to Michael is not by him, it might have been attributed to him because of its use of Aristotle.

these may have been the one ascribed to Michael and printed in Professor Thorndike's volume. Michael died in or before 1235.

Now this commentary, which is in the form of lectures given probably at the University of Paris, makes extensive use of Aristotle. But it has only one mention of the great Commentator, and this would be surprising if the author had just translated his works. Four facts must be established if we are to use this evidence for the early date of lectures which make use of the *libri naturales*:

(*a*) That Michael, who was employed by the Emperor Frederic II during the years he could have delivered the lectures, had leave of absence to go to Paris for a year or less. This is quite possible, though there is no positive evidence. Frederic, sending the commentaries of Averroes to the universities of Europe, as we know he did, could easily have sent Michael himself as his emissary.

(*b*) That there was a course being given at the University of Paris either before, or beginning at, this time, on the *Sphere* of Sacrobosco. Thorndike has not produced evidence for this, and such evidence as we have (for instance, the professor's vade-mecum, dealt with below) seems to be negative. However, as this professor was concerned with philosophy, he would not necessarily mention the *Sphere*, though he does mention other text-books than Aristotle, e.g. the *De motu cordis* of Alfredus Anglicus.[1]

(*c*) That lectures could be given making extensive use of the forbidden *libri naturales*. It is possible that a distinction might be made between lectures on what was officially a different subject, and the *libri naturales* themselves.

(*d*) That the commentary, in fact, is by Michael. Thorndike does not find his authorship assured, but he does demonstrate from internal evidence that it is early, and, indeed, the earliest commentary known on the *Sphere*.

So while all these desiderata may be satisfied, I do not think the evidence in its favour can amount to even a probability that it was such a work as this that Bacon had in mind when he said that Michael Scot introduced the natural philosophy of Aristotle.[2] His work as a translator was of far greater importance, and Bacon's reference to Averroes and Michael's connection with the translation is fully sustained. But there is no reason to suppose that Averroes was lectured upon yet, any more than the *libri naturales*; though private

[1] Incidentally, I have found no reference in Bacon's works to the *Sphere*. But nothing can be inferred from this as Bacon seldom, if ever, quotes from his contemporaries.

[2] Thorndike, *The Sphere of Sacrobosco* . . . p. 22.

reading of the Commentator would begin to produce its effect gradually, culminating in the extensive use of him as an authority by the late 1240's. And such evidence as I have examined and considered does not seem to confirm the tacit lifting of the ban. On the contrary, it seems to have been fairly well observed as long as Gregory IX was alive.

Grabmann says that we cannot deduce from the fact that the expurgation was not carried out that lectures were at once given on the *libri naturales* and the *Metaphysics* at Paris.[1] He mentions some verses of John of Garland which refer to the use of Plato and Aristotle at Paris, and can be dated with certainty as 1234, but does not think they are decisive.[2] Philip the Chancellor (died 1236) undoubtedly used the books, as did William of Auvergne. Roland of Cremona wrote a *Summa* with 672 quotations from Aristotle about 1229, but in it Averroes is neither named nor used.[3] In any case, Roland taught at Toulouse during the period Paris was closed down. But quotation, however extensive, proves nothing about public lectures at the university. Moreover, these men, of high position and well advanced in life, would not at this time be studying. So the evidence is not really valuable for the question of public lectures in the Faculty of Arts.

Much more decisive is the vade-mecum spoken of earlier and described by Grabmann. Here the anonymous professor says specifically in his preamble that he is intending to deal with questions containing much difficulty and required for examinations in 'the different faculties'.[4] Can it be suggested that this would *not* include the *libri naturales* if they were being lectured upon, when surely the most serious questions of all were concerned with these? And yet the professor does not deal with them except merely to mention the books in a few lines. A half column is devoted to the huge *Metaphysics*, in which he speaks of the number of books, and gives in some cases the incipit and a brief note on the contents. He adds: 'Take notice that metaphysics, since it treats of the general principles of things, is superior to all other sciences . . . the subject of metaphysics can be called first being'. He then says how it is to be regarded

[1] Grabmann, *I Divieti* . . . (1941), p. 109.

[2] *Ibid.*, p. 110. The poem is in the Municipal Library of Bruges.

[3] Grabmann, *I Divieti* . . . pp. 111–12.

[4] 'Nos gravamen quaestionum plurimarum et difficultatem attendentes in quaestionibus, que maxime in examinibus solent fieri, eo quod nimium sunt disperse et in diversis facultatibus contente nullum de eius habentes ordinem vel continuitatem, dignum duximus in quadam compenditate huiusmodi quaestiones cum suis solutionibus pertractare'. Grabmann, *I Divieti* . . . p. 114.

(*univocum in ratione*) and at once concludes with: 'And *hoc modo* it can be said that being in general is the subject of metaphysics'. That is as far as he gets with metaphysics. On the *libri naturales* there is one page, including indications of one or two minor problems to which he devotes two or three lines each. That is all.

But the *Ethics* (a permitted if not required book since 1215) is gone through carefully book by book, as also the whole content of the *Organon* that was in use.[1]

Grabmann then attacks the problem from another point of view.[2] If the *libri naturales* were not being used, this must have left a considerable gap in the curriculm. How was it filled? And he gives the suggestion that it was filled by a greatly increased study of logic and grammar. He finds that the quantity of logical works which can be exactly dated in the 1220's and 1230's greatly exceeds that of any other period. The very important *Summae logicales* of Peter of Spain, later Pope John XXI, may date from this time.[3] George Sarton remarks that in the study of grammar, and particularly in the work of John of Garland, 'there is a tendency to give the subject a greater philosophical depth. John was one of the first speculative grammarians or *modistae* whose efforts tended to lift grammar up a to higher philosophical level'.[4] Bacon approved of John of Garland[5] and, of course, had a great interest in grammar, and wrote in his Parisian period a *Summa grammatica*, which has been printed.[6]

The evidence of questions asked in Paris from 1225 to 1235 supports Grabmann's contentions. O. Lottin has printed a list of such questions contained in MS. Douai 434. None of these questions, nor the incipits of those not included, seems to give even a hint that the *libri naturales* or the *Metaphysics* were being discussed during those years, though, of course, such negative evidence cannot in itself be conclusive.[7]

Bacon's own evidence on this subject is interesting, but we cannot place any actual date on the dropping of the prohibitions from these particular remarks, since they come from the *Communia naturalium*, which was composed over a long period of years, and was revised and added to after his works to the Pope. 'The natural philosophy of Aristotle', he says, 'which has been lectured on for barely thirty

[1] Grabmann, *I Divieti* . . . p. 125. [2] *Ibid.*, pp. 127–28.

[3] Prior, at least, to Peter's departure for Siena in 1246, where he taught natural philosophy. His logical work belongs to his Parisian period. Van Steenberghen, *Siger de Brabant* . . . p. 422.

[4] G. Sarton, *Introduction to the History* . . . (1931), II, 530.

[5] *CSP*, p. 453. [6] Steele, Fasc. XV, 1–190.

[7] O. Lottin, 'Quelques *quaestiones* . . .' (1933), pp. 79–95.

years (*vix a triginta annis* always means *less than* thirty years) and by few men, and these have not written on him, still cannot be known *apud vulgum*'.[1]

Dom Lottin has also discovered in later researches the increasing influence of the logical and ethical works of Aristotle in the Faculty of Theology at this period, and concludes that there was an interplay between the two faculties as a result of their mutual interest in philosophy, however much it may have been officially frowned upon.[2] It is quite possible that a percolation of the ideas of the Faculty of Arts into the Faculty of Theology did dispose the latter to modify its oppositions, which may not have been altogether of its own making, but more as a result of pressure put upon it by Pope Gregory IX and its own more conservative theologians.[3]

I have been impressed by Professor van Steenberghen's suggestion that there would have been much comment in Paris that the foremost university of the world should be behind its English competitor in the matter of public lecturing on the works of Aristotle,[4] and that the opposition in Paris is likely to have gradually collapsed, the conservative theologians having enough trouble of their own, between the older generation of scriptural exegesists and 'Augustinians' and the younger generation who wanted to use their philosophy. Moreover, the Bishop of Paris, as we know, found nothing specially wrong with

[1] Steele, Fasc. II, 12.

[2] Lottin, 'Psychologie et morale . . .' (1939), pp. 182–212.

[3] From Davy, *Les Sermons universitaires* . . . esp. pp. 292, 340, it can be seen how the reigning theologians severely rebuke those of their own number who mingle theology and philosophy. In the Faculty of Arts during these years was Alexander of Hales who, according to Bacon (*Opus Minus*, p. 326), did not know the *Metaphysics* of Aristotle because it had not yet been translated. This, of course, is not true, but Bacon is never very sound on events that happened before his day, and, in fact, the *Metaphysica Vetus*, which he uses himself, had been translated already in the twelfth century. Actually Alexander had a considerable acquaintance with Aristotle, including the *Metaphysics*, though he objects to the use of him as an authority, and thinks Anselm and Augustine should be more believed. He tries himself to set up a system of metaphysics free from the impure physics and astrophysics which are typical of the work of Aristotle in this field. See especially the December 1945 issue of *Franciscan Studies*, which is exclusively devoted to Alexander of Hales. P. Boehner, in one article on the metaphysics of Alexander, concludes that the *Summa Minorum*, that part of the *Summa Theologiae* which can with probability be ascribed to Alexander himself, is 'truly Aristotelian' (p. 414). In the article by M. M. Curtin in the same number, the author thinks Alexander has been too favourable to Aristotle, that he uses the scholastic conception of the *intellectus agens* and the *intellectus possibilis* unnecessarily, and tries without success to reconcile it with the philosophy of St. Augustine.

The work of Albertus Magnus in the Faculty of Theology is probably too late to be of importance at the period under discussion and is dealt with below in Appendix B.

But it is clear from a fuller consideration of these faculties in the 1220's and 1230's that the old contention (especially propagated in the works of E. Gilson) that the theological faculty was Augustinian, while the Faculty of Arts was Aristotelian is too bald a distinction to be seriously maintained to-day.

[4] Van Steenberghen, *Siger de Brabant* . . . pp. 429–30. I have considerably expanded his few brief sentences.

Aristotle, although he advised a cautious attitude towards him; and he was ignorant of the dangers of Averroes. Everyone must have realized that the prohibition could not be kept in force indefinitely. Even Toulouse, which had been founded as a bulwark against heresy, was free of restrictions till 1245.[1] The university authorities had probably given up hope that a suitably expurgated edition of Aristotle would ever be made, since no progress had been visible along this line in years, and apparently no one was working on it. But in the University of Paris any such innovation as public lectures, in direct contravention of the official decree, could not pass unnoticed.

From what quarter could opposition come? Surely only from one place, the highest seat of authority in Christendom—from Pope Gregory IX, who was now in his nineties[2] but not lacking in vigour, as can be seen from his stubborn fight against Frederic of Hohenstaufen, the Emperor. This Pope had always looked upon Paris as the apple of his eye; and, as we have seen, he had been an uncompromising opponent of Aristotle as long as his works had not been expurgated. It would still not be safe for the Parisian authorities to tangle with him, or back might come one of those terrible letters, or even the thunders of excommunication.

But at last, in 1241, Gregory died, and Frederic shut up the Cardinal electors in an Italian castle until they could agree on a successor favourable to himself. They elected one, but he only survived his ordeal for a few days, and again the throne was vacant. Not until June 1243 was Innocent IV finally elected. And in spite of his former friendship for Frederic—it is impossible for a pope to be a Ghibelline, said Frederic—he found it necessary to oppose him, and by a stratagem he fled from Italy to a safer place. So, with his hands full with his own affairs, Innocent could pay little attention to the curriculum of the University of Paris. Not until 1245 was he free to give it a little thought, and then he merely repeated, in essentials, Gregory's letter of 1231, promising the expurgation but not appointing any scholars for the job, and then extending the prohibition for the first time to the University of Toulouse.[3] But by this time the damage had been done. For nearly four years all initiative had rested in the hands of the local authorities, and they had taken full advantage of it.

This line of argument seems to me to be as convincing as anything in history for which there is only circumstantial evidence. The times,

[1] *Chartularium* . . . I, 185–86.

[2] Born in or about 1147, according to *Dictionnaire de théologie Catholique*.

[3] *Chartularium* . . . I, 185–86.

the intellectual atmosphere, the personnel available, were right. And we know that if not in 1241–44, at least very soon afterwards, Bacon was lecturing publicly on Aristotle at Paris, and using the *libri naturales* and the *Metaphysics*. There is no evidence, of course, that he was the first to lecture on the scientific works of the period, though as yet no earlier commentaries or *quaestiones* are known. But the arguments given at the close of the previous chapter may show why Bacon might have been invited or offered himself. It is enough if he is thought of, as might in any case be inferred from his remarks quoted above, as among the pioneers.

Against this hypothesis is to be set Bacon's own date of 1237, given in the last year of his life when he was in the seventies.[1] If this date be accepted, and there is nothing positive against it,[2] then there was no special event as far as we know that was responsible for the re-introduction.

The second part of this chapter will try to show why Bacon was a good man for the post.

II

The question of Bacon's fitness for undertaking the delicate work of interpreting Aristotle in a manner likely to cause as little offence as possible requires the serious consideration of those statements of Aristotle and his commentators which had been objected to, and had been at least partly responsible for the prohibition. A whole detailed work could be written upon this, and it would in any case greatly exceed the space desirable to be expended on it in this study. So only an outline of a few of the more important arguments, together with Bacon's replies, will be attempted here.

1. *The materialistic-pantheistic argument of David of Dinant.*[3]

There is a well-known passage in the *Opus Majus* where Bacon tries to demonstrate by mathematical (i.e. geometrical) means that the statement that matter must be one in number and the same in all things is untrue. He agrees that if this were so, then the doctrine would be 'very close to heresy or wholly heretical', as the necessary

[1] *CST*, p. 33.

[2] The vade-mecum must be after 1230 since the writer is aware of the 1230 Arabo-Latin translation of the *Metaphysics*, and it should be before 1240, since he is unaware of the new translations of the *Ethics* by Hermann the German (1240) and Grosseteste (1240–43). Van Steenberghen, *Siger de Brabant* . . . p. 416.

[3] See above, pp. 35–36.

consequence would be that matter is God and Creator.[1] Bacon chooses this argument as an example of how to reason mathematically 'though reasonings from nature and metaphysics are abundant and efficacious, concerning which elsewhere a long disquisition can be made.'

I have not found any direct discussion of this problem in his Parisian *Quaestiones*, at least not in connection with its logical consequence that matter equals God. There are many discussions on the nature of matter, and he recognizes that this is a question of extreme difficulty.[2] But the gist of these is that the question is suitably solved by Aristotle with his distinctions of *per se* and *per accidens*, and potentiality and actuality. Matter, says Bacon, is something incomplete, most imperfect and ignoble; therefore it cannot be 'una numero, tamen est numerositate essentie'.[3]

Perhaps it was Albert's attack on the unknown Baldwin that caused Bacon to take the question more seriously, and hence led him to deal with it directly in the *Opus Majus* and other works in his later life. Bacon, of course, does not give this potential heresy as one of the reasons for the prohibition of Aristotle.

2. *The question of plurality of forms.*

This question does not become of real importance until the latter part of the century. Though it had not yet perhaps in Bacon's period at Paris reached the status of a problem, nevertheless there was already considerable disagreement on it, and this had originally stemmed from Aristotle.

'The main point is whether the attributes of the soul—understanding, opinion, desire, and the like, appertain to the soul as a whole, or whether each operation is dependent upon a particular part: that is, whether the soul thinks as a whole, or whether one part thinks, another perceives, and another desires'.[4]

[1] *Opus Majus*, I, 143–46. Cf. also Brewer, *Op. Tert.*, p. 127, and Steele, Fasc. II, 55.

[2] 'Nunc ad perscrutationem arduam et difficilem cause materialis accedamus'. Steele, Fasc. XI, 53. In his latest commentaries on the *Physics* (Steele, Fasc. XIII, 49 ff.), Bacon asks the question: 'Queritur quomodo materia est una, an numero vel genere vel specie'. And he goes on to ask how prime matter, if it were one in number, could still be prime matter when universal and particular forms are received, but the universal forms first, which are not one in number. It is to this objection that he gives the answer above: 'Sic non est una numero, tamen est numerositate essentie'. Cf. also the other discussions on the nature of matter, Steele, Fasc. X, 59–71; XI, 53–62; XIII, 44–56. See also Sharp, *Franciscan Philosophy* . . . pp. 132–33, but her account is incomplete since in 1930 she only had Fasc. VII and Fasc. VIII of the *Quaestiones* at her disposal.

[3] Steele, Fasc. XIII, 49.

[4] This admirable definition is from Callus, 'Two Oxford Masters . . .' (1939), p. 420.

Aristotle does not divide the soul into parts located in different organs. But whether there are one or more substances in the soul he does not determine. He holds that the intellectual soul in man is the perfection of the sensitive soul, the sensitive in turn of the vegetative soul. The soul, according to Aristotle, is 'una subjecto, multiplicitas secundum virtutes'. Averroes, enlarging this in the sense indicated by Aristotle, concluded that there was one soul 'secundum subjectum' and many 'secundum virtutes'.[1] The question adumbrated by the Franciscans in particular, later in the century, especially by John Peckham,[2] was whether there were separate substantial forms—as against Thomas Aquinas who insisted there was only one.[3]

Various opinions had been put forward on this question early in the century. It was, in fact, certain to be discussed in the study of theology because of the importance attached to it by Peter Lombard in his book of *Sentences*, the standard text-book in faculties of theology everywhere.[4] It has an obvious theological importance because of the immortality of the intellectual soul, and the relationship of this to the vegetative and sensitive souls possessed by animals as well as by man, and the lack of immortality prescribed for these. Furthermore, the question of the resurrection of the body, with vegetative and sensitive souls, is closely related to it.

[1] Callus, 'Two Oxford Masters . . .' (1939), p. 420.

[2] Sharp, *Franciscan Philosophy* . . . pp. 186 ff.

[3] On this whole discussion see also M. de Wulf, *Histoire de la philosophie* . . . II, 255–58, though there are many scattered references to the subject throughout the volume, which are not always easily linked together. De Wulf has always been especially interested in this problem, I think, since his first published work on Giles de Lessines in 1901 (*Les Philosophes Belges*, Vol. I).

It is an interesting commentary on Bacon's remarks about the unavailability of the best works of the Arabs that Avicenna's views on the soul were not at this time fully known in the West. Gundissalinus in the twelfth century had purloined many of Avicenna's views and included them in his *De immortalitate animae*, a work so highly thought of by William of Auvergne that he reissued it, with hardly a change, under his own name. But even Gundissalinus, working in Spain, still did not have the full works of Avicenna, or else he did not understand him enough. (For this see Gilson's study, 'Les Sources greco-arabes . . . (1920–30), pp. 1–158.)

A recent and very valuable little study has been made on Avicenna's real thought on the soul from Arabic sources (M. Amid, *Essai sur la psychologie* . . . (1940)). Avicenna insists that the soul is one, and a substance; and unlike most of the Latins who dealt with the subject, he draws upon his considerable medical experience to prove his theories. Man has a 'corporeal soul' and a 'specific soul', the latter only being immortal, and, of course, peculiar and individual in each person. After death there is no further use for the corporeal soul, and it disappears with the body; but the specific soul is immortal. In Avicenna, as with the pluralists, there is a hierarchy of forms, each one embracing the one higher in the scale of being, but the whole forming a complete unity, as with Aristotle. This theory of the corporeal soul comes from Simplicius, the sixth-century Greek commentator on Aristotle, who evidently felt the need for a more complete account than the Master had given. The medievals were more interested in the *functions* of the soul, and so paid more attention to the *intellectus agens* and the *intellectus possibilis*, and Avicenna's views on these are objected to by them. But Avicenna as a medical man was more interested in the *nature* of the soul, and his more important work is devoted to the specific and corporeal souls in themselves, a work unknown to the Latins.

[4] O. Lottin, 'L'Identité de l'âme . . .' (1934), pp. 191–210.

Peter Lombard had insisted on the unity of substance in the soul, as Albert and Thomas equally insist later, and as William of Auvergne and Philip the Chancellor do in our period. The theologian, Richard Fishacre, who taught at Oxford *c.* 1236–43, states the difference of opinion bluntly, and gives three possible views that may be held on the subject.[1] He concludes by expressing no personal opinion of his own on which is true (diffinire non audeo). Adam of Buckfield, an early Oxford commentator on Aristotle who taught there after 1243, is inclined towards the pluralist interpretation.[2] Richard of Cornwall, who lectured on the *Sentences* at Oxford, 1250–53, and at Paris, 1253–55, and was regent master of the Oxford friars from 1256, with whom, as we have seen, Bacon violently disagreed on other matters, regards the theory of the plurality of forms as contrary to the teachings of the saints.[3] Among all the masters of theology who were really considered authorities, only William of Auxerre, one of those appointed by the Pope in 1231 to expurgate Aristotle, gives pluralism his full support.[4]

Albertus Magnus points to the existence of a real problem in his commentary on the *De anima*.[5] But much earlier, in his *Summa de creaturis*, written in the 1240's, he had already said that no reputable philosopher upholds the plurality of forms, and he mentions the names of Avicenna, Aristotle, Boethius, and St. Augustine as being against it.[6] This position is also taken by Richard of Cornwall.[7] Robert Grosseteste and Thomas of York had, however, implied pluralism without definitely stating it.[8]

Potentially it is clear that the problem was an explosive one. And it did explode in the time of St. Thomas, and during the archiepis-

[1] The opinions are as follows:

'1. Estimant enim aliqui, quod vegetabilis et sensibilis et rationalis sunt una et eadem forma, et variantur tantum secundum operationem.

'2. Alii posuerunt quod in homine est anima unica forma numero.

'3. Tertii ponunt quod sunt tres formae et tria haec aliquid in hominibus a quibus sunt istae tres operationes—cui plena contradicit Magister Augustinus'. Quoted by Martin, 'La Question de l'unité . . .' (1920), pp. 107–112.

[2] See Callus, 'Two Oxford Masters . . .' (1939) for a fuller account, pp. 420–24.

[3] Callus, 'Two Oxford Masters . . .' (1939), pp. 424 ff.

[4] Lottin, 'L'Identité de l'âme . . .' (1934), also 'La Pluralité des formes . . .' (1932), pp. 449–67.

[5] 'Hunc errorem . . . sequuntur quidam Latinorum philosophorum . . . qui dicunt esse diversas substantias et animam unam in corpore hominis, adducentes Aristoteles viditur dicere in sexto-decimo librorum suorum de animalibus'. Albertus Magnus, *Opera* . . . V, 184 (Lib. I, *De anima*, Tr. I, cap. xv). He deals with this problem by speaking of the analogy of the light of different candles in one house.

[6] Albertus Magnus, *Opera* . . . XXXV, 97 (Pt. II, *Summa de creaturis*, Tr. I, Qu. 7, Art. 1). The *Summa de creaturis* is dated 1240 or 1241 by O. Lottin, 'Note sur les premiers ouvrages . . .' (1932), p. 82.

[7] Callus, 'Two Oxford Masters . . .' p. 432.

[8] Sharp, *Franciscan Philosophy* . . . pp. 28 ff., 83–85.

copates of Robert Kilwardby and John Peckham in England. And, since it does arise in its acute form from the study of Aristotle and Averroes, it may already in Bacon's day have had to be considered in connection with his work. Unfortunately, the discussion would be likely to arise during the study of Aristotle's *De anima* and *De animalibus*, and though, as we shall see, Bacon seems to have given courses on these books, his questions or commentaries have not been preserved.[1]

In Bacon's extant lectures there is no direct discussion of the problem; the arguments for and against plurality might have been most interesting. In the absence of specific statements we are forced to fall back upon arguments that seem to indicate the view he held. One of the beauties of scholastic reasoning is its consistency and logic, so that it is usually possible to see in what direction an argument is tending, and then transfer it to another subject matter, and reach conclusions which the master himself would probably have reached by the same methods.

Thus in the first series on the *Physics* Bacon states that there are certain animals, to wit men, whose perfection is the intellectual soul, but with vegetative and sensitive souls also. Of these beings a double distinction must be made. If we consider 'material dispositions', that is, vegetative and sensitive, then men in this sense are natural beings and derived from nature. As far as the intellectual soul is concerned, its substance and essence and capacity for willing are not 'natural'. But as far as its existence in a body is concerned, it *is* natural, not because it is produced by nature, but because it is the actuality and perfection of the natural body.[2]

Here, of course, Bacon is not speaking of the soul as a substantial form, but of the capacities of the soul. There is a distinction between the soul itself and its capacities, like the Thomistic distinction between God and His attributes. But under this definition the capacities do not each require a substantial form, as under the theory of pluralities.

Finally, in what its editor considers the latest series of extant lectures, on the pseudo-Aristotelian *De causis*, Bacon does for a few lines deal directly with the soul. 'The corruptible and the incorruptible', he says, 'are not in communication in any simple subject, . . . but they can communicate in a composite substance, as in the soul of man. For the soul of man is made up of a sensitive and vegetative soul which are corruptible, and an intellectual soul which is incorruptible—and yet from these is made one soul *secundum subjectum*,

[1] Steele, Fasc. XIII, xxx–xxxi.

[2] *Ibid.*, Fasc. VIII, 52–53.

which is the perfection of man and is one composite essence, not a simple one; and it happens to be essentially composed of matter and form, and is one, though it is of diverse simple essences . . . as in the second book of *De anima* it is proved that there are three simple essences, and yet from these there is one composite, not simple, which is the soul of man and his perfection'.[1]

While this might leave room for the plurality of forms, it is far from being stated. So we cannot say without the lectures on the *De anima*, in which the problem could hardly be avoided, what were Bacon's complete views at this time. On the other hand we do know what they were at the time of the *Communia naturalium* (perhaps 1260–63, or later, according to the version); he has become much more definite, and seems to come right out for at least the main features of the current theory of plurality. Now he says that there must be matter corresponding to the various differences in form, e.g. *forma corporalis*, *forma corporalis non celestis*, *forma animalis*; but these are all moved and controlled by the *forma intellectiva* which completes the whole.[2]

The conclusion that must therefore be drawn is that we do not know enough about Bacon's Parisian period to be certain what his views were on this question—but that later he would be in sympathy with the preponderant Franciscan position of the day. It is, however, unlikely that the question was yet of enough moment in the 1240's for an orthodox and unorthodox position to have established themselves, of which he would have had to take account when delivering these lectures.

3. *Specific objections to Aristotelian doctrines put forward by William of Auvergne, Bishop of Paris.*

It has already been said that William objected to Aristotle on several grounds. Some of these will now be considered. He himself states so admirably the principle he intends to use in his criticism that it may be quoted in full: 'Although Aristotle must be contradicted in many things, as, indeed, is right and just, he must be regarded suspiciously in all his sayings in which he contradicts the truth, and he must be sustained in all those things in which he is found to have been of the correct opinion'.[3]

[1] Steele, Fasc. XII, 158. A more thorough treatment of Bacon's attitude to this problem is given in Crowley, *Roger Bacon* . . . pp. 136–52, which had not been seen when the passage in the text was written.

[2] Steele, Fasc. II, 58 ff., 83. See also Sharp, *Franciscan Philosophy* . . . p. 134.

[3] William of Auvergne, *Opera* . . . II, Supp. p. 82 (*De anima*).

(*a*) In his *De universo* William attacks the view of the 'followers of Aristotle', as he calls them, that creation was carried out by intelligences and not by God Himself.[1]

This is one of the questions on which Bacon adopts a position with which it would be difficult to quarrel. When he is dealing with the problem from the standpoint of physical and natural philosophy, like Aristotle himself he sees no need for creative intelligences, and there seems no room for them. When he deals with it from the point of view of natural theology, he uses his *belief* that there are intelligences or subsidiary causes, in order to show that power may be communicated from one being to another under the Creator's direction.

In his questions on the *Physics* he says that 'the movers of the inferior orbs are naturally apt to obey the movement of the superior orb . . . although the orbs are discontinuous, yet because the virtue which moves the first orb is of infinitive potentiality, so it can move the other orbs'.[2] This is a straightforward scholastic position, and deals with communicated motion. So there is no question of any possible creation by the inferior orbs.

But in his questions on the *De causis* Bacon has now to deal with a neo-platonic position which he still believes to be Aristotelian.[3] The argument, however, is quite familiar and to be expected. Much of the *Liber de causis* is devoted to the relationship between primal and subsidiary causes, and we are therefore out of the realm of strictly physical arguments, and dealing with a group of ideas amongst which the relationship between the first cause and its subsidiaries would take a natural place. Bacon always insists that the influx of power from the primal cause is the deciding factor in creation. Is a medium needed, he inquires, between the first cause and the inferior created things, either (*a*) for the operation of creating, (*b*) for the production of inferiors, or (*c*) to continue them in operation?

The answer Bacon gives to this is that the medium is not necessary. The Creator is in no way impelled. But He *may*, from His goodness, make use of a medium between Himself and His inferiors. If, therefore, there is a medium, this will merely be for the sake of order,

[1] William of Auvergne, *Opera* . . . I, 618–22 (*De universo*).

[2] Steele, Fasc. XIII, 420–21.

[3] This series of *Quaestiones*, found, like the others, in MS. Amiens 406, is as clearly Bacon's as any other, even though it is not directly named as his in the MS., which is in any case very defective. There is a little more use in it of his theological beliefs, but the emphasis is dictated by the different nature of the subject matter. The manner is exactly the same, and many of the arguments; and he quotes several times from his own earlier *Quaestiones* (e.g. pp. 64, 97, 113, 138). It can only be supposed, therefore, that Little places it among Bacon's doubtful works (*Essays* . . . p. 408, item 40) because he had not in 1914 yet been able to examine the text of the MS. which was not printed till 1935.

and not 'on account of weakness or powerlessness or any defect on the part of the Creator'. He could produce without a medium if He wished; but He does not wish. And not only would He communicate His goodness to His creatures, but would even communicate more so that they could hand it on. Likewise He could keep creation going by Himself if He wished. But 'I say that in some operations He acts through a medium for the sake of order . . . and not only can He Himself rule, but even one creature can rule another. But no creature could bridge the infinite gap between something and nothing'.[1]

(*b*) William objects to what he calls the 'cultus stellarum', and all who say that the world or stars are ensouled. He complains of Avicenna, who said that the world was an animal obedient to God, and of 'Aristotle and all his followers who claimed that the heavens were animals, and allowed them to be of a separate substance and endowed with intelligence'.[2]

Bacon is quite specific on this point, discussing the two questions directly since they arise out of the text of the pseudo-Aristotelian *De plantis*. Is the sky a 'noble animal', as his text says, or has it life? In favour of this idea is his text, and many other philosophers, as he tells us. Aristotle also says in his *Physics* that self-motion is animal motion; the sky moves by itself, therefore it is an animal motion. Against this theory is the argument that the animal is only an animal because of its capacity for sense-perception which the sky does not have. Bacon defends Aristotle by saying that he is not here giving his own opinion, but the opinion of others. And for the rest, the sky does not move by its own power, but by communicated motion from a created or an uncreated intelligence. On the question of its life, the same answer is given. It is its movement that makes us say it has life; but it is the most noble life of *its* mover that communicates motion to it, and the sky itself is only an instrumental cause of the further movement of inferiors.[3]

William does not like the idea that it is a 'natural' thing for human beings to have a soul, and that it came into existence *per generationem*, and not by a special creation.[4]

On this point again we have a specific treatment from Bacon. 'Substantial form', he says, 'is induced immediately, but we can speak of a generation which is the last transmutation and introduction, and this takes place in an instant'. There is a 'successive transmutation in

[1] Steele, Fasc. XII, pp. 105–7.
[2] William of Auvergne, *Opera* . . . I, 77 (*De legibus*).
[3] Steele, Fasc. XI, 190–91.
[4] William of Auvergne, *Opera* . . . II, Supp. p. 65 (*De anima*).

time before the sudden introduction of substantial form'. Nature operates in accordance with its own power and the nature of things, but there is an *intensio potentiae ex nichilo* when creation takes place, and this is what happens in the case of the introduction of substantial form or the soul.[1]

The above are a few of William's objections. With a more thorough examination of his very extensive work, more would no doubt be uncovered. But this, while possibly an interesting study in itself, lies outside the scope of this study, and would altogether unbalance it, to the neglect of Bacon's own work in which we are primarily interested. It has only been intended to show how well Bacon conformed at this period of his life to the standpoint of the Bishop of Paris, and how far he was from any views that could be considered heretical or dangerous, and thus how suited he was for a position as pioneer lecturer in the natural philosophy of Aristotle; and how impossible it is that he could be considered, at this time, as a rebel against authority and his scholastic contemporaries.

4. *The value of dream interpretations.*

Bacon himself states that the books of Aristotle were banned on account of the arguments for the eternity of the world, and because of Aristotle's remarks in the third book of the *De somno et vigilia.*[2]

Before coming to the great question of the eternity of the world it may be mentioned that there might well have been objections to Aristotle's writings on the divination of dreams which occur in this book, but it is difficult to think that the whole of the natural scientific work of Aristotle could have been banned for such a small reason. Aristotle argues in his naturalistic way that 'it is not easy to take dreams seriously and to believe them'. They are merely natural movements, and if they happen to correspond to what actually occurs later, this is better to be explained as coincidence. It is clear from observation that animals have them, and the weak-minded person is more likely to have them than the wise. If, then, it had been God who sent them, for a definite purpose, why would He not have chosen to give them more to the wise, and in the daytime? It seems an inefficient method of revealing the future if that had been God's intention. Dreams are a confused picture of ordinary daytime events, like pictures we see mirrored in water, and the best interpreter is one who is able to relate them to the daytime experiences on which they

[1] Steele, Fasc. XIII, 29–30. [2] *CST*, p. 33.

are based, or, as Aristotle calls it, the confused 'motion' to the actual 'motion'.[1]

Such brilliant common sense must have been hard to take in the medieval world which, on the whole, believed so strongly in the divinely-sent dreams of the biblical characters, if not in their own. The practice of divining the dreams of contemporary men is sometimes supported and sometimes condemned by the writers of the twelfth and thirteenth centuries. Albertus Magnus defends Aristotle's view as superior to other opinions on dreams, though he also finds it 'naïve, unphilosophical and imperfect'. But he does not suggest that ordinary dreams come from God, preferring to take the side of Aristotle in this.[2] He finds that Aristotle was too sceptical of dream interpretation since certain dreams can be interpreted. According to Professor Thorndike, Albert 'seems to have had no particular objection, either moral or religious, to the interpretation of dreams even if it is a branch of magic'. It seems, however, unlikely that punitive action would have been taken against the whole of the Master's works for such slight reason. There would be much disagreement with Aristotle's views amongst the strict upholders of biblical inspiration; but it would be easy to say that Aristotle, being a pagan, could not know about the rare occasions when dreams were sent by God. Though I have found no specific comment on the subject in Bacon, I believe this would be his attitude—if he did not content himself with saying that the *De somno et vigilia* was either incomplete, or too badly translated to be of value in ascertaining Aristotle's real views!

5. *The eternity of the world.*

There can be little doubt that this was the central problem of the time, and remained so until 'Averroism', the doctrine of the single intellectual soul for all human beings, came into importance during the second half of the century. It was the chief obstacle to any belief in the infallibility of Aristotle. If anyone held that the world had not been created, then it followed that the book of Genesis was not true—which belief was heretical. There is no doubt that it was the general opinion in the thirteenth century that Aristotle had, in fact, denied creation. And this appears even in the famous 'Platonic' passage in *XII Metaphysics*, where Aristotle hypostasizes the logically necessary first mover as God, and proceeds to predicate qualities of him. But he

[1] Aristotle, *De somno et vigilia* iii, 462*b*–464*b*.

[2] Thorndike, *History of Magic* . . . II, 575–77. The question is also discussed in connection with several other thinkers of the period. See index, sub. Dreams.

still does not become a creator, and the other famous passage in *VIII Physics* seems even more definite.[1]

William of Auvergne is most forthright on the matter. 'Whatever may be said, and whoever may try to excuse Aristotle, this undoubtedly was his opinion that the world is eternal and that it never had a beginning, that he thought likewise about motion, and Avicenna after him, and they adduced reasons and proofs of this. Similarly other expounders of Aristotle'.[2] After devoting several pages of argument to refuting these views and others to be deduced from them, William proceeds to give ethical and moral reasons against the eternity of the world. He spends more space in attacking this than upon any other problem in his *De universo*.

Albertus Magnus in his commentaries on the *Physics* and *Metaphysics* never actually says that it was the opinion of Aristotle that the world was *ab eterno*, but by using Aristotelian methods and arguments he tries to show that it is not necessary to accept this eternity. Nothing, he says, can come from nothing *per generationem*, but something comes from nothing *per actum causantis*. Generation is always *per accidens*, which presupposes a prior generation *per se*; prime matter cannot take on form without an agent, though it is in potency *per se*. But the chief Peripatetics do not deny that the essence of prime matter and substantial form is 'drawn forth into being by God', and even Aristotle in his (?) book *De natura deorum* says that the world was created by 'God the Artisan' (a deo opifice).[3]

Elsewhere Albert says that on this subject we should not proceed from things proved, or known *per se*, but we should rather 'transcend' those things which cannot be comprehended by reason—such as creation, and the method of creating everything at one and the same time. The physicist must prove that *naturaliter* motion must begin, and *naturaliter* it will never come to an end.[4] Then Albert promises that in his book on the *Metaphysics* he will show by good arguments (verisimilibus rationibus) that 'the world was created and not ab eterno'. But in the relevant passages in his commentaries on the

[1] Michael Scot is careful to dissociate himself from the views of Averroes and Aristotle, whom he had translated. In his general preface to three treatises on astrology he says: 'Ob hand causam dicunt multi quod mundus sit ab eterno . . . et quod mundus non sit eternus patet aperte'. Quoted by Haskins, *Studies in the History* . . . (1924), p. 285.

[2] William of Auvergne, *Opera* . . . I, 690 ff. (*De universo*). Cf. I, 34 (*De legibus*): 'Error Aristotelis quo posuit aeternitatem mundi.'

[3] Albertus Magnus, *Opera* . . . III, 530 (VIII *Phys.* Tr. I, cap. iv).

[4] Albertus Magnus, *Opera* . . . III, 524 (VIII *Phys.* Tr. I, cap. i–ii). 'Non procederemus et probatis vel per se notis, sed potius transcenderemus ea quae ratione non valent comprehendi. . . .'

Metaphysics[1] he refers back to the *Physics*, and as far as I have been able to discover he never makes his proof. Thomas Aquinas, on the other hand, admits freely that creation cannot be proved *naturaliter*, but only through revelation.[2] Bonaventura and Philip the Chancellor, while believing in creation themselves, thought Aristotle did also, and Bonaventura in particular strongly defends Aristotle from those who claimed that he had posited a world *ab eterno*.[3]

Bacon also thought that Aristotle actually allowed creation, though frequently in the course of his long discussion of the subject it might seem to a twentieth-century reader that the opposite is shown by the very passages of Aristotle that he quotes. In the course of the arguments he valiantly tries to stick to his philosophy, but every now and then he inserts illegitimately arguments into the discussion that are drawn from his religious beliefs. His students, if it was indeed the actual students who expressed the doubts and queries, give him little peace; and the considerable space that Bacon devotes to the discussion shows how important the problem was, and how necessary it was to deal with it exhaustively. His anxiety to save the letter of Aristotle is everywhere apparent, and remains with him through his later life, though, as we shall see, in later years his reasons were different. In the process Averroes, who had taken it for granted that Aristotle had denied creation, comes in for some severe criticism, and is made the scapegoat for Aristotle's errors. Later Bacon is able to blame the translations, but this magnificent idea has not yet occurred to him.[4]

Though the problem is touched on lightly in several other passages, the main discussion, as might be expected, occurs in the consideration of the text of Aristotle's *Physics*, book VIII. In Bacon's earlier series of comments on the *Physics* he does not reach the eighth book, so that we have only one set of comments on the eternity of the world. But fifty-eight of the pages in Steele's edition are devoted to it, and nearly every argument that could be thought up seems to be used.[5]

It is impossible in this study to go into the whole discussion and Bacon's attempt to handle it, extremely interesting though it is, and revealing the vitality of Bacon's reasoning power at this time, the

[1] Albertus Magnus, *Opera* . . . VI, 611 (XI *Met.*, Tr. II, cap. i).

[2] Thomas Aquinas, *Summa Theologica*, I, Q. XLVI, Art. ii.

[3] See the passages quoted by F. Delorme in Steele, Fasc. XIII, xxxvi, and the special study of Bonaventura contained in Van Steenberghen, *Siger de Brabant* . . . pp. 446–58.

[4] 'The Commentator speaks falsely and does not understand Aristotle because he always imposes on Aristotle that he meant the world was eternal which is false. Because the world was made and is not eternal. 'Non tamen recipitur, si factus est, in vacuum nec in plenum sed in nichil, et ideo mundus non est eternus secundum Aristotelem et veritatem'. Steele, Fasc. XIII, 223.

[5] Steele, Fasc. XIII, 370–428.

depth of his faith, and the bewildering variety of arguments at his disposal. What are we to say of this argument? If God created the world at all, why wasn't the reason for creating it always there? Doesn't this make it a creation *per accidens*? If He couldn't create it in a determined time, then this detracts from His omnipotence. *Quod concedendum est*! The principle of sufficient reason. If there was sufficient reason for creating the world at all, this reason always existed, and so why not the world? To which Bacon can only reply that this principle only applies *in naturalibus*, and is not valid in cases that involve the will, nor must a cause of God's will be sought.[1]

Again he gets into trouble on eternity and time. Creation supposes non-being before being. But time is the measure of motion, as the point of transition took place in time. 'If non-being terminated in being, then being is subsequent to non-being. When there is a before and an after, then there is time'. If there is time then there must be motion, because motion is the measure of time. So time was before motion. Time then must be eternal.'[2] One cannot escape the conclusion that Bacon had a real problem on his hands, and the 'students' for the most part seem to have the best of it. If only he could have been allowed a world *ab eterno* one thinks he would have been far happier—in his reason if not his faith! This argument on time he clinches for himself by saying that if nature came into being, it must be in time; this must be understood to refer to the things which can be measured, not to the measures themselves (i.e. time).

As to whether the world will last for ever, Bacon says that for anything to have an infinite duration it must have an infinite 'virtue', and this the world does not have—though the primal cause, if it continues to fill it with 'virtue', *could* make it possible. But the eternity of the primal cause does not extend to created beings. So the world receives 'virtue' *modo finito*; it cannot last for ever, but it can be prolonged indefinitely. The primal cause could cease now to move the world, though it does not—and here Bacon inserts illegitimately an argument from Scripture that it will cease when the number of the elect is complete.[3]

Finally he comes to Aristotle. 'It is seen', he says, '*per intentionem eius* that he has suggested nothing against the faith. For he says there

[1] 'Non valet in voluntariis nec est querenda causa sue voluntatis'. Steele, Fasc. XIII, 376–79.

[2] Steele, Fasc. XIII, 380.

[3] Steele, Fasc. XIII, 382–83. This argument about the elect has already been used to show that generation is not perpetual either (*ibid.*, p. 377). The number of the elect, of course, refers to the 144,000 of the Book of Revelation (chap. vii). Presumably there is no limit to the number of the damned who will comprise all the remainder.

will have been no motion when there was no time; so he only meant that motion did not begin in time, which is true. Aristotle argues elsewhere that there must be a first of everything or there would be no later things, so why not a beginning of the world? It is a natural deduction from his *Metaphysics*. But no one can blame Aristotle or any philosopher for saying there is no end to the world or motion, because this is not to be proved philosophically, though they do assume a beginning'. On the other hand, Bacon goes on—and this is his supreme piece of apologetics for the Master—Aristotle does say in his *Ethics* that 'we shall be happy like the angels, but not in life, for happiness is after death . . . this can only be if we posit the resurrection of the body, and this will not be until the number of the elect is filled. So', he concludes triumphantly, 'it is clear that Aristotle well understood that motion comes to an end!'[1]

Even now the 'students' will not let him go. Assuming that the world is not *ab eterno*, nor motion, nor even time, might it be possible, they ask, that the world *could* have been from eternity although it was not, according to the truth![2]

But even to this temptation Bacon will not yield. Everything, he says, came from either something or nothing. Which raises the question, what was this something? It, too, must come from either something or nothing, and so *ad infinitum*. So ultimately only one thing can be from eternity, and more are impossible. It is not only by faith that we are led to this, but even by reason. And this it was that Aristotle and the other philosophers meant, and Aristotle did not put forward reasons for showing the world or motion was eternal, except against those who said that motion began in time.

After considering the care with which Bacon has gone over this argument I cannot think that it is only an apologetic. He believed in creation, and, in spite of his lapses from philosophy to faith, was prepared to defend it publicly by philosophical and metaphysical arguments, from which even later philosophers of greater renown shrank. It is surely possible that Bacon was permitted to teach Aristotle publicly just because he had a philosophical answer. In his old age, as we have seen, he picks out just this eternity of the world as the main reason for the prohibition. Could it be that it was fixed in his mind as the central point in his own teaching, and the reason for his appointment?

[1] Steele, Fasc. XIII, 389.

[2] Steele, Fasc. XIII, 390. It is this really outrageous question that tempts me to think that these were real students, and not only the *döppelganger* of the professor.

III

As a result of a careful examination of the works they edited in their fine edition of the hitherto unedited works of Bacon, Steele and Delorme came to the conclusion that at least twelve series of lectures on the *libri naturales* and *Metaphysics*, including the pseudo-Aristotelian books on plants and 'causes', were given by Bacon in Paris. Eight have been printed, and the other four are only known from cross-references, and no MSS. are known for them. But these editors have also printed another work, which was not ascribed to Bacon in any bibliography, and does not bear his name on the MS.[1] It is not a series of *quaestiones*, but a regular textual commentary on Aristotle's *De sensu et sensibili* (or *sensato*, as Bacon calls it), and appears, not in MS. Amiens 406, like the *Quaestiones*, but in BM Add 8786. Except for the *Perspectiva communis* of John Peckham, all the other works in this MS. are by Bacon. A discussion of the genuineness of this work, the reasons why I attribute it to Bacon, and some of its characteristics, are given in Appendix C below.

Steele, in his introduction to this work, tentatively places it as 'later than the *Quaestiones* of Amiens 406, but before the first draft of the *Communia naturalium*, and most certainly before his *Perspectiva*, as shown by the much greater range of quotation in the corresponding parts of the latter'.[2] While not minimizing the significance of the greater range of quotation, for reasons given in the Appendix I am inclined to put this commentary even earlier, and actually within the Parisian period. There are no other certainly known commentaries of Bacon, as distinct from series of questions, but Little in his bibliography draws attention to the fact that there used to be in St. Augustine's Abbey at Canterbury a commentary on the *De somno et vigilia* of Aristotle, and this was attributed in the MS. to Bacon. Unfortunately the MS. has now disappeared.[3] We do not know therefore whether it was, indeed, a commentary by Bacon or whether it was Albert's more well-known commentary of the same title. But it may have been Bacon's.

Now there is no real reason to suppose that the Parisian books referred to by Bacon in his various series of *Quaestiones* were actually books of questions at all. In his cross-references Bacon always calls

[1] Steele, Fasc. XIV, 1–134.
[2] *Ibid.*, Fasc. XIV, v.
[3] Little, *Essays* . . . p. 408, item 41. The tract is No. 834 in the catalogue of M. R. James.

them 'books'. There may well have been a commentary on the *De generatione*, on the *De animalibus*, or the *De coelo et mundo*, or on each of these. Delorme, in his list of the Parisian courses, calls them *Quaestiones supra librum de generatione*, etc., but this is his own inference from Bacon's remarks. He could have written commentaries, as well as *quaestiones*, for his Parisian lectures.

If Bacon did, indeed, write a number of close textual commentaries of the type of the *De sensu et sensato*, this could supply a reason for the omission of some of his Parisian material from the huge MS. Amiens 406 which contains the *Quaestiones*. The ex-student or scribe who collected the *Quaestiones* from the booksellers of Paris and had the copy made[1] might have been only interested in the *Quaestiones* because he attended the lectures. The commentaries fall into a different category, far less lively, if no more closely worked out. The missing four books are all on the shorter works of Aristotle, nearer to natural science and further from metaphysics. It is quite possible that Bacon chose a different method for dealing with these shorter works, and wrote commentaries rather than *quaestiones* on them. Though this is only a hypothesis and cannot be confirmed until some of these missing works are discovered, I am tentatively changing Delorme's list of the courses given by Bacon on the *libri naturales*, and making a separate one for the missing books and the known commentaries. The chronological order has been compiled by Delorme from internal evidence, especially cross-references.[2]

1.	Quaestiones prime supra libros Physicorum.		(Fasc. VIII, 1–266)
2.	,,	supra undecimum prime philosophie.	(,, VII, 1–122)
3.	,,	,, IV libros ,, ,,	(,, XI, 1–170)
4.	,,	altere supra XI libros ,, ,,	(,, VII, 125–51)
5.	,,	,, ,, libros Physicorum.	(,, XIII, 1–428)
6.	,,	,, ,, ,, prime philosophie.	(,, X, 1–336)
7.	,,	supra librum de plantis.	(,, XI, 173–252)
8.	,,	,, ,, ,, causis.	(,, XII, 1–158)

The commentaries would then be as follows. The order can be placed by references in the *Quaestiones*, except for the *De sensu et sensato*, and the *De somno et vigilia*. There are, however, in the former commentary two apparent references to what seems to be Bacon's book on the *De generatione*, and not to Aristotle's book of the same

[1] For this hypothesis of Steele's see below, p. 63.
[2] Steele, Fasc. XIII, xxx–xxxi.

name.[1] This would establish a relative date, placing the *De sensu* after the *De generatione*.

1. Commentarium supra librum de generatione et corruptione.
2. " " XVIII libros de animalibus.
3. " " librum de anima.
4. " " " de coelo et mundo.
5. " " " de sensu et sensato.
6. " " " de somno et vigilia.[2]

In addition to these scientific works there is reason to suppose that several works on logic and grammar, required courses for the degree in the Faculty of Arts, were also given by Bacon at this time. The following seem to belong to this period: the *Summa grammatica*,[3] the *Sumulae dialectices*,[4] and the *Summa de sophismatibus et destructionibus*.[5] These courses may have been given at any time during Bacon's career at Paris. Steele places the *Sumulae dialectices* as the last work of Bacon's university career, though he does not state his reasons.[6] It might be considered more likely that he would give at least the elementary courses in logic and grammar before natural philosophy, since this was the usual *cursus studiorum* at Bologna and other universities.

Without knowing the length of the missing works, nor what others there may have been that have not yet been found or examined, it is impossible to determine how many years' work was needed for all these courses. But it does not seem likely that it can have been fewer than seven, and it might have been spread over more than a decade.

The method of treating problems adopted by Bacon[7] had developed

[1] See Appendix C below, p. 232.

[2] The first four of these are not at present known, the fifth has been printed by Steele in Fasc. XIV, and the sixth has been lost, but was formerly at St. Augustine's Abbey, Canterbury.

[3] Steele, Fasc. XV, 1–190. This course is obviously given in connection with the required study of Priscian's *De constructionibus*. The first *quaestio* of the book begins with the definition of the central theme *De constructione*. Priscian himself is quoted on the first page.

[4] Steele, Fasc. XV, 193–359. There have been doubts of the authenticity of this logical discussion. But an interesting argument *De appelatione* recalls, as its editor suggests, Bacon's later treatment of the same problem in connection with Richard of Cornwall (xx–xxii); and there are no special reasons otherwise for doubting it. Bacon will in any case have been expected to give lectures on logic at Paris.

[5] Steele, Fasc. XIV, 135–208. This book gives instructions on how to deal with one group of *sophismata*, those universal distributive propositions which have an indefinite extension. There are many interesting discussions in the book, such as on equivocal and univocal propositions, composition and division, etc. I noticed a specially valuable one on the uses of the word *omnis*. But I have not, for the purposes of this study, considered any of these logical and grammatical works in detail.

[6] Steele, Fasc. XV, xx.

[7] The method is formally discussed in Bacon's *Summa de sophismatibus et destructionibus*. Steele, Fasc. XIV, 135–208.

in the European schools over a period of more than a hundred years. First a question is posed or a doubt raised. Then the argument begins with a 'quod sic videtur' or 'quod non videtur'. If there is more than one argument on the same side they are tabulated in order, item . . . item, with perhaps an occasional 'nota'. Then follow the arguments on the other side (contra). If these are accepted, the master gives a 'quod concedendum est', followed by an answering of the objections raised on the other side. Or, if there is something to be said on both sides, nothing is conceded, but a *solutio* is given, and objections are answered.

There is an extraordinary intellectual honesty about this approach, which is difficult to reconcile with the prevalent idea that medieval scholars were slavishly subservient to authority. While the solution of the master no doubt had to be accepted, it was certainly not for the want of considering the arguments put on the other side. A thirteenth-century student might prefer the arguments brought forward by the prosecution, and we to-day may think in some instances that the master's solution was not the best of those suggested. It looks, however, as if the student had a remedy; he could put the next question, and force a restating of the arguments in slightly different form. It may be added that in Bacon's *Quaestiones*, though authorities may be quoted on either side, they are never decisive, and it is always the argument itself and not the master who propounded it that must prevail.

In reading the commentaries of Thomas Aquinas one does not have the same impression as with Bacon's that students were actively participating. St. Thomas seems to be creating his own opposition, and sometimes allows himself to have too easily the best of the argument. But one can feel the pressure being put upon Bacon by intelligent and experienced students, and sometimes, rather patently, he does not have the best of the argument. In a discussion on the soul of plants that will be given below in some detail as an example of Bacon's method and ingenuity, it is clear that he had to change his original views in response to the new questions that were fired at him. I do not think there can be much doubt that these *Quaestiones* consist of actual discussions, no doubt, as Delorme says, 'revu par le professeur et mis au point',[1] but substantially as they were delivered, and not as they were lucubrated in the silent study or cell of the master. This is confirmed by the frequency with which Bacon drops into the vocative case (tu obicis); and I think there is a difference also between

[1] Steele, Fasc. VIII, vi.

the formal 'queritur' and the less frequent 'dubitatur' The latter seems to cover cases where more doubt may have been expressed on the problem by the students themselves. And some of the questions are so amusing (as, for instance, the one mentioned on p. 58 above) that only the students can be blamed for them, preserving their doubts for posterity. They are, in short, just the questions you or I would ask in a similar class if we wanted to push the professor into a corner! On the other hand the students can hardly have had as much detailed information on the works of Aristotle as is contained in the various questions, or they would not have been still students in a fairly elementary course. So the editing by the professor must have been considerably more than mere revision for publication. My conclusion would, therefore, be that the form and substance of the original discussions have been retained, but that the professor took care to increase their value for the scholarly public by adding copiously from his own erudition.

Reference was made above (p. 63) to a suggestion of Steele that the huge MS. Amiens 406 was compiled towards the end of the thirteenth century by an ex-student of Bacon who had remembered his master's courses with gratitude, and went round to the Parisian booksellers picking up any copies that were still available, and collecting them within one MS. This would account for the incompleteness of several of the series, especially the *De causis*, since by that time some of the works could not be found. The existence of the MS. must in any case be explained by some hypothesis, and this would fit all the known facts excellently.[1] There is no reason to suppose that Bacon's philosophical opinions were ever taken very seriously by the important scholastics of the time, and he certainly never became an authority in the schools. He was only one of many masters teaching the same subject, and he was still young and probably of only local reputation. These *Quaestiones* cannot be shown to have ever been quoted elsewhere; but Bacon's own pupil might have remembered them. There is certainly no other series available in print which gives so much the impressive of actual discussion in the classroom, and they constitute a mine of information on the methods and subjects discussed there in the first half of the thirteenth century. It is, therefore, perhaps for the history of education that they offer the most material for study.

As for the master who gave them, they show us first his really outstanding knowledge of Aristotle, even if he has not always

[1] Steele, Fasc. XII, xv.

understood him,[1] but not so wide a knowledge of his commentators as he later acquired.[2] On the other hand it was hardly necessary for him to know, say, the *Canon* of Avicenna for his classes in philosophy, and there are a few quotations from the first book in his commentary on the *De sensu et sensato* where such knowledge would be valuable. His vitality of mind and his ingenuity are most stimulating, though this was probably a characteristic of the period, and a natural result of this particular kind of education.

I have, on the other hand, noticed very few references to his own experience, though they are not altogether missing. In one argument on astronomy, for instance, he says that something is 'according to sense and Aristotle'.[3] His knowledge of things of common observation in the plant world is brought in not only in his special philosophical discussion of plants, but in his examination of the powers of nature.[4] He has a few interesting things to say on astronomy, and shows some knowledge of this science, though nothing on astrology. As Steele points out in his essay on the science of Roger Bacon, his astronomy uses only the oldest authorities, which were already out of date by the time of his lectures, and is unaware of those used by his supposed master, Robert Grosseteste.[5] This is partly remedied during the course of the lectures. In the second series on the *Physics* there are several discussions on light, as also in the later *De causis*, while they are missing in the first series on the *Physics* which covers the same material.[6] In fact, this second series in is every way better, fuller, more interesting and authoritative than the first, and shows considerable development in the powers of the master over the years, and justifies his own later statement that he 'had always been studious'.

In conclusion it is perhaps worth while going into some detail on Bacon's manner of dealing with a subject which obviously offers interesting possibilities, and has already been referred to briefly (p. 23). When a plant is grafted, what happens to its vegetative soul,

[1] The references are very accurate, as befits a teaching master, and greatly superior to what we find in the works of his maturity.

[2] The quotations from Averroes increase in the later lectures; the second series on the *Physics* (Fasc. XIII) has many more than the first (Fasc. VIII).

[3] Steele, Fasc. XIII, 420.

[4] For example, the delightful discussion of whether a sport (monstrum) in a plant is the result of sin, and if the plant can, in fact, sin. (It can't!) The students, to judge by the questions Bacon answers, have a similar knowledge of common animals, reminding us of the usual rural background in this age.

[5] Steele, 'Roger Bacon and the State of Science ...' (1921), pp. 130–31.

[6] Steele, Fasc. XIII, 206, Fasc. XII, 52. In another place, commenting on the *Metaphysics* (Fasc. X, 153), Bacon states on one side of the question that Al Hazen and Aristotle are more to be believed than Boethius and Augustine, and then proceeds to show that the problem is also to be solved in the sense of Augustine.

and what kind of a soul has the new plant? The difficulty has a certain added spice because Bacon has no Aristotelian or even pseudo-Aristotelian authority to fall back upon.

The first question asks whether it is possible to insert a part of one plant into another, so that both continue living.[1] Bacon answers that he knows from experience that it can be done, and Aristotle agrees—though part of an animal cannot be inserted in the same way into another animal. Parts of animals, say Aristotle and Bacon, unaware of facial surgery, lose their life when separated from the original organism. But the plant still has roots and organs which make it possible for it to continue its life afterwards.

The Opposition (students or döppelganger): Does the graft, then, receive a new soul? It can't retain its old one, or there would be two souls in the new plant. If so, when? After it has been inserted, and before the fruit and flowers? On the other hand, as the effects are the same, it must come from the same cause—i.e. it keeps its old soul.

Bacon sustains the objection. The old plant would die if the climate were too different or it were transported too far. But, then, this would be the fault of the new locality and not of the change *per se*. As it does not, therefore, lose its old life, it cannot need a new soul.

The Opposition: What about the plant into which it is inserted? Does *it* need a new soul? The trunk is now going to produce a new species of fruit. How can it do this, with its old soul? On the other hand, the trunk would make its own fruit without this interference, and the graft makes its own. Both are bearing at the same time from the same tree.

Bacon concedes this point also, but doubt remains. 'Dubium est tamen in aliquibus'. The solution follows. The formal cause is two-fold. Either the true form which gives actuality to the material is its own, in which case the matter is transformed into a new species, and then the trunk is not the true matter; or the formal cause is not the form and perfection of the tree on which it is grafted, but it is only called the formal cause *per appositionem*. And thus we must not say that such material is transformed into another species, but rather that the trunk has its own form and material, different from the form of the graft.

The Opposition refuses to accept this. One of the souls, either of the graft or of the trunk, must be corrupted. A fundamental conception of Aristotle is urged against the professor. 'Everything which is

[1] Steele, Fasc. XI, 243–51.

received in something is received according to the mode of the receiver and not the thing received'.[1]

At this point it looks as if the master begins to flounder. At all events his arguments fall thickly one after the other. A staggering blow is received from the student, if he was a student, who reminds him that 'the slave receives from the master and vice versa. The graft receives from the trunk as from a servant, and from the root. The trunk alone is a servant, and receives from the graft as from a lord! So—is the nature of the trunk turned into the nature of the graft?' Aristotle's *Metaphysics* is quoted. 'The living does not come from the dead except through resolution into prime matter'—which does not happen in this case. So how can the old, dead trunk get a new soul without such resolution? On the other hand, no new branches of this kind will spring up if the graft is not inserted.

Bacon hedges. 'Prime matter', he says, 'may only mean proximate matter', and not *omnino remota*; and the old tree is only received into *materiam communem proximam*, which is common in the transmutation of the dead and living, and as happens, indeed, in the transmutation of elements.

The Opposition again offers the *Metaphysics* in rebuttal. 'Out of matter and form is made one thing *per essentiam*'.[2] The trunk is the material. Can the shoot be the only form required for the new substance? And where has the first form gone to? Are they not both form, and both *in actu*, the old and the new alike?

Bacon at last gives way; but it is certainly not what he said so easily at the beginning. There always remain, he says, two forms which make diverse fruits and leaves 'vel secundum speciem vel secundum numerum'. Both retain their own soul, when one is not fully converted into the other's nature.

This decision Bacon sticks to, in spite of some further efforts by the Opposition. The new formula he has found, whatever the philosophical difficulties, seems to have been forced upon him by the facts, and it even suffices to cover the grafting of different species of plants altogether. The master has changed his mind.

[1] 'Omne quod recipitur in aliquo recipitur ad modum recipientis et non per modum recepti.'
[2] 'Ex materia et forma fit unum per essentiam.'

CHAPTER V

THE PROMISED LAND—VISION OF A UNIVERSAL SCIENCE

IN the twenty years or less between Bacon's departure from the University of Paris and the writing of the *Opus Majus*, only one work can be dated with certainty, the *Computus*, in which Bacon mentions 1263, 1264, and 1265 as being the current year of writing.[1] Other works we know were written in these years, and in a later chapter we shall attempt to establish a chronology for them. The total activity of these years must be pieced together from Bacon's own statements written in 1267 and afterwards. We also know from the *Opus Majus* that he saw the leader of the Pastoureaux rebels in Paris in 1250 or 1251;[2] but we do not know from this whether he was teaching or had just finished teaching there. It certainly is not possible to infer that he had *remained* in Paris because he was able to witness this event'.[3]

In order to build a possible chronology it is proposed here to take into consideration not only the works which can with confidence be ascribed to this period, and not only his own direct statements, but the psychological probabilities which may serve to show *how* he could have written his works—the intellectual and spiritual development in the man himself and the influence of external events in his own life and the life of the time. This procedure must necessarily be based on our understanding of his total character as it is shown by his works. We have no contemporary evaluation of him. There are, in fact, no references to him in any contemporary writer except one trivial anecdote by an unknown chronicler of no importance.[4] An occasional remark in the works of Albertus Magnus has been taken to apply to him. But the reference is by no means certain, and Bacon is not mentioned by name.[5]

[1] Steele, Fasc. VI, 17, 32, 165, 192, 196.

[2] *Opus Majus*, I, 401.

[3] Bridges makes this inference. *The Life and Work . . .* (1914), pp. 25–26.

[4] Anon, *Liber exemplorum*, p. 22.

[5] Bacon's name does not appear in the published letters of either Adam Marsh or Robert Grosseteste, whom he reveres; nor in local English chronicles or the more elaborate histories of Matthew Paris; nor yet in the list of the important figures (personae valentes in saeculo) who joined the Franciscan Order in the thirteenth century, published by Brewer, *Monumenta Franciscana* (1858), I, 541–43. The curious misprint (?) in Luard's edition of Grosseteste's

Bacon himself sometimes referred to his contemporaries by name when he was attacking or praising them. But this was by no means the usual medieval practice outside the chronicles and histories. Much more usual is the plain 'quidam'. The vast bulk of our knowledge of medieval personalities comes from their own work, and is a matter primarily of inference. Later legend is particularly unreliable in regard to Bacon, because before very long all real knowledge of him seems to have been lost and he was regarded as a necromancer and magician; and fancy and subjective opinion took the place of fact.

Perhaps the one important inference to be made from this lack of contemporary information is that Bacon was a person of no particular importance to his contemporaries. He was one of many regent masters in the Faculty of Arts in Paris, he was a rather obscure student of sciences at Oxford, and then a friar who was certainly not treated as of any consequence—totally unlike Alexander of Hales who, according to Bacon's own account, was treated with such exaggerated respect by the Order and whose entry brought it such renown.[1] Bacon may have been well enough known in the universities, though we have only his own word for it;[2] but, as so many academicians at all times, not so well known to the public and to chroniclers and historians.

If it is urged that he was well enough known in small circles to receive the honour of a request from Pope Clement IV for his opinions, this may well have been the result in the first instance, as will be shown later, of an initiative taken by Roger himself. His proposal was transmitted through a personal friend who happened to be in the employ of Cardinal Foulques, as he then was before becoming Pope. This resulted in a request from the Cardinal with which Roger was unable to comply. But when the Cardinal became Pope, Bacon again took the initiative, this time sending his message through an English envoy who was presumably known to him. The Pope was still interested, and sent Bacon the important mandate which he obeyed in due course.[3]

letters (p. 64) may be mentioned here. It is impossible that the text, which reads 'fratre Rogero Bachun' can be correct, as the letter refers to Grosseteste's recent appointment to his bishopric (meae novitati), and Bacon is quoted in the passage as an authority, and called 'frater', which he cannot possibly have been in 1236. Robert Bacon was surely meant, and, indeed, Luard gives 'Robert' for this passage in the index.

[1] *Opus Minus*, p. 326.

[2] He speaks of himself as exiled in his convent, from his former University fame. 'Jam a decem annis exulantem usque ad famam studii, quam retroactis temporibus obtinui.' Brewer, *Op. Tert.*, p. 7.

[3] Little, *Essays*, p. 10. Gasquet, p. 500. See below, pp. 146 ff.

None of this gives us any grounds for believing that the Cardinal would ever have heard of Bacon by reputation. Indeed, we can be reasonably sure that he would never have become known at all in such high ecclesiastical circles if it had not been for his own initiative and that of his friends. I do not wish to imply that Bacon was deliberately neglected, much less opposed, by the great men of his time, with a possible exception which will be mentioned later. He was simply a relatively obscure Englishman, working in a field which did not bring him into much notice. And it is usually a private demand from a friend or relative that calls forth his writings.[1] Indeed, it will be suggested that the desire to obtain more recognition and assistance was one of his reasons for becoming a friar.

For it is clear from all his work that he was not meek or retiring by nature. He liked being a teacher, and he thought himself a good one, much better than his contemporaries.[2] As suggested earlier, he wanted desperately to be considered an authority, and was jealous of everyone who was accepted as such. He was proud of his ability, and like most writers of the time, had a profound contempt for the 'common run of students and philosophizers' (vulgus studentium et philosophantium). It is our contention that he ruined his chances of fulfilling his ambitions by not choosing the one academic study that he believed could have brought him into real prominence; and that the substitute he chose, however strongly he advertised its value, did not bring him the fame he sought. This, more than all the difficulties he had from his poverty and neglect and possible persecution within the Franciscan Order, made him the embittered man he was in 1272 when he wrote the *Compendium studii philosophiae*, which should have been the masterpiece of his life, but is in its present form nothing but a

[1] His *Liber de retardatione accidentium* was written at the suggestion of two acquaintances as being something in which an elderly pope and prince would be interested (*supra*, p. 24, n. 4), and he states that he would have composed books for his brother the scholar, and many other dear friends if, as a friar, he could have communicated freely (Brewer, *Op. Tert.*, p. 13), and he did compose 'a few chapters on one science and another at the insistence of friends' (Gasquet, p. 500).

I cannot agree with Professor Thorndike that his writings, instead of being neglected by his age, 'are so valued that they are pirated before they are published' (*History of Magic* . . . pp. 626–27). What Bacon says is that it is unsafe to let scribes handle the work because they 'transcriberent pro se, vel aliis, vellem nollem, sicut saepissime scripta per fraudes scriptorum Parisius divulgantur' (Gasquet, p. 500). Surely Bacon is here speaking of the current practice; and he cannot risk this, not because his writings are so popular, but because the Pope has asked for them to be sent secretly. He does not say 'scripta mea', but just 'scripta' in general.

[2] See especially his remarks on the speed and efficiency with which he could teach languages that had taken him years to learn (Brewer, *Op. Tert.*, p. 65); and on the teaching of geometry. He claims to be able to teach more in two weeks than his competitors in ten or twenty years, because they 'are ignorant how to teach usefully' (Gasquet, p. 507).

scurrilous and unfair attack upon his contemporaries in every rank of society.

But in the 1240's and 1250's he may not yet have been embittered. For some unknown reason he ceased to teach in the University of Paris, and turned his attention to the natural sciences. The immense knowledge that he acquired of the scientific writings of the Arabs, the by no means negligible contributions of his own on many scientific subjects, including his extensive monograph (the *De multiplicatione specierum*) on a subject of especial interest to the Arabs, above all the fervour with which he pleaded the cause of science as 'pulcherrima et utilissima', testify to the tremendous emotional drive he put behind his study. It is not really to be wondered at if his friends marvelled that he was able to live under such pressure of work, both in *alio statu* and afterwards.[1]

The inferior and derivative nature of his medical works written at this time show also that the new knowledge was not being properly assimilated and thought through. This is just what was to be expected of such a thoroughgoing student who had left his philosophical training behind.[2] And even by the time of the *Opus Majus* the assimilation is not yet complete.

What, then, was the nature of this emotional drive, and what led to the decision at the conclusion of his Parisian teaching?[3] There was an old medieval academic saw which says 'non est senescendum in artibus'. One should not grow old in the arts. This maxim Roger probably felt with peculiar force. He had lectured on almost every course in the curriculum. He had read and mastered the relevant authorities; and it was not part of his particular talent to try to see the wider application of this kind of learning. To build it into a *Summa Theologica* would have been as beyond his powers as it was alien to his desires. Besides, he did not know formal theology, and such an undertaking would necessarily have to be fitted into the current formal framework. The famous book of Al Hazen on optics, though he had read it, had only so far been pressed into service as an aid to

[1] 'Nullus in tot scientiis et linguis laboravit, nec tantum; quia homines mirabantur in alio statu quod vixi propter superfluum laborem: et tamen postea fui ita studiosus sicut ante.' Brewer, *Op. Tert.*, p. 65.

[2] As Little has pointed out (*Essays* . . . p. 9), it would be bad for Bacon's reputation if his competence in philosophy were to be judged only by the published fragment of his *Metaphysica* (Steele, Fasc. I), a work subsequent by many years to his Parisian teaching. The *Quaestiones* on the *Metaphysics* (Steele, Fasc. X and XI) are greatly superior from every point of view.

[3] I should like to suggest that he took his two years' vacation at this time (Gasquet, p. 507; Brewer, *Op. Tert.*, p. 65); but, of course, there is no evidence for this, unless his statement in the *Liber de retardatione* (Steele, Fasc. IX, 39) that he has at some earlier date been 'in partibus Romanis' could be considered such.

philosophy. It had not yet become for him the fundamental text-book for his favourite science as it has by the time of the *Opus Majus*.[1]

As a man Bacon was evidently of the disposition that the medievals called irascible, or choleric. Though potentially a man of action, he had, for unknown reasons, turned early to the study of books. But he attacked books in the same way he would have attacked problems in the outer world. It was not enough for him to acquire a little learning and fit into a niche as a minor scholar in the medieval academic world, but he must be an authority. He couldn't look with a tolerant eye on the vagaries of his contemporaries. He felt deeply about them, about everything. He felt called upon to offer his opinions publicly in the dispute between the Orders, pointing out not only the errors of the other Order, but of his own. And he tries to show (by logic!) that their quarrels are the signs of the coming of Antichrist, only to meet the retort: 'Quite right—so *you* must be a heretic and a disciple of Antichrist'. But they don't see, he insists with the pathetic confidence in the justice of his own viewpoint so characteristic of his kind, that the conclusion follows from the premises, and 'I have found no one who can dissolve the argument!'[2] 'I am always talking', he says again, 'about the condition of regulars and seculars, and how Judas was in the highest order, and yet was most imperfect and, in fact, altogether evil'.[3] His intellectual arrogance and conceit in his own knowledge are also shown by the way he amuses himself in Paris by setting geometrical problems that no one can solve,[4] and again he tells us how he confounded a lector who was speaking on the law of Moses. The lector, according to Bacon, made five statements about the chirogrillus of which four were wrong. Bacon publicly told him so; but this was mild treatment, since Bacon tells *us* that all five were in fact wrong.[5]

He was not an easy man to get along with, and surely not one to make friends in high places, though he speaks warmly about his own devoted circle of *familiares*.[6] A sense of diplomacy so noticeable in the great churchmen of his day, for instance, his own Robert Grosseteste and Adam Marsh, was not a part of his make-up. Nor

[1] 'Si pulchra et delectabilis est consideratio quae dicta est, haec longe pulchrior et delectabilior, quoniam praecipua delectatio nostra est in visu, et lux et color habent specialem pulchritudinem.' *Opus Majus*, II, 2.

[2] *CSP*, pp. 429–30.

[3] *Ibid.*, p. 431.

[4] Brewer, *Op. Tert.*, p. 139. It is significant that this conceit in one's own supposed knowledge (presumptio mentis humanae) should appear in Bacon's works as the famous fourth and worst cause of error. 'Illum modicum quod scit vel estimat scire, licet nesciat, gaudet imprudenter ostentare.' Brewer, *Op. Tert.*, pp. 69–70.

[5] *Opus Minus*, p. 354.

[6] Brewer, *Op, Tert.*, p. 16.

was the ability to criticize himself. It is clear that he had no thought of applying his remarks to himself, however appropriate they must have been, when he said of the angry man: 'It is the vice by which man loses himself, his neighbour, and God, which forces him to break peace with all, even with his dearest friends. He disparages everyone with insults and assails everyone with injuries, and he does not omit to expose himself to all perils, and is not afraid to blaspheme God'.[1]

But, as another passage from Parisian days seems to show—and his life, indeed, was a witness to it—Bacon could himself be neither broken nor coerced. In a discussion of the distinction between necessity and violence, and the realms in which they operate, he says: 'Man, in so far as he is man, has two things, bodily strength and virtues, and in these he can be forced in many things; but he has also strength and virtues of soul, that is, of the intellectual soul. In these he can be neither led nor forced, but only hindered. And so, if a thousand times he is thrown into prison, never can he go against his will unless the will succumbs'.[2]

So when we watch him later making his attempt to storm the fortresses of science, we must not expect him to do it half-heartedly. Nor perhaps in his lifetime to find some little stone to add to the building that is slowly rising, constructed out of many little stones. No, nothing is fitting for him but a knowledge of *all* the sciences. While this may not have been an unusual desire in the Middle Ages, Bacon's insistence that a man's knowledge is worthless unless it is complete is surprising, even for his age. The unnamed master, though he has written a few useful books, is ignorant on the whole because he has not learned the science of *perspectiva*; so, according to Bacon, 'his building cannot stand'.[3] A mere part cannot be known (nisi in suo toto cum aliis), and he quotes Cicero as having held the same view. All sciences are connected, and help each other, 'as the eye directs the whole body, and the foot supports the whole body'. The part is useless without the whole, 'like an eye which has been plucked out, or an amputated foot'.[4]

This, I think, is Bacon's personal credo, and the key to his whole work. And I think it must have been this vision of a universal science which inspired him to begin his study and to pursue it so unfalteringly. In spite of its exaggerated expression, it is one of the few things of value of which Bacon can still remind our modern

[1] Little, *Op. Tert.*, p. 60.
[2] Steele, Fasc. X, 106.
[3] Brewer, *Op. Tert.*, pp. 38, 42.
[4] *Ibid.*, pp. 17–18.

scientists. And Bacon's viewpoint gains more adherents in the twentieth century than in any period since science first became 'modern'.[1]

But the idea cannot have sprung fully armed from the head of Bacon like Athena from the head of Zeus. Did he learn it painfully as he progressed? Or did he find it somewhere and it set him on fire with enthusiasm? I think he had it from the beginning, and it was this that gave him the impulse for the work of the rest of his life.

As a philosopher he knew Aristotle as the prince of philosophers, the 'master of those who know'; but he did not in 1247 know quite the full scope of his knowledge. Above all he did not yet know the knowledge itself as *utilissima*. He was not aware of the other Aristotle, the adviser of kings—the philosopher and scientist who from his profound wisdom could tell the greatest monarch of the world how to win battles, and how to rule conquered countries by 'changing the air so that the *complexiones* of the inhabitants would be altered and they would become more pliable'.[2] He did not yet know that in the past this unity of knowledge had once existed but was lost owing to sin. He must have known the story of the gift of wisdom bestowed on Solomon, but without associating it with the secrets of science; nor that, long before Solomon, the sons of Seth and his descendants the patriarchs had also had these secrets revealed to them, and God had granted them their long lives so that they might meditate upon this knowledge and assimilate it. And Bacon had never before realized that Aristotle himself had learned his knowledge from the Hebrews by way of the Egyptians and Chaldeans, though his understanding had been limited because he was a pagan and lacked the gift of grace and was ignorant of Christian revelation.

This precious knowledge Bacon owed to the *Secret of Secrets*, one of many so-called secret works which had flourished among the Arabs, but which differed from others in so far as it was generally believed to be from the hand of Aristotle himself. A new and more complete translation of this work into Latin was made by Philip of Tripoli, according to Steele's calculations, in 1243'.[3]

[1] 'Si enim particularem scientiam et propriam cuiuslibet primo petit, tunc de necessitate ingenium obruetur difficultate, memoria fragilis confundetur multitudine et ejiciet sicut recipit lubrica, et abominans evomet quodcunque receperit.' Brewer, *Op. Tert.*, p. 19.

[2] 'Ut . . . elicerent bonos mores.' *Opus Majus*, II, 216.

[3] Steele, Fasc. V, xx (*Secretum secretorum cum glossis et notulis Fratris Rogeri*). Incidentally, if this date of 1243 is correct, then Bacon cannot have written the *Liber de retardatione* as early as 1236, since it contains many quotations from the *Secretum* which are not to be found in the earlier translation of John of Spain.

The passage on the handing down of this knowledge occurs in the *Secretum* in a much simplified form (p. 64). Bacon must then have gone to the sources and found the passages in

But this recovery of the knowledge that had once been possessed by Aristotle and the pagans and the ancient Hebrews was still not enough for Bacon. For there was one significant and all-important difference between their time and his own—the coming of Christianity. All was now changed. It was possible for a Christian, as it had not been for a pagan, to know *all* science if he were granted the grace of God. Time and again Bacon makes it clear that the moral character of the recipient determines the extent and truth of the revelation; and though this idea was a commonplace of medieval thought, Bacon gives it a new emphasis. 'For this reason', he says, 'true philosophers have laboured more in morals for the honour of virtue, concluding in their own case that they cannot perceive the causes of things unless they have souls free from sin. Such is the statement of Augustine in regard to Socrates in the eighth book of the City of God. For it is not possible that the soul should rest in the light of truth while it is stained with sins, but like a parrot or magpie it will repeat the words of another which it has learned by long practice'.[1] Elsewhere Bacon jeers at the unnamed master, saying that he could not have received a revelation entitling him to be ranked as an authority, because he had not lived in the right manner.[2]

'Virtue, therefore,' Bacon goes on, 'clarifies the mind so that a man may comprehend more easily not only moral but scientific truths. I have proved this carefully in the case of many pure young men who because of innocency of soul have attained greater proficiency. . . . The bearer of the present treatise is quite young, not a man of great genius or of retentive memory, and there can be no other cause than the grace of God which, owing to the purity of his soul, has

Josephus that have a bearing on it, since he quotes Josephus whenever he makes the statement. But even in Josephus the statements are very brief, and in at least one case, the handing down of the knowledge to the sons of Seth, Bacon deliberately changes the sense of Josephus who only said that the sons of Seth had founded the science of astronomy (*Ant.* i. 2). But Josephus does say that 'God afforded the patriarchs a longer time of life on account of their virtue and the good use they made of it in astronomical and geometrical discoveries which would not have afforded the time of foretelling the periods of the stars unless they had lived for six hundred years. For the great year is completed in that interval' (*Ant.* i. 3). The third thing of importance that Josephus said was that 'Abraham communicated to the Egyptians arithmetic and delivered to them the science of astronomy; for that science came from the Chaldeans into Egypt and thence to the Greeks' (*Ant.* i. 8, all translations by W. Whiston (1839)). Neither in Josephus nor in the *Secretum*, therefore, are to be found specific statements that the knowledge itself was revealed by God. This is Bacon's own contribution, as is the use he makes of his authorities, as will be discussed later. In one passage he says, with truth, that 'most philosophers are unaware of this revelation' (Little, *Op. Tert.*, p. 4).

[1] This passage (*Opus Majus*, II, 170) is considerably enlarged a few years later when Bacon goes into detail as to the means by which sins of all kinds prevent the attainment of wisdom, the nature of each of these sins, and how they affected learning in his day. *CSP*, pp. 408–12.

[2] Brewer, *Op. Tert.*, p. 31.

granted to him those things which, as a rule, it has refused to show to all other students'.[1]

Bacon does not, however, think there is any need for a special revelation from God; only that philosophy cannot be understood by the unworthy, as he shows in one of his most eloquent passages. 'As God wishes all men to be saved and no man to perish, and His goodness is infinite, He always leaves some way possible for man through which he may be urged to seek his own salvation. So that he who would wish to consider this way may have the power to do so; and thus urged may see clearly that he ought to seek those things which are needed beyond this way, that he may know through it that revelation is necessary for him and for the whole world. . . .

'Every man may come to this grade of the truth, but no further. For this reason the goodness of God ordained that revelation should be given to the world that the human race might be saved. But this way which precedes revelation is given to man, so that if he does not wish to follow it nor seek a fuller truth, he may be justly damned at the end. . . . Therefore this way, which precedes special revelation, is the wisdom of philosophy, and this wisdom alone is in the power of man, yet supplemented by some divine enlightenment (illustratione) which in this part is common to all; because God is the intelligence active in our souls in all cognition, as was earlier shown. This is what moral philosophers teach . . . and show that a revelation is necessary, by whom it must be revealed and to whom. And it is not surprising that the wisdom of philosophy is of this kind since this wisdom is only a general revelation made to all mankind because all wisdom is from God. . . . But we assume a special revelation when we say that revelation is made outside philosophy'.[2]

So we see that there is a philosophy which includes all sciences, and there is a higher knowledge which completes this. And this 'philosophy', as he is never tired of telling us, is not only what in his time was called philosophy, the scholastic discipline including

[1] *Opus Majus*, II, 171. The translation of this and the preceding passage is drawn from Burke.

[2] Little, *Op. Tert.*, pp. 64–65. It will be noticed that the quotations giving Bacon's thought are taken from any of his works. The principle used in selecting quotations is simply to choose the passage where it seems to be best expressed. Since both the *Opus Minus* and the *Opus Tertium*, and to a lesser degree the *Compendium studii philosophiae* and the *Communia naturalium* restate what has already been said in the *Opus Majus*, this seems a legitimate procedure, unless I am trying to show development of thought between the writing of these works. As it happens, many passages are better expressed in the *Opus Tertium*, which is to be expected since much of it was apparently written under less trying conditions, and after Bacon had had a little more time to put his thoughts in order. For Bacon's belief in revelation, Carton's monograph *L'Experience mystique . . .* (1924) may be consulted.

'physics' and metaphysics, but all the sciences which have since been called empirical. All have their contribution to make to the gaining of what he called 'integritas sapientiae'. Aristotle and others had what was possible to them, but since the coming of Christianity the crown is now *revealed science*, which comes from God. I do not think it altogether accurate to say that Bacon wanted to use the sciences for theology; this is too rigid a distinction. All forms of knowledge, including the knowledge of God which was to be obtained from theology, were part of the *integritas sapientiae*.[1] It is to be practical and speculative. 'Either we contemplate the splendour of wisdom *in studio*, or we experience its power in operation while we make it ready for the Church and the other three uses'.[2]

This, then, was the vision he glimpsed, and to him, and surely to all unprejudiced people, it was a noble, and, as Bacon calls it, a 'most beautiful and magnificent' one. Writing of its value for the human being, Bacon says, though, of course, the sentiment had been a commonplace even in the time of the Old Testament, and had been stated eloquently in the Proverbs: 'The unspeakable beauty of wisdom naturally attracts and holds our minds with full admiration. Its magnificence and dignity force us by its infinite virtue to tread in its footsteps (adhaerere vestigiis eius) . . . whatever is natural to man, whatever becoming, whatever useful, whatever magnificent, whether in this material or another, is altogether worth while to be acquired in the pursuit of wisdom'.[3]

The vision was only to take form after the study of years; but Bacon seems never to have despaired until the very end. The rest of his life he was fighting against time. His complaints to the Pope that he had nothing ready for him, the way in which he offers different sets of excuses each time he writes, only show that it was impossible for him, with all his enthusiasm, to translate his still chaotic thoughts into convincing words. The lack of scribes, the lack of money, the weariness and sickness, his slow working, the demands made upon him by his superiors, all these may have been perfectly true in detail; but they only served to mask his inward understanding that the task that he had set himself was impossible, that he had perhaps got as far as anyone could in his time, but that

[1] 'Integritas eorum quae ad sapientiam completam requiruntur.' *CSP*, pp. 393, 396.

[2] *CSP*, p. 394.

[3] *CSP*, p. 396. It is significant that in this very passage on the value of wisdom he should once again show what was in his mind by saying that Alexander the Great, by the counsel and wisdom of Aristotle, in spite of an army much inferior in numbers, yet succeeded in subduing the kings of the Orient. *CSP*, p. 395.

no one could achieve such an illusory end, the end only a perfectionist could have offered to himself. He had read everything he could lay his hands on, he had made desultory experiments, he had thought through part of his synthesis—but only part. Everything could not be put in its place. Those parts of his great series of *Opera* that he had thought through, of which he was certain, he includes in every work he writes. In every work of his maturity appears his statement on the transmission of philosophy to the patriarchs that he first found in the *Secret of Secrets*, which he has nailed to his masthead to remind him of his goal; in every work appear in slightly changed form the causes of error; in every work come his general statements on the necessity of studying the sciences. And those sciences he knew best and their relation to the study of God are never missing. Who else would have written the *Opus Minus* and the *Opus Tertium* merely on account of the perils of the road? He could not bear that this chance of a lifetime should fail through the lack of any effort on his part. The heart of the work must be offered again to the Pope in case the great man had been too busy to read the first. Then both works must be supplemented by things he had forgotten, or written too quickly to include. This is the compulsive activity of a man who has had a prophetic vision which he must communicate while he has the chance, but which may fail to convince because it is not perfect. It may lack the one touch that would make all the difference, the magic word that would touch the heart of the Pope and spur his action. Every perfectionist clings to this pathetic belief to account for his failure.

No other work of the Middle Ages is, as Thorndike rightly remarks,[1] quite like the *Opus Majus*, nor has there been one like it since. There never can be another like it, because no one believes now that we shall ever have a universal science that can be known by one man. Even Aristotle, who laid the groundwork for all sciences, who really did the work for his own day to which Bacon aspired, would probably not have believed that science would ever be complete—an 'integritas sapientiae', or 'scientia perfecta' as Bacon conceived them. Perhaps no one in the Middle Ages would have imagined it possible if it had not been for their Platonic heritage and their belief in Universals, a Universal Church, a Universal Cure (the elixir of life or the philosopher's egg), as well as the Universal Wisdom of Roger Bacon.

And Bacon himself might never have acquired his belief if he had

[1] Thorndike, *History of Magic*... II, 678.

not read in a book he thought was by Aristotle that this knowledge had once been held in the early days of mankind by the sons of Seth, who was the son of Adam, who was the son of God.[1]

II

The book of the *Secret of Secrets*, ascribed by Bacon and Albertus Magnus to Aristotle,[2] is, from many points of view, a most interesting work. Professor Thorndike has analysed it,[3] showing that it is by no means a 'wretched compilation of philosophical mysticism and varied superstition' (Steinschneider), and mentions the instructions in king-craft as displaying shrewdness and common sense. Of its medicine he makes the dry remark that 'one would infer that the art of healing at first developed more slowly than the art of ruling in the world's history'.[4]

Our interest here is focused on a different feature of this work—its persuasive power on a medieval scholar who, up to this time, had been one-sidedly interested in philosophy. As Faust, in Goethe's poem, had come to the end of all earthly knowledge, and had decided that life was no longer worth living, and then was recalled from the fatal potion by the sound of the Easter bells; so perhaps Bacon awaited a revelation and received one. As Mephistopheles came to show Faust the way to the world of beauty and sense that he had never known, and above all showed him a vision of endless activity, so perhaps did Bacon awake to a new world. The reading of the *Secret of Secrets* may well have awakened his dormant sense of wonder. He had a vision of what was to be the activity of his life, and he found it 'beautiful and useful'.

In this section we intend to show in some detail the use Bacon makes of this book in his later years; and by a study of the work itself as it has come down to us in Philip's translation with Bacon's personal glosses, we shall try to show what there was in it that could have so stirred him.

We have seen that the book states that there are secrets of knowledge in all fields of science which have been withheld from those who are not qualified to receive them. Aristotle himself only divulged them to Alexander because 'God has granted you such grace in your understanding, quickness of invention and reading of the sciences', and because Alexander has been a good pupil in those things which

[1] Luke iii. 38. [2] Steele, Fasc. V, xviii. Thorndike, *History of Magic* . . . II, 268.
[3] Thorndike, *History of Magic* . . . II, 267–78.
[4] *Ibid.*, II, 273.

he has been able to give him in the past.[1] And if God wills, his fervent desire to know will lead him to his desired end.[2] Even now Aristotle tells him that he must speak partly in secrets and enigmas; but the most glorious and wise God will illuminate his reason and clarify his understanding so that he may perceive the 'sacrament of knowledge' —the mystic word *sacramentum* would be likely to appeal to the religious fervour of Bacon's nature—and he may truly become his own successor in wisdom.[3]

This is not new knowledge, but knowledge that was long ago known when God revealed it to His holy prophets, and to those whom He had chosen and illuminated with the spirit of divine wisdom.[4] Some say that Enoch had it in a vision, and this Enoch was the same as that Hermogenes (Hermes) whom the Greeks greatly commend and praise, and they attribute to him all secret and heavenly science.[5] And Enoch, as Bacon would at once remember, was taken up into heaven without seeing death.[6] Moreover, it was even said by the Peripatetics that Aristotle himself did not see death, but was carried up to heaven in a column of fire.[7] This last statement Bacon cannot accept without question. In his gloss he remarks that only those who are either Christians or were instructed by prophets can be saved. But Aristotle had also believed in a Trinity (even if it was only the natural trinity of beginning, middle and end) and we cannot assume the damnation of some most worthy men, because we are ignorant of God's actions.[8]

This, then, is the kind of authority that the supposed writer of the *Secret of Secrets* possessed. He writes it in a secret book which, although it is published, yet will not be understood by the *vulgus*, but only by those who can by the power of their soul penetrate its secrets. What are these secrets, and how do they make their appeal to the naïve philosopher that Bacon then was?

The world is one, says the pseudo-Aristotle. 'The substance of the world is one . . . its *differentia* is only in accidents; its existence is in form and colours'. If, therefore, there are no real differences, such differences as there are are not substantial but accidental. Whatever we see in the corruptible world is divided into parts, that is, the four elements. Whatever change there is from the original form, the cause of this is the universe itself. It therefore appears that lesser

[1] Steele, Fasc. V, 40. [2] *Ibid.*, Fasc. V, 41. [3] *Ibid.*, Fasc. V, 42.
[4] *Ibid.*, Fasc. V, 64. [5] *Ibid.*, Fasc. V, 99. [6] Gen. v. 24.
[7] Steele, Fasc. V, 36.
[8] *Ibid.*, Fasc. V, 37. Cf. Brewer, *CSP*. p. 423, where Bacon repeats this, in order to show how superior in every way the pagans were to moderns who claim to be Christians.

forms are ruled by supercelestial spherical spiritual forms—and this is the reason for the validity of incantations (music of the spheres). The things of the world receive impressions from without, according to their susceptibility. Whatever is found in inferior things comes from impressions of superior bodies, hence astrology.[1] Plants and stones also partake of this power, but this is hidden from men.[2]

All things are generated from a single substance. 'I will tell you, Alexander, the greatest secret of the stone which is not a stone, which is found everywhere and in every time and in every man; it can be converted into every colour, and in it are contained all the elements. So it is called a lesser world' (minor mundus).[3] 'Each kind of plant has its own disposition . . . and imitates the disposition of one planet, and has another property which is associated with the virtues of two or more planets. And the rational soul gathers together all these properties and they are combined with it and changed by it'.[4]

The crown of all this is man. 'There is not found in the universe any animal or vegetable, or simple mineral, or heaven or planet or sign or any single being of all kinds of beings which has anything of its own that is not found in man'.[5] It is for this reason that he, as well as the philosopher's egg, is called a 'minor mundus'. The very organism of man is compared with a state, and political wisdom comes from this understanding. He has five chamberlains, the five senses, each with a different office and different means of communication.[6]

Into this world-conception astrology fits naturally, since man is a *minor mundus* and earthly bodies are affected by heavenly bodies.[7] The heavenly bodies leave their impress upon the pregnant woman,[8] a theory which is expanded at considerable length by Bacon in his famous passage in the *Opus Majus* on the reasons for the study of astrology.[9] 'Consider the disposition of the firmament', says 'Aristotle', 'and the ascending signs . . . and compare this operation with the generation of human beings or other animals, plants, and stones. Make a scheme of the heavens, and you will see that it will be of great advantage to you'.[10]

It cannot be emphasized too strongly that the enormous difference

[1] Steele, Fasc. V, 157–58.
[2] *Ibid.*, Fasc. V, 114.
[3] *Ibid.*, Fasc. V, 114–15.
[4] *Ibid.*, Fasc. V, 120.
[5] *Ibid.*, Fasc. V, 143. But cf. also p. 130: 'Convenerunt in eius compositione omnia universe res que pariuntur et inveniuntur in entibus simplicibus et compositis quia homo est ex corpore denso commensurato et ex anima que est simplex substantia spiritualis'.
[6] Steele, Fasc. V, 132.
[7] *Ibid.*, Fasc. V, 157.
[8] 'Ydeas et similitudines rerum et earum formas.' Steele, Fasc. V, 157.
[9] *Opus Majus*, I, 396 ff.
[10] Steele, Fasc. V, 161–62.

between what Bacon now learns from the book of *Secrets* and all that he had previously studied was that the knowledge now acquired is practical. Aristotle is shown as a practical man advising kings; Bacon in his vision sees himself also as a practical man, though within the framework of the ideas of his time. It is possible, he still thinks, to change the air and govern peoples by this means, and it is possible to defeat armies by using a certain kind of stone. We know he thought so, because this is what in later life he advises the Pope to do.[1] It is practical to use judicial astrology—the greatest error in medicine, he tells us, is that it does not use astrology enough, or, if it is used, the theory on which it is based is neglected.[2] Alchemy explains inorganic medicine.[3] All the secret cures advised by 'Aristotle' may be used to preserve the life of princes and popes.[4]

As we have tried to show earlier, Bacon wanted to be, and was temperamentally fitted to be, a practical man. Secret knowledge not possessed by the *vulgus*, practical knowledge that could be used to shape events, a view of the interrelationship of all the phenomena in the universe which lent intellectual respectability to these secrets—these, I think, appealed with irresistible force to the visionary in Bacon, and to his own suppressed longing for power. And above all it gave him a goal, a wider, 'more beautiful and useful' goal than the endless discussions of the book of *Sentences* in the Faculty of Theology. This did not mean that he had discarded theology as worthless. He was to return to his first love, in which he had been thwarted; but not at once. Only over the years will the vision take full shape—the utility of the natural sciences for theology.

I think the words addressed to Alexander by Aristotle will have sounded with peculiar solemnity in the ears of Bacon, supplying the motive impulse that sustained him through the years of frustration and overwork that lay ahead. 'Those who have been of quick understanding and have a good mind for acquiring knowledge, and who have investigated what was hidden from them by what was clear to them, have confirmed for themselves things whose knowledge was certified by authority. . . . And after they have learned and investigated its utility and permanence they have concealed and hidden it, so that those who have not such an apprehension and knowledge should not share it with them, since the divisions of the All-Highest, whose power and gifts are glorified in those of His creatures who live according to His own disposition, will, according

[1] *Opus Majus*, II, 216–17.
[2] Steele, Fasc. IX, 168 (*De erroribus medicorum*).
[3] *Ibid.*, Fasc. IX, 169.
[4] *Ibid.*, Fasc. IX, 1–83 (*Liber de retardatione*), *passim*.

to His wisdom, be bestowed upon those whom He has willed and approved. And the glorious God will not debar you from the number of those who have this knowledge since you are one of those who desire to acquire it and who long to gain the victory. . . . How many secrets and how much occult knowledge of universal things and their details do men pass by, and they are not known because their minds are turned to other things and their objectives are different!'[1]

But Bacon is a Christian. He holds certain beliefs from his religion. And all the time he was reading the book and it was speaking to him, like any medieval he will have been thinking: 'This pagan knowledge is still not enough. We are a part of a peculiar community, and through our revelation we know more than pagans. Is it likely to be true? There is so much that is strange in it—could it be the work of demons? Astrology and alchemy, are they contrary to Christian teachings?' Did he have any doubts on the authenticity of the work?

These would be merely idle speculations if it were not that we happen to have Bacon's own edition of the work, and his own glosses. These are probably the earliest of his scientific works, with the possible exception of the *Liber de retardatione*, and the glosses may be even earlier than this. It seems certain that they are earlier than the introduction to the *Secret of Secrets*, in which there is a reference to a comet of 1264, and which is one of Bacon's more learned and complete scientific expositions; while the glosses show almost no specialized knowledge of the material, such as is acquired later. The glosses serve to give us a most valuable insight into the workings of Bacon's mind, and his reception of the work. It may be mentioned at once that he has no doubt of the authenticity of the book, though he is aware that it has been questioned. He has a very sarcastic note on people who try to deny Aristotle's handiwork, and reminds us that according to Pliny and Censorinus there were even three genuine Aristotles.[2]

[1] Steele, Fasc. V, 158–59. The influence of this passage and the general tone of the *Secret of Secrets* is to be seen in the remarkable precautions Bacon took to maintain secrecy when he sent his alchemical formulae to the Pope. 'Since, therefore', he says, 'the works of this science contain the greatest secrets . . . they must not be written openly in case they should be understood by those who are not worthy of them. For when Alexander of Macedon asked Aristotle about these things, and blamed him for hiding them from him, the chief of philosophers replied to him in the book of *Secrets* that he would be the breaker of the heavenly seal if he revealed this to unworthy people. And so he wrote most obscurely so that no one who had not listened to his oral teachings could understand him. Take this stone which is not a stone, etc.' Little, *Op. Tert.*, p. 80. The hiding of alchemical formulae, as a form of esoteric knowledge, was a long established custom, and requires no hypothesis of persecution to account for it. Surely Aristotle himself was not supposed to have been in danger of persecution from his pupil! The above is only one of many instances of Bacon's imaginary identification of himself with Aristotle. We shall meet others in the course of this study.

[2] Steele, Fasc. V, 93.

Bacon's first gloss of importance, already referred to, claims Aristotle as at least a possible Christian before the time of Christ, and allows that he may not have been condemned to hell since we cannot know what God may do. He reminds us also that Avicenna preached the resurrection, and Democritus (this last on the authority of Pliny).[1]

In another long gloss he explains that the effect of changing the air and water of a territory will only be to change the 'complexions' of the inhabitants, and does not coerce their will; it only inclines it by virtue of the change in their physical organism. Bacon, unlike some later astrologers, is always careful to make this point and bring it into accord with Christian teaching on the freedom of the will.[2] Later on, in another gloss, he emphasizes the same point'.[3]

In a prohibition of murder for the sake of revenge the text says: 'vengeance is mine, I will repay'. Bacon reminds us that Aristotle had read the Old Testament and the prophets. Plato used the same name for God as Moses ('I am who I am'), and Avicenna accepted the authority of Scripture. Bacon is very anxious indeed to give the pagans a certificate of Christian respectability.[4]

The text gives some information on the number of planets and fixed stars. Bacon reminds us that the pagan philosophers did not discover these sciences, but the Hebrews (who are unaccountably not mentioned in the text!). He quotes Albumazar, Josephus, and Ptolemy to prove that Noah knew these sciences and taught them in Babylonia.[5]

When Alexander is exhorted to take the author's counsel so that he may have comfort and riches, the Christian moralist glosses, 'that is, necessary but not superfluous riches, because they induce too much care for their multiplication, and fear that they may be lost, and very great sorrow when they are lost—and these three are the worst things of all'.[6]

When the author carelessly speaks of a 'virtutem superiorem universalem', Bacon adds, 'scilicet, through the virtue of God and the angels, and through universal nature'.[7] Later on, he inserts another note when intelligences are mentioned, and says this means angels (though, in fact, angels are not in Christian theology ascribed such powers as the text gives to these intelligences).[8]

[1] Steele, Fasc. V, 36–37.
[2] *Ibid.*, Fasc. V, 38–39. Bacon emphasizes the same point in *Opus Majus*, I, 391 ff.
[3] *Ibid.*, Fasc. V, 121.
[4] *Ibid.*, Fasc. V, 56.
[5] *Ibid.*, Fasc. V, 62–63.
[6] *Ibid.*, Fasc. V, 95.
[7] *Ibid.*, Fasc. V 119.
[8] *Ibid.*, Fasc. V, 132.

The anonymous author has gone into some detail on the ages of life, and the time of the entry of the *anima sensibilis* into the body.[1] This happens to be something on which Jerome and Gregory have expressed themselves, and Bacon has a definite Christian teaching at hand. He says that the distinction between these ages is drawn chiefly from Scripture and the teachings of science and philosophy, 'but it would be too long to explain authorities and reasons'. But the truth is that the passage Bacon is glossing is clearly of Platonic inspiration and assumes the pre-existence of the *anima sensibilis* which comes from *that place* to the habitation of men. But Bacon either deliberately or unwittingly glosses the words 'de illo loco' with a 'scilicet, de utero', a meaning it surely cannot bear.[2]

Almost at the end of the book comes what is, perhaps, Bacon's most important gloss if we are looking for evidence of his attitude towards this new knowledge. The author has explained that it is possible to detect the true nature of a man from his outward appearance, with the assistance of astrology.[3] Bacon says that this is a science of the utmost beauty and utility; but there is a limit to its application to Christians because the grace of God can conquer an evil disposition of soul to which all the other things in the body's complexion might lead them. So the wise man will only consider the natural disposition, and hesitate to give a final judgment until he knows of his conversion to good morals. Bacon adds with his usual tact that kings and great men should know this science when they choose their friends and ministers, because, although they were good men when first elected to the courts of kings and prelates, they are quickly depraved by riches and pleasures, honours and gifts (never, of course, by the cares of office, which would not occur to a man of Bacon's stamp). Presumably it can be seen in advance whether they would be likely to deteriorate under such temptations.

These, then, are the lines along which Bacon's mind has been working, and his glosses are mainly directed to the purpose of convincing his readers that there is nothing unchristian in the book of the *Secrets*. For the rest, they are the immature comments of a recent

[1] Steele, Fasc. V, 130–31.

[2] 'Operatio ergo hujus vis generative . . . tunc transmittit ipsam animam animalis sensibilis de illo loco usque ad egressionem ad habitaculum, scilicet hominum, et adquirit aliud regimen usque ad complementum .4 annorum'. Steele, Fasc. V, 130–31.

[3] Steele, Fasc. V, 155–66. I fear that if this is true, the famous modern statue of Roger Bacon at Oxford would never be recognized by any of his contemporaries! A photograph of this statue appears as the frontispiece in Burke's translation of the *Opus Majus*. The predominant expression is one of calm serenity.

convert. The positive correlation of this new material with Christianity, the tremendous use of all this scientific knowledge to constitute a wholly new understanding of Christianity itself, must have been a conception that grew slowly with the years. In his minor medical opuscula[1] only the *Liber de retardatione*, which may have preceded in time even the glosses, contains extensive quotations from the *Secret of Secrets* (twenty-five in all).[2] The remainder make occasional, but not excessive use of it. But in his great *Opera* the influence is everywhere apparent, only at a different level. Bacon speaks of the value of extracting the allegorical meanings from astronomy and astrology for the deeper understanding of the scriptures,[3] of the value of speculative alchemy for understanding such mysteries as the composition of the bodies of Adam and Eve after the fall.[4] There is no sign of any such use of his scientific knowledge by the time of the glosses.

In the introduction to Bacon's edition of the *Secret of Secrets* most of the space is given to an exposition of astrology that goes far beyond anything in the book itself or the glosses, and Bacon has now discovered in the works of Ptolemy the words *experimentalis scientia* of which we shall hear so much later.[5] At the time of the glosses he is unable to add much in the way of information to what is included in the text, confining himself to a few elementary calculations, and remarks on the history of the Amazons.[6]

Many other items might be quoted showing the specific use Bacon makes of the book of the *Secrets* in his major works, right up to his very last book on theology; but it is not the details that are important so much as the general application of the whole body of ideas and their practical nature. The suggestion of powers to be gained by all who will follow the path was a potent inspiration to one who, like Bacon, was at this time probably almost waiting for just such a vision to give meaning to his life. And if it could be a path that was in some ways original and interesting, something different from the theology of the schools but yet potentially useful to it, something that would give him a Weltanschauung appealing to his seeking soul, that was all that could be asked of a vision. I think this book gave it to him.

[1] These are all printed together in Steele, Fasc. IX, edited by Little and Withington.

[2] This leaning on the authority of 'Aristotle' in the *Liber de retardatione* was to be expected, in view of the fact that he is again in the position of a layman instructing a potentate, and he can identify himself with Aristotle addressing Alexander. This gives Bacon the opportunity to write very impressively on the great value of what he is saying.

[3] *Opus Majus*, I, 183 ff.

[4] *Opus Minus*, pp. 367–75.

[5] Steele, Fasc. V, 9.

[6] *Ibid.*, Fasc. V, 155.

His whole later life and the emotional intensity with which he pursued it can be traced to the impact of this book.[1]

So for these reasons, even without corroborative evidence, I am offering the hypothesis that towards the end of his life in Paris, or perhaps after he had finished and was taking his two-year vocation, someone put this book into his hands. And it proved as epoch-making for him as when Descartes spent his sleepless night from which came the vision of analytical geometry, when Rousseau heard that a prize was offered for a composition on the place of science in civilization and sat down and wrote his first book and won it, or when St. Augustine heard the child's voice saying: 'Take and read!'

[1] There is one further point of interest in these glosses. Bacon has continual difficulty with the Arabic words in the text, which evidently infuriate him. Several times he says that he has had to consult other MSS. but without result, and on other occasions had to consult the doctors who used the drugs given in the text in Arabic. This may be the dawning of the idea that other works of Aristotle had been mistranslated, an obsession of which we hear much later in his career.

CHAPTER VI

'TWENTY YEARS HAVE I LABOURED...

WHEN Bacon finally made his decision to undertake his study of science he probably, though not certainly, returned to England at once. In England were men who were interested in science, the older generation of scientists so highly praised by Bacon, of whom Grosseteste was chief. After resigning his chair at the University of Paris I think Bacon's first impulse would be to leave the city and go back to his native land where he presumably had friends from his youth and could find an atmosphere congenial to his studies. Even if he did not as yet know the scientists personally, he would have been aware of their worth and reputation. Moreover, at least one brother in England was still rich,[1] and could help him if Roger had no patrimony of his own.

Writing in 1267, Bacon tells the Pope that from his youth he has laboured 'in scientiis' (his philosophical studies could be classed as scientiae), but that during the twenty years in which he has made a special study of wisdom by unusual paths he has spent more than two thousand pounds for secret books, experiments, tables, etc.[2] This would seem to indicate a definite change to a specialized and unusual study about the year 1247. Even taking into account Bacon's habitual use of round numbers, the change can hardly be placed later than 1250, and in my view probably coincides with his return to England.

Now, though Bacon may have been a hardy beggar, as Little calls him,[3] and as he shows himself later when trying, as a friar, to raise a mere fifty pounds from his friends,[4] it seems impossible that he could either have begged or borrowed any such sum as two thousand pounds. This can only have come from his family or have belonged to Bacon as his own patrimony. I think he probably decided, as soon as he determined on his study of science, to spend this money in equipping himself with the tools of his new profession. This meant,

[1] Brewer, *Op. Tert.*, p. 14

[2] 'Jam a juventute laboravi in scientiis, et linguis et omnibus praedictis multipliciter . . . per viginti annos quibus specialiter laboravi in studio sapientiae, neglecto sensu vulgi . . .' (Brewer, *Op. Tert.*, pp. 58–59). The statement that he had studied languages also from his youth may only refer to the French and English vernaculars in addition to Latin.

[3] Little, *Essays* . . . p. 6.

[4] Brewer, *Op. Tert.*, pp. 16–17.

in particular, the purchase of great numbers of books, some of them perhaps very expensive. And, as we know, he also searched for classical MSS. such as the *De republica* of Cicero, which he did not find,[1] and the *De ira* of Seneca, which he ultimately did.[2] It seems very possible that the expenditure of all his private funds was one of the reasons for his putting himself later under the protection of the Franciscan Order, though perhaps not the most important one, as will be shown.

Though we do not know for certain that Bacon returned to Oxford as soon as he left his Parisian chair, we do know that he was there when he came to write the glosses for the *Secret of Secrets*. For he speaks of having just found at Oxford four mutilated *exemplaria* of the book, whereas in Paris he had had perfect ones.[3] We know also that he heard Richard of Cornwall lecture on the *Sentences* at Oxford about the year 1250.[4]

It is interesting to note the names of Bacon's associates in England and France, as they are occasionally revealed in his scientific writings, and it seems to me that they throw a little light on his period of studying and working in each country. In the first recension of the *Communia mathematica*[5] the mathematicians whom he praises are Robert of Lincoln, Adam Marsh, and one John Bandoun.[6] For various reasons, as will be shown later, this recension should, in my view, be dated in the late 1250's. In the *Opus Tertium*, which can be dated with certainty as from 1267 to 1268, Bacon speaks of only two first-class (perfecti) mathematicians, John of London (perhaps the same as John Bandoun) and Peter de Maricourt. Not as good as these, but still good, are Campanus of Novara and Master Nicholas.[7] Now we know how much he admired Peter de Maricourt; and it seems very unlikely that he would not have been included in the list in the *Communia mathematica* if Bacon had been aware of Peter's work when he wrote it. I conclude, therefore, that Bacon only met Peter de Maricourt when he went to France later as a friar, but that the *Communia mathematica* was written in its first draft before he left England, or soon afterwards, and at a time when he only knew the

[1] Brewer, *Op. Tert.*, p. 56.

[2] *Opus Majus*, II, 323. Incidentally, this successful search, even though made by one of his friends, shows that Bacon was not, even as a friar, entirely without access to funds.

[3] 'Exemplaria quatuor que nunc inveni Oxonie non habuerunt illa, nec similiter multa alia, set Parisius habui exemplaria perfecta'. Steele, Fasc. V, 39.

[4] *CST*, pp. 52–53. This is actually an inference, but an almost certain one. Bacon knows the contents of Richard's lectures, and says he knew Richard well.

[5] Steele, Fasc. XVI, 71–135.

[6] *Ibid.*, Fasc. XVI, 118.

[7] Brewer, *Op. Tert.*, p. 34.

older generation of English mathematicians. Of English mathematics he merely says: 'There are few who study in this science, and Latin students have the greatest difficulties in overcoming the obstacles'.[1]

Throughout Bacon's works the names of Robert Grosseteste and Adam Marsh continually reappear. Both are considered great scientists and mathematicians, as well as examples of saintly lives. Since we have not conceded that Bacon studied under Grosseteste before his stay in Paris, and he shows no signs of having been influenced in thought by the great Bishop by the time of the Parisian lectures, at what period in his life did he meet him and study with him, if at all? Grosseteste died in 1253.

Now it is a striking fact that in all his eulogies of Robert Grosseteste, Bacon never speaks as if he had known him personally. He is 'the Bishop of Lincoln of happy memory', or 'of sacred memory',[2] but there are never any revealing anecdotes of the kind he relates about Adam Marsh.[3] But he does know a good deal about his works, enough to say, with some exaggeration, but with substantial truth,[4] that 'he neglected altogether the works of Aristotle and his method, but followed his own way of experimenting, using other authorities'.[5] Bacon knows, of course, that Grosseteste brought translators to England, and he tells us in 1272 that some of them are still living,[6] but this was doubtless common knowledge at the time in academic circles. Though he knows that in Grosseteste's theology classes the biblical text was used rather than the *Sentences*, this again will have been well known to any interested outsider.[7] Elsewhere Bacon says that Grosseteste knew enough languages to be able to understand the works of the saints, philosophers, and wise men of old time, that he knew mathematics and optics, and that he did not know enough Greek and Hebrew to translate himself, but had many helpers.[8] He

[1] Steele, Fasc. XVI, 118.

[2] *Ibid.*, Fasc. XVI, 118; *CSP*, pp. 469, 474.

[3] Brewer, *Op. Tert.*, p. 186.

[4] See above, pp. 14 f.

[5] *CSP*, p. 469. This opinion is supported by Aegidius of Lessines in his work on comets. 'Expositio autem Alberti videtur conveniens textui Aristotelis secundum translationem que de arabico est, sed expositio Lincolniensis fundatur super exemplum experimentale de resplendentia radiorum solis. . . .' Thorndike, *Latin Treatises on Comets*, p. 109.

[6] *CSP*, p. 434.

[7] *CSP*, p. 329. Cf. also Grosseteste's own letter to the Faculty of Theology at Oxford in which he advises this procedure. Grosseteste, *Epistolae* . . . pp. 347–48.

[8] *CSP*, p. 472. S. H. Thomson, in his recent study of the known, doubtful, and spurious writings of Grosseteste (*The Writings of Robert Grosseteste* (1940)) says that it is extremely unlikely that Grosseteste knew Hebrew himself, as he can find no trace of such knowledge in his writings, where it would have been of the greatest value to give the original text (pp. 38–39) If Bacon really implied that Grosseteste knew Hebrew, as Thomson suggests, it might be an important argument against Bacon's close knowledge of Grosseteste's capacities. But if there is any such implication, it can only be that Grosseteste knew a little Hebrew, as much, perhaps, as he might pick up from his personal translators.

mentions the names of Grosseteste's works, though as a rule under different titles from those given in the extant MSS. of Grosseteste.[1]

We have already seen that it is improbable that Bacon attended any of the lectures given by Grosseteste to the Franciscans, which in any case were on theological subjects;[2] and prior to 1229, when Grosseteste ceased to give lectures at Oxford and devoted himself instead to the Franciscans, Bacon was certainly too young to have listened to him with understanding. Though there are some works of science that can definitely be attributed to the later years of Grosseteste's life when he was a bishop, his letters written in these years show that his time was very much taken up with his diocese; and there is no sign at all that he was lecturing. Bacon says that *perspectiva* was lectured upon twice at Oxford to his knowledge, but never at Paris.[3] If the lecturer had been Grosseteste, I feel sure that Bacon would not have omitted to record the fact.

It is possible that Bacon did in these years meet the great man personally, but it seems to me unlikely.[4] Such an admirer of the work and sanctity[5] of the bishop would hardly have failed to improve on the occasion by referring to it. But it seems more probable that Bacon became acquainted with his work, firstly by his reputation which will have been familiar to all Oxford students in the 1230's, and then with his actual writings. The influence of Grosseteste's work upon Bacon's is adequately explained, in the case of a student like Bacon, by his familiarity with the bishop's writings. It seems possible that even this familiarity was not acquired until he became deeply interested in the subjects on which Grosseteste had written; and this may not have been before he became a friar. As a Franciscan he will have had access to Grosseteste's own library which the great bishop bequeathed to the Franciscan convent at Oxford,[6] for this was almost certainly the first convent Bacon entered when he joined the Order.

[1] Thomson, *The Writings* . . . pp. 93, 101, 107, 109.

[2] Thomas de Eccleston, *De adventu* . . . pp. 60, 114, 123. As a contemporary, Eccleston would surely have known of, and noted in, his chronicle, a matter of so much interest as scientific lectures to friars. For the whole question of Grosseteste's lectures to the Franciscans, and the supposed courses on scientific subjects, see Appendix A below.

[3] Brewer, *Op. Tert.*, p. 37.

[4] In the *Opus Majus* Bacon does say 'vidimus aliquos de antiquis qui multum laboraverunt sicut fuit dominus Robertus (I, 73), but this need not mean more than that he was aware of Grosseteste's work. In any case there is no reason why he should not have seen the great man on occasions, but this does not mean an acquaintance. The present writer has *seen* the English King and his father, three Presidents of the United States, and a Shah of Persia, but claims no personal acquaintance with them. Cf. *CSP*, p. 428, where Bacon uses the same expression. He may, of course, have heard Grosseteste preach, as the bishop of his diocese.

[5] 'Cuius vitam pauci prelati imitantur.' *CSP*, pp. 431–32.

[6] Grosseteste, *Epistolae* . . . lxxiv and note; Little, 'The Franciscan School . . .' (1926), p. 836.

The presence of these books may indeed have been a contributing factor in his decision to become a friar. In the relative peace of his first years in the Order, Bacon will have had time to study these works fully, and the influence of Grosseteste upon his own studies can thus be fully explained. As we have seen, Bacon's first interests in science were probably medical, in accordance with the suggestions he received from the *Secret of Secrets*. Mathematics, required for astrology, and optics which was connected with geometry, may well have come later. Mathematics and optics were the chief scientific interests of Grosseteste; he could have been of little help to Bacon in his medical studies.

Bacon's relations with Adam Marsh are in some respects more mysterious. There is no doubt that Roger knew him personally, and what he says about Adam must therefore be considered seriously. This does not mean that we must unconditionally believe everything he says about him. For it is extraordinary that if Adam had really possessed all the learning in mathematics and languages, even in *scientia experimentalis*, that Roger attributes to him, this knowledge should never be exhibited in any of Adam's extant works, and no one else should ever have attributed it to him. Grosseteste's erudition and interests appear in his letters, but Adam is remarkably successful in concealing his from public view. A great many of Adam's letters have been preserved,[1] for he was a very busy and important personage, but they are prolix in the extreme, their style is tortuous, and they do not exhibit the clarity and lucidity we might expect from an accomplished scientist. However, this is, perhaps, not a fair argument, since even in our own time scientists may not always carry their scientific lucidity over into their own private and official correspondence. But Bacon in one place even goes so far as to imply that Adam assisted Grosseteste with his books,[2] a suggestion that Russell in a recent study of Grosseteste's helpers believes must be discounted.[3]

It is difficult to see how and where Adam could have found the time to acquire his learning in science and languages, since he was so fully occupied, at least in his later life during which he was friendly with Bacon, with public affairs. It is possible that he studied with Grosseteste before entering the Franciscan Order (latest date 1232), but such early studies would hardly merit Bacon's encomia on the perfection of his knowledge, which should surely have emerged in some written masterpiece. We cannot, of course, deny categorically

[1] Brewer, *Monumenta Franciscana*, I, 77–489. [2] *Opus Majus*, I, 106.

[3] J. C. Russell, 'The Preferments and Adjutores . . .' (1933), pp. 167 ff.

that he ever wrote such a work, but there is no record of it; his extant writings, apart from his letters, are exclusively theological.[1] Matthew Paris calls him 'senex et literatus', which, of course, he was,[2] and we know that he was learned enough in theology to break the Franciscan tradition that their lectors or regent masters in theology at Oxford should be appointed from outside the Order.[3] A letter of Grosseteste's shows that, if he had desired it, Adam could have had the most important chair of theology at Paris reserved to the Franciscans, previously held by the great Alexander of Hales.[4]

Since, therefore, none of the known facts of Adam's life support Bacon's statements, is it possible that he exaggerated, and if so, why? It is noticeable that on the only two occasions when Adam appears in Bacon's work without having his name coupled with Grosseteste's, it is in his capacity as an authority on theology. On the first occasion some friars ask him the nature of the *intellectus agens*, and Adam answers that it is 'the raven of Elias',[5] and on the other occasion it was another question, this time put personally by Roger, on whether demons can be in hell and on earth at the same time.[6]

The most probable explanation is that Adam did in his youth indeed study the sciences with Grosseteste before he entered the Franciscan Order; but after entering the Order he specialized in theology. As it happens, there is a record of his having gone abroad with St. Anthony of Padua to study theology after admission to the Order, but this evidence is not trustworthy, coming from the sometimes unreliable *Chronicle of the Twenty-four Generals*.[7] The story may, however, be true; though, if so, we should have expected Eccleston himself to have mentioned it, as he was a contemporary, and Adam appears frequently in his pages.

It is, however, certain that Adam had taken holy orders before becoming a Franciscan,[8] and we should have expected a man of his scholarly attainments and capacities to have undertaken the long and strenuous study of theology at an earlier age, since in any case he was destined for the Church. It is extremely unlikely that he collaborated with Grosseteste in books written during the latter's episcopate; but prior to his entry into the living of Weirmouth in the 1220's he may for some time have been one of Grosseteste's favourite pupils and

[1] Little, 'The Franciscan School . . .' (1926), pp. 836 ff.
[2] Matthew Paris, *Chronica* . . . V, 619.
[3] Thomas de Eccleston, *De adventu* . . . pp. 63–64.
[4] Grosseteste, *Epistolae* . . . pp. 334–35.
[5] Brewer, *Op. Tert.*, p. 75.
[6] *Ibid.*, p. 186.
[7] Thomas de Eccleston, *De adventu* . . . p. 23 and note b.
[8] Eccleston, *De adventu* . . . p. 23, note b.

assistants at Oxford. This may, indeed, be the beginning of the long friendship which is so fully attested by the letters of each. In this case we must merely assume that any letters written by one to the other on scientific subjects have not been preserved. As to the matter of languages, there is no need to connect Adam's studies with those of Grosseteste in this field. He may have acquired them when Grosseteste invited his Greek scholars to England. Or it is possible that he may have made special studies at the time when he planned to go as a missionary to the East, an ambition with which Eccleston credits him.[1] There is simply no information on any of these points.

But it is also possible that Bacon had an ulterior motive for singing the praises of Adam. He may have been a personal friend, perhaps Roger's only friend in high places. He had been a famous enough man for his name to carry weight with the Pope, and Roger may not have thought it would do him any harm to mention his personal acquaintance with him.[2] Adam died in 1258 or 1259, long before the works to the Pope, and it was quite safe to praise him, use him as an authority for his opinions, and even to ascribe to him an excellence he did not possess in life. On the whole it seems to me probable that Adam has gone down in history as a great scientist as well as a great churchman and theologian largely by the lustre reflected on him from the association with Grosseteste and from the praise bestowed on him by Roger Bacon for reasons not necessarily connected with his real excellence. Unfortunately for Bacon, Adam had no prevision of his posthumous fame, or Roger would have rated at least one entry in Adam's voluminous letters, which remain as silent as if Roger Bacon had never been born and never made inquiries on the ubiquity of demons.

It is possible that Bacon made acquaintance with Adam after his return from Paris. Adam lectured in theology at Oxford until 1250, and Bacon could have been greatly impressed by his lectures and the scientific examples, culled from his earlier studies, that he used after the manner of Grosseteste. We know that Adam did have a remarkable influence upon another student, Thomas Docking, though this was in the stimulation of theological rather than scientific researches.[3] But this attendance at theological lectures must have occupied only a small portion of Bacon's energies at this time. Grosseteste's scientific influence had persisted at the university, and many thinkers in the

[1] Eccleston, *De adventu* . . . p. 23.

[2] Bacon's two references to his personal acquaintance with Adam are both to be found in the *Opus Tertium*, a work destined for the Pope.

[3] Little, 'Thomas Docking and his Relations to Roger Bacon . . .' (1927), p. 301.

thirteenth century, especially among the English Franciscans, were attracted by his theories on light, as was Bacon.[1] Bacon, therefore, could have begun his studies on optics. But his interests in medicine, already aroused by the *Secret of Secrets*, were also important to him, and he mentions in one of his glosses that some drugs are not obtainable in England and must be procured from Montpellier, which suggests that he was engaged in some medical research.[2] He may also have lectured himself at Oxford, perhaps on philosophy, though there is no evidence for this. I think it psychologically improbable in view of the urgent nature of his new interests and the fact that he had given up a position in Paris to devote himself to them. He would not yet be sufficiently well qualified to lecture on his new studies, even if there was a place for them in the curriculum. The mathematical disputes already referred to took place in Paris at a later period of his career.[3] Before considering in greater detail in the next section the work Bacon accomplished during his 'twenty years' labour', a sidelight on his possible university activities will be presented in the form of a hypothesis concerning his relations with Richard of Cornwall, which may help also to explain partly the neglect that Roger suffered later when he entered the Franciscan Order.

We have already noted that Richard of Cornwall came out strongly against the plurality of forms, and that Bacon admitted his high reputation among the vulgar, though he was 'the stupidest of men in the opinion of the wise'.[4] In the same work Bacon gives us some details about Richard's teachings, and his philosophical doctrine from which the theological deduction can be made that Christ was a man for three days before the resurrection, which idea could be considered heretical. Bacon tells us also that Richard was able to make his doctrine stick, as it was still flourishing in Oxford forty years later. Now this teaching is by no means new, having had a long and chequered history. A considerable article on the subject[5] manages to discuss it without reference to either Richard or Bacon. Moreover, Bacon says that at Oxford, Richard was followed and accepted, while at Paris he was 'reproved'. On the other hand, Eccleston says that Richard had the brightest reputation both at Oxford and Paris,[6] and on another occasion that at Paris he 'was considered a great and

[1] Sharp, *Franciscan Philosophy . . . passim.* [2] Steele, Fasc. V, 106.
[3] Brewer, *Op. Tert.*, p. 139. *Supra*, p. 114.
[4] *CST*, 52 ff.
[5] A. M. Landgraf, 'Das Problem utrum Christus fuit homo in triduo mortis in der Frühscholastik,' *Melanges Auguste Pelzer* (Louvain, 1947), pp. 109–58.
[6] 'Tam Oxoniae quam Parisius fama clarissimus.' Eccleston, *De adventu* . . . p. 24.

admirable philosopher'.[1] Evidently, if Richard was reproved at Paris, Brother Thomas had not heard of it. Adam Marsh, as we shall see, also had a high opinion of Richard's capabilities, and put himself to much trouble on his behalf. We know that Bacon already in his Parisian days disapproved of Richard's philosophical views on this particular problem on logical grounds, though at this time he did not ascribe it to Richard;[2] but it is a different matter to say that everyone else agreed with his estimate and that wise men considered Richard a fool for holding it. It would appear that the opinion was at least an arguable one, and not formally heretical, whatever Bacon may have thought. Yet Roger even in his last book remembers it against Richard, and reserves for him some of the choicest language of his entire career. It certainly looks as if there were some personal animosity on Bacon's part which cannot be entirely accounted for by a mere disagreement with Richard's theological and philosophical opinions.

Not a great deal is known, at present, about Richard of Cornwall. D. A. Callus, in his study of MS. Balliol 62, a commentary on the *Sentences* given by him during his Oxford period, remarks, however, on the special character of his disputing. Richard's aim, he says, is to stress opposition between the different outlooks on the plurality of forms, rather than to reconcile divergence of opinion. He busies himself more with denouncing the tendency of philosophers to expound views in conflict with theological truths, than in giving information on what they actually say. He 'shows independence of mind, is outspoken, and ready to criticize'—in short, a character not unlike Bacon's own.[3]

We have also some information about Richard from the letters of Adam Marsh. From the first letter, written in 1248. it appears that Richard has received permission from the Minister-General of the Franciscan Order to go to lecture in Paris on the *Sentences*. But now he does not want to go, and Adam is begging the Provincial Minister to excuse this change of mind and allow him to stay. Oxford will be delighted to keep him. The reason given is Richard's poor health.[4]

In the second group of letters, which is still full of praise for Richard, Adam asks the Minister to allow him to go to Paris after all. These letters are dated by Little 1252 or 1253.[5] This time the reason

[1] 'Magnus et admirabilis philosophus judicatus est.' Eccleston, *De adventu* . . . p. 65.
[2] Steele, Fasc. XV, xxi–xxii.
[3] Callus, 'Two Oxford Masters . . .' (1939), p. 431.
[4] 'Propter multimoda valetudinum suarum discrimina.' Brewer, *Monumenta* . . . I, 330.
[5] Little, 'The Franciscan School . . .' p. 842.

is 'ob vehementiores perturbationum occasiones'. Richard, says Adam, has come to an 'inexorable' and 'irrevocable' decision that he must go, in accordance with the permission of the Minister-General previously granted. He adds that it is 'very urgent'.[1] Elsewhere Adam refers again to Richard's 'inexorable intention', and asks for the assistance of the Minister in providing necessaries for him.[2]

Now this is all very extraordinary if, as the Catholic *Encyclopaedia* suggests,[3] the 'perturbationes' were merely local riots in Oxford. Why should Richard be so urgent to leave? The only reason that seems feasible is that in some way he personally was mixed up in the riots, or that they were directed against him, for it is clear that no one else is trying to escape from Oxford, and Adam himself, though he is doing his best to help, does not approve of the decision. If Richard had been in any real trouble Adam would have concurred in it.

Professor Little once threw out the suggestion that perhaps Bacon was involved in these disturbances, but he did not pursue the matter.[4] Could Bacon have publicly challenged the doctrine of Richard that he so much detested? In 1252 and 1253 he was certainly at Oxford, and he was an accomplished disputer. He may have been glad of the opportunity to deflate a master of theology, a class of person he disliked on principle. In his attack on Richard in his last work he says that Richard was teaching this detested doctrine from 1250, and that he knew him well.[5] All these facts are consonant with a public challenge about the year 1252.

If Bacon had publicly attacked him, Richard, being the kind of character he was, might have felt so gravely insulted, especially if Bacon had had some support among the students who created a disturbance, that he would want to leave at once and go to Paris, where he would be more appreciated. This might explain the urgency of his pressure on Adam Marsh, and Adam's apparent reluctance to indulge a personal whim which he felt was not in the best interests of Oxford. The use of the words 'irrevocabile' and 'inexorabile' suggests that Adam had tried to talk him out of it. So Bacon may have enjoyed a brief triumph, and in due course Richard received his permission and went to Paris.[6] Here Bacon says he was reproved,

[1] 'Insipiens factus sum; postulantis urgentia me coegit.' Brewer, *Monumenta* . . . I, 365.

[2] Brewer, *Monumenta* . . . I, 360.

[3] Art. Richard Rufus of Cornwall.

[4] Little, 'The Franciscan School . . .' p. 842.

[5] 'Optime novi pessimum et stultissimum istorum errorum autorem.' *CST*, pp. 52–53.

[6] Eccleston, in giving his account of the original profession of Richard, says that he entered the Order in Paris; but in the disturbances caused within the Order at that time over Brother Elias, Richard came to England and professed 'calmly and with devotion'. It would look as if Brother Richard had a special dislike for disturbances. Eccleson, *De adventu* . . . p. 65.

while Eccleston says he gained a high reputation. It is possible that Richard did get into some trouble in Paris since in the mid 1250's the struggle between the religious and seculars was raging, and for a time both Orders of friars had to suspend their lectures. But this can have had little to do with Richard's opinion on the three days during which Christ was a man. And we do know that Richard was recalled to Oxford in 1256 to take up the position of regent master of the Franciscans in theology, the highest academic position in the gift of the Order, and a definite promotion. In this position, which he held until his death, it is just possible that he was able to be a considerable nuisance to Roger Bacon who was by 1257 a friar, and subject to discipline within his Order. Richard's influence may have been one of many that prevented him from rising to any degree of dignity within this Order in spite of his intellectual attainments.

Though this hypothesis may have no direct evidence to support it and must therefore be considered gratuitous, it does satisfactorily explain a few definite facts, such as the sudden decision of Richard and the long continued enmity of Bacon. There is nothing inherently improbable in it. On the contrary, it fits Bacon's character excellently —he was never a man to keep his opinions to himself—and it is in accord with the little we know of Richard. I think that a man capable of changing his mind so suddenly and putting pressure on his friends and superiors, if it was for the personal reasons I have suggested, would have been quite capable of turning his personal attention to Bacon within the Order and helping to ensure his continued subordinate position. This fact in my view does need some additional explanation, for, if he had been nothing else, at least Bacon had been a *magister regens* in the Faculty of Arts at Paris, and this, though not a very high academic position, was superior to any held by the majority of his fellow-friars.

I

After an undetermined time as a secular student of the natural sciences, Bacon entered the Franciscan Order. His relations to this Order, his reasons for joining it, and the effect it had upon his work will be studied in the next chapter. There can be no doubt that if he had remained a secular master and student of the sciences, supporting himself and his research out of his private means and giving occasional or regular lectures to augment his income, then the corpus of his work would have been entirely different, and it is doubtful if even his great *Opera* to the Pope would ever have been written.

At all events he did join the Order, and his writings were modified accordingly. But for the purposes of analysis, and the establishment of a chronology for the twenty years' work prior to 1267, this influence will be arbitrarily ignored in this chapter, and Bacon as a writer and student will alone be examined.

It has always been difficult to establish the chronology of the works of most ancient and medieval writers from external evidence. Though astronomers and astrologers, working in a field where exact dates are important, usually take the trouble to state the year and even the month when they are writing, the remainder do not seem to have thought that posterity would be interested in such information, and it would already be known to their contemporaries. A speech of Isocrates or Demosthenes may be successfully dated, but not the contemporary works of Plato and Aristotle. It is only in comparatively recent times that another approach has been utilized which takes account of the fact that a man does not necessarily think the same thoughts at the end of his life as in his early twenties. This may be called the 'genetic' approach, and it tries to trace the development of thought, and does not confine itself to the thought when it has reached its highest point of maturity.

The tremendous work of Werner Jaeger on Aristotle in our own century was a pioneer effort in this direction,[1] even though Jaeger was by no means the first to realize that the method was applicable to Aristotle. Others followed in his footsteps, questioning many of his findings, especially in the fields where they were more competent than Jaeger.[2] In 1914 Dr. Grabmann attempted a similar service for the commentaries of Thomas Aquinas on Aristotle, and much of his work has been accepted by subsequent scholars.[3] There are two distinct schools of thought on Albertus Magnus, some (with Mandonnet) putting his scientific work early in his life, while others, with Pelster, attribute it to his last years.[4]

In the case of Aristotle the work had to be accomplished almost entirely by the use of internal evidence. Even if the result is not historically accurate, this procedure serves its main purpose, to point out that there was a distinct change in the method of dealing with his material, and that apparent inconsistencies could be explained by

[1] W. Jaeger, *Aristoteles—Grundlegung einer Geschichte seiner Entwicklung* (Berlin, 1923). English translation (2nd edit.; Oxford, 1948).

[2] E.g. F. Nuyens, *L'Evolution de la psychologie d'Aristote* (Louvain, 1948).

[3] M. Grabmann, 'Les Commentaires . . .' (1914), pp. 229–31.

[4] P. Mandonnet, 'La Date de naissance . . .' (1931), pp. 253–56; F. Pelster, 'Zur Datierung einiger Schriften . . .' (1923), pp. 475–82; 'Um die Datierung Alberts des Grossen . . .' (1935), pp. 143–61.

the assumption of a real deepening of thought and its application to a wider range of phenomena. This, with Aristotle, was connected with a progressive emancipation from the persistent influence of Plato, his master. For a student only interested in the thought-content of a philosopher or scientist, it is invaluable to know what was his 'latest' thought. This gives him a solid foundation. When characterizing his subject's thought he can relate all the transitional opinions to this one. He can then re-imagine the process by which he arrived at the final stage of his thought, and place his earlier tentative efforts in relation to it. He can even make use of the mathematical procedure of 'interpolation' and suggest further transitional stages which may not even be represented by extant works.[1]

But when the historian is also trying to reconstruct a biography and relate the production of different works to known events in his subject's life, it is essential that he should have at his disposal at least some indisputable facts—for Aristotle these are very scarce and doubtful—and some works which can be dated with certainty. For Bacon, most fortunately, we have the solidest *point d'appui* we could wish for. There is no doubt at all that the great masterpieces of his life were written between 1264 and 1268, and these represented the culmination of his thought. In the early part of his life we have the Parisian lectures which can be dated to within a few years. This alone might justify the use of the 'genetic' method; but there are also various single works such as the *Computus* and the *Compendia* of philosophy and theology which have internal evidence of their dates. There are also other works which provide dates before which they could not have been written, such as the introduction to the *Secret of Secrets*, which mentions the comet of 1264. Finally there are works which must be placed as subsequent to others because of unmistakable references in the text to the earlier ones.

Nevertheless, these materials are far from sufficient for the establishment of a convincing chronology for the whole twenty years between the Parisian teachings and the *Opus Majus*, and we are forced to examine the development of Bacon's thought, the various subjects on which it was exercised, and to re-imagine his method of working and see how it was ever possible for him to write the *Opus Majus*, and what were the stepping-stones to this crowning achievement.

Bacon's biography is also complicated by one factor which is also true of Aristotle and Albertus Magnus, though not perhaps to the

[1] The importance of the commentaries on the *Sentences*, given in their early years of study by so many who later became masters of theology, has already been pointed out.

same degree—the difficulty of knowing for certain which works are authentically his, and the rarity and poor conditions of his manuscripts. Later legend attributed to him many works which were certainly not his, and others are probably his, though without definite manuscript attribution to him.[1] Even to-day several important fragments have not yet been published, and this writer has had no access to them, though he has made inquiries from the prospective editors on several important points. No one who has not worked with Bacon can realize the tremendous job done by A. C. Little in his appendix to the *Commemorative Essays* of 1914,[2] which, though there may be disagreement in detail, must remain the basis for any subsequent study. Little here has attempted to compile a bibliography of the works actually written by Bacon, though we do not possess them all, even in MS. He uses Bacon's own references to works intended and written, and gives his opinion as to whether they remained only in his mind or were actually started or completed. But he attempts no chronology, and only gives the dates of those works which can be indisputably established, and suggests a few others from internal evidence. P. Glorieux, who included, in my view mistakenly, Bacon amongst the masters of the Faculty of Theology of Paris, repeats this bibliography, but adds very little to it,[3] and his new dates seem to me highly doubtful.[4]

I believe enough biographical and literary material is available on Bacon to make feasible a further refinement of the genetic procedure. This has already been suggested, and to some degree used. But a formal statement at this point may be of value. I have attempted to infer Bacon's psychology from his writings. I shall now take this psychology as my initial postulate, add body to this by drawing on such knowledge as is available on the psychology and work-methods of later writers and thinkers, and see how this may explain certain other features of Bacon's writings prior to the *Opus Majus*, and such indisputable facts as we possess. It is recognized that this is a tentative and delicate procedure, and can give rise to no certainty. But once the 'prediction' is made it is possible that confirmation of certain particulars may come from MSS. as yet undiscovered and unedited. In continued working with the material after the hypothesis had been

[1] An example is the commentary *De sensu et sensato* which I, like its editor, believe to have been written by Bacon. See Appendix C below.

[2] Little, *Essays* . . . pp. 375–419.

[3] Glorieux, *Répertoire des maîtres* . . . (1933), II, 60–76.

[4] Glorieux states, as if it were an undisputed fact, that the date of the *Liber de retardatione* was 1281 and that it was dedicated to Pope Nicholas III (*Répertoire* . . . p. 64). His variations from Little seem to be based on Vanderwalle's monograph, *Roger Bacon dans l'histoire*. . . .

framed, various passages which had hitherto appeared unimportant already tended to confirm it, and gave some assurance that it approximated to the truth.[1]

The following facts need some explanation:

1. Bacon was a thoroughly competent philosopher by the time he left Paris, fully equipped to deal with disputed questions in the current scholastic manner. Yet he shows himself in the fragment of the *Metaphysics*, undoubtedly written after his Parisian days, as apparently unequipped to deal with philosophical questions.[2] And though the whole of this work is not yet published, there is sufficient philosophical matter in the fragment printed by Steele[3] for a judgment to be formed on his method. Yet in the treatise *De multiplicatione specierum* sent to the Pope,[4] Bacon shows himself once again thoroughly competent to deal with scholastic terminology and method and to apply them to a field of inquiry in which he had made considerable observations.

2. Although he wrote several medical works after his Parisian teaching, Bacon never makes any attempt to deal with this subject in a philosophical manner. He is usually naïve and credulous, though he thinks his work to be of great importance, and even originality.[5] Only in one medical work does he attempt to think through his subject matter and relate his knowledge of other sciences to the science of medicine, and even in this work the credulity is still very noticeable.[6] Furthermore, although he has tried in the 1260's to teach his favourite pupil John everything he knows, he makes no reference to medicine as part of John's curriculum.[7]

3. It has been frequently pointed out how Bacon repeats himself *ad nauseam* and incorporates material from one writing into another, usually verbatim.[8] This was not the customary medieval practice. Even when a writer uses the same material for a second time, as in many of the great *Summae*, in the later work the subject matter has undergone considerable transformation according to the new purpose.

4. Many of Bacon's works were apparently left unfinished, and

[1] I am aware that this procedure commits the logical sin of 'affirming the consequent'—if A then B; B is the case; therefore A is the case. But even in the physical sciences to-day this is customary, and accepted, with reservations, as permissible. F. S. C. Northrop, *The Logic of the Sciences and the Humanities* (New York, 1948), pp. 146 ff.

[2] Little already pointed this out in 1914. *Essays* . . . p. 9.

[3] Steele, Fasc. I. The MS. from which he worked, however, is very defective, and before much can be said on this subject we must await the publication of the whole *Metaphysics* promised by Mgr. Pelzer.

[4] Printed by Bridges with the *Opus Majus*, II, 407–552.

[5] Steele, Fasc. IX (*Antidotarius*), p. 117.

[6] *Ibid.*, Fasc. IX (*De erroribus medicorum*), pp. 150–79.

[7] Gasquet, p. 506.

[8] Little, *Essays* . . . p. 22; Thorndike, *History of Magic* . . . II, 630.

several manuscripts of the same work are often known, usually with substantial variations. The latter may be accounted for in part, as Bridges suggests, by Bacon's practice of making several copies of each before he was satisfied.[1]

5. Even in his major works there is evidence of a very unequal grasp of his subject matter. In places there is extensive direct quotation without any attempt to correlate this with his own thought and philosophy, while elsewhere in the same work it is clear that the subject matter has been fully assimilated. The most notorious example is the section on moral philosophy in the *Opus Majus*, which is greatly inferior to the rest of the work, though Bacon regarded moral philosophy as the highest and most dignified form of knowledge.

6. There is an apparent discrepancy between Bacon's statement that prior to 1267 he had only composed 'a few chapters, now on this science and now on that',[2] and had finally 'decided to compose no more',[3] and the actual fact that there is a fairly extensive body of work that must be allotted to this period.

We think that all these points can be satisfactorily explained, and in the process we shall hope to cast some light on Bacon's method of working which should prove consistent with what we have been able to infer of his character.

Most writers of imagination and vision at all periods of history have not developed in a uniform manner, but experienced intervals of retrogression. This, I think, depends to a considerable degree upon the enthusiasm with which they undertake their work, and how they deal with their rare moments of vision and inspiration. A prolonged effort of thinking and imagination, warmed by enthusiasm, leads them to a certain point of vision where they are able to reach out beyond themselves and write something which in later years they cannot see how they were ever able to accomplish. All the world's masterpieces have not by any means been the latest to be written by their authors. Dante's *Divine Comedy*, which he even claims to have been an actual vision on the night of Good Friday, 1300, was undoubtedly a work of supreme vision which he was unable to match later; the first part of Goethe's *Faust*, while perhaps surpassed in depth and understanding by the second part, cannot be considered inferior in poetic inspiration. Rimbaud used to be ashamed of his early *Une*

[1] *Opus Majus*, III, xiii–xiv.

[2] 'Proculdubio nihil composui nisi quod aliqua capitula nunc de una scientia, nunc de alia.' Gasquet, p. 500.

[3] 'Decrevi quod omnino cessarem de componendis scripturis.' Gasquet, p. 500.

saison en enfer, and even in his later life deny he had written it, because it was the product of youthful inspiration. The process may be seen at work even in modern novelists, who may be persuaded by a publisher's insatiable demand to try to repeat an earlier success. But it is impossible merely to dot the i's and cross the t's of their earlier work; they find they cannot stand still because the vision recedes with the effort to recapture it, and the retrograde movement begins. But Bacon did not lose his vision; it continued to increase until the great *Opera* to the Pope. And he did not lose confidence in the value of what he was doing except for a few years during which external events were proving too much for him, and which, as we shall see, he describes so eloquently in one of his prefatory letters. Even then it was not so much that he ceased to believe in himself as that he could see no means of interesting anyone of authority in it, and research was not worth the trouble if nothing came of it in the end.

I think, therefore, that there was a real development in his work, and that the apparently inferior writings that he occasionally produced are more to be explained by a temporary lack of familiarity with the method and subject. If for years we concentrate very seriously upon a subject and even master it, we cannot at once turn back to it with an equal facility when our attention in later years has been absorbed in another field of activity. One can observe a retrogression after the great *Opera* to the Pope have failed of their main purpose, but this is understandable. Many obvious reasons may be used to explain it, and we shall attempt to give some of them in due course.

But when he left his chair in Paris, Bacon could not foresee the future. He had read the *Secret of Secrets*, caught the vision of a universal science, and he set to work. If we imagine what it was like to study natural science in the thirteenth century, with no preparation but a specialized training in scholastic philosophy, we may appreciate the extent of Bacon's researches in the following years. At first, being above all a writer and a teacher, and having no frame of reference to work with, his writings came out in much the same way as they were taken in. They are not much more than compendia of his readings, with innumerable quotations of passages that seemed interesting to him as he read. There is a perfect example of this kind of work as late as the *Opus Majus* itself. Here he tells the Pope that he had only recently discovered the *De ira*, *Ad Helvium* and other works of Seneca for which he had searched from his childhood. Since his exalted reader might not have seen these books himself, Bacon gives the gist of them at inordinate length without troubling to assimilate them to his own thought.[1] I believe the *De retardatione* was a work of the same kind, relying heavily on his recent reading of the *Secret of Secrets*, and the medical works of Avicenna and the Arabs.

As the shape of the synthesis he hopes one day to perfect takes hold of his mind, certain parts of his readings become assimilated, and he is able to write without so much direct quotation. He is learning to penetrate his material with his imagination and perceive its 'useful' implications. First he is able to perceive how science can be useful for the spreading of Christianity—changing the air, and thus the 'complexions', of its enemies, enabling them to be governed; the use of burning glasses to win battles,[2] the prolongation of life and health. The second stage is to see how scientific teachings can be reconciled with Christian thought, what is wrong with present-day thought and method (his work on astrology, the *De signis et causis ignorantia modernorum*, the *Metaphysics* which is concerned with the errors of theologians), and, of course, how these things should be improved. The last stage in his purely scientific development would be the ability to use the scholastic method on a totally new set of ideas from those dealt with in the schools, a procedure not so easy as it sounds.[3] His most fully thought-out piece of scientific work is surely the *De multiplicatione specierum* which he himself also thinks is his best.[4]

[1] *Opus Majus*, II, 276–365.

[2] Brewer, *Op. Tert.*, p. 116.

[3] There is great difficulty for anyone to relate the theoretical prime matter of St. Thomas and the scholastic hylomorphists with *actual* prime matter which no one has ever seen or ever will see, and is, indeed, *ex hypothesi* invisible and imperceptible to any of the senses. Heisenberg has shown in modern times that no 'physical' prime matter is capable of being perceived by any instrument. In both cases prime matter is a theoretical or mathematical entity. But the medieval alchemist was dealing with perceptible data, trying to 'transmute elements' and not merely theoretically postulated entities. Hence when the question arose as to whether this transformation took place only *via* prime matter, it was clear that this was impossible if prime matter was only a theoretical entity. Change, as Bacon saw, did take place; so there must be some real substance, which was not prime matter, but had some of its theoretically postulated characteristics, e.g. more or less unlimited potentiality. It is this extraordinary difficulty of equating theoretical conceptions with visible objects that has occupied so many philosophers of science, even in our own time, and has made it difficult to say whether the 'multiplication of species' of Bacon and his contemporaries is the equivalent of the 'propagation of force'. (*Opus Majus*, I, lxv–lxix.) And even 'force' is not a physical entity. One remembers how Clerk-Maxwell tried to make models to fit his field theories of physics which had been worked out theoretically first, but failed to do so. The problem is a fascinating one, but obviously cannot be entered into here.

[4] 'Per haec aperta est via sciendi omnia—in omni scilicet actione, sive in visum, sive in auditum, sive in tactum, sive in alios sensus, sive in intellectum, sive in totam mundi huius materiam' (Brewer, *Op. Tert.*, p. 117). It is clear that Bacon's work in this field has been greatly influenced by Al-Kindi, 'the first and only great philosopher of the Arab race' (Sarton, *Introduction* . . . I, 559), to whom, as far as we know, the theory of the propagation of force in rays should be credited. Indeed, Bacon gives him this credit, though the use he makes of the theory himself is all his own. See especially Part II, ch. ix, of the *De multiplicatione*, printed by Bridges with *Opus Majus*, II, 494–96, and Thorndike, *History of Magic* . . . I, 642–46.

It is clear that his penetration of the science of optics, even though much had been done on it before and the lines had been laid down for his own researches, was more thorough than anything else he did. Though he regards his *scientia experimentalis* as more important, in so far as it occupies a key position in 'universal science', he does not do much constructive work in it, and, indeed, the most important section of his work on this 'science' in the *Opus Majus* is only an extension of his work on optics. The last stage in Bacon's development, then, is the production of his synthesis, and the use of *all* his scientific knowledge, and the relation of the particulars to the whole. His last word on optics is probably the long passage in what appears to be the last revision of his *Opus Tertium*, where he links up this science now with the powers of the soul, taken from another study, and carries it one stage further beyond the separate study on optics in the fifth part of the *Opus Majus*.[1]

A man like Bacon beginning this kind of research would at once come up against the language difficulty. Already from his *Secret of Secrets* days he had found himself impeded by his ignorance of Arabic medical terminology, and, as was pointed out before, he had to have recourse to practitioners who were often as ignorant as he.[2] This probably set him to thinking over the problem of Aristotle, and the inadequacy of his translations, which he had not troubled about in his lecturing days in Paris. So Bacon set himself the task of learning at least enough Greek to enable him to understand the original Greek works. In later years when he has his synthesis fairly clear, he knows that he is going to need Hebrew also for his study of biblical texts, and the full interpretation of certain passages in the light of his scientific knowledge. Probably his language studies were pursued at the same time as his other activities, since they were to be only the tools of his research. His urge for writing would not compel him to write a grammar unless he actually needed it for a useful purpose; he did not need a written grammar for his own work, and it would mean neglecting his scientific studies for the time necessary to write it. So, if he wanted to share his grammatical and linguistic knowledge with the public, we should expect him to prefer to wait until he had sufficient leisure. External and internal evidence from the grammars he did write suggests that they were, in fact, composed after the great *Opera*. In the *Opus Tertium* he makes it clear that he has not yet composed a satisfactory one, if he has even composed one

[1] Little, *Op. Tert.*, pp. 23 ff.

[2] *Supra*, p. 86, no. 1.

at all,[1] while he still has it in mind to compose a dictionary later, at the time he is writing the so-called 'Oxford' grammar.[2]

I expect, therefore, that Bacon at once sought out teachers of Greek, and that he continued this study side by side with whatever branch of science occupied him at the time. The only way in which he could achieve the amount of work that he did, and write as much as he did, was to concentrate upon one branch at a time, whether it was medicine, astronomy, geometry, alchemy, mathematics, or optics—and his urge for teaching and writing would lead him in every case to crown his efforts with a book, or several books, on his speciality of the moment. These I should not expect to be finished or perfect productions, nor perfectly digested. Such a book as the first recension of the *Communia mathematica* would be the result of a prolonged period of study of this kind.[3] Then if he had the time and interest later in his career he would go back to it and improve it, reveal new uses for the science which he had perceived since the first draft. The result would be that he produced a far more finished piece of work. And this has certainly happened in the case of the *Communia mathematica*. The first pages printed in Steele's edition, which are evidently later in date, are much more fully thought out.

This procedure left him with a large number of more or less unfinished works on hand at any given time. We learn from Bacon himself that he did not always keep all his manuscripts, and could not at once have access to them. Presumably they would circulate within the scientific circle of which he was a member, and they might or might not be returned to him. He needed them all when the Pope requested a *scriptum principale* from him. Raymund of Laon, who, according to Bacon, misunderstood his message to the Cardinal, who later became Pope Clement IV, and told his master that Bacon had writings ready, could easily have been deceived when he saw so many smaller manuscripts (*aliqua capitula*, as Bacon called them) circulating amongst his friends.[4]

Writing in this manner, his interest in a subject he had studied a few years before would necessarily wane as he branched out into a new field; and he could not return to it at once with his old enthusiasm nor his old facility. When the Pope or a friend asked him for

[1] Brewer, *Op. Tert.*, p. 88.

[2] Nolan and Hirsch, *The Greek Grammar of Roger Bacon* . . . (1902), p. 68. There are two different versions of Bacon's Greek Grammar, which the editors call the 'Oxford' and the 'Cambridge', from the libraries where the extant MSS. were discovered. Since a passage in the earlier 'Cambridge' grammar corrects a philological error in the *Opus Tertium*, both may be placed subsequent to the latter. (*Ibid.*, xxxiii–xxxiv.)

[3] Steele, Fasc. XVI, pp. 71 ff.

[4] Gasquet, p. 500.

some work in a discarded field there was only one thing to do—pick up the earlier work and add a few touches, or a prologue if there was time; or, if not, then send it off just as it was. This is not a piece of laziness. He might very well not know any more on the subject than he had when he had done his research many years before. Yet it was a part of the *integritas sapientiae*, and could not be omitted in a *persuasio* that claimed to be complete. When a friend asked him for a book on baths, he wrote it[1] because he had some knowledge of what authorities had said on the subject; when a friend suggested to him that the Pope, a secular prince, or 'my brother E.'[2] might value some advice on how to live longer, Roger dutifully obliged. But when the Pope asked for his opinions on the value of science for theology, this meant putting all the scientific knowledge he had into it. Naturally he felt pressed for time. And there was only one thing to do—incorporate everything he had ever done, and try to think out some of the implications as he went along. His earlier work on optics is probably incorporated without a change.[3] The *De multiplicatione specierum*, as Bacon himself tells us, was sent in two different versions, as a separate work from the *Perspectiva*, although it covered much of the same ground.[4] Much of his *Metaphysica*, poor as it is, is included in Part VII of the *Opus Majus*.[5] Bacon sent four treatises on alchemy to the Pope, two of which were inserted in the *Opus Minus*, as he thought he had not said enough on this subject in the *Opus Majus*. The greater part of these are still awaiting publication by Mgr. Pelzer, though the fourth has already been printed by Little as part of the *Opus Tertium*.[6] A separate treatise, *De laudibus mathematicae*, appears to have been included also in *Opus Majus*, Part IV.[7]

From the foregoing it will be seen that I am inclined to explain the

[1] Steele, Fasc. IX, 96–97 (*De balneis*).

[2] *Ibid.*, Fasc. IX, 120 (*Liber de conservatione juventutis*).

[3] Many MSS. exist of part V of the *Opus Majus* alone (*Perspectiva*), and it was published at Frankfort in 1614 as a separate treatise before there was any printed text of the *Opus Majus* as a whole. In this edition there is an introduction evidently not addressed to the Pope, which is printed by Bridges (*Opus Majus*, II, 1–2), who wants to place this introduction as subsequent to the *Opus Majus*. In it Bacon speaks of the *De multiplicatione* as already finished, and required reading if the *Perspectiva* is to be understood. I should prefer to place both of these works as prior to the *Opus Majus*—the *Perspectiva* incorporated in it instead of being re-written, and the *De multiplicatione* sent separately. We know that the *De multiplicatione* was composed before the *Opus Majus*, so there is no reason why the *Perspectiva* should not have been another of the 'chapters' Bacon had made. Since the *Opus Majus* itself, long as it is, was not a *scriptum principale*, but only a *persuasio*, we can have some idea of what Bacon thought of as a book, and what as a chapter.

[4] Brewer, *Op. Tert.*, pp. 38, 99. Bacon also started a third version of this work, which, according to Little (*Essays . . .* p. 386), was to have formed part of the *Communia naturalium*. which he regards as Bacon's projected *scriptum principale*.

[5] Little, *Essays . . .* p. 407.

[6] *Ibid.*, p. 393, item 14.

[7] *Ibid.*, pp. 393–94.

duplication of so much of Bacon's work by the hypothesis of the incorporation of earlier unfinished attempts into the later masterpieces rather than by the alternative hypothesis that some copyist or literary pirate, or even Bacon himself, made extracts from these masterpieces and published them separately. Both hypotheses are, of course, equally possible, and, indeed, the truth may lie between the two. Both processes may have been at work. But the first explains so many more known facts and apparent discrepancies—above all, the speed with which the *Opus Majus* was composed—and seems so much in accord with what Bacon himself says about his activity in the years prior to 1266 that I am adopting it. Let us now see how this helps in establishing a chronology, by imagining exactly how Bacon worked during these years.

He learned his languages, as has been already said, and at the same time he devoted himself to the principal study suggested by the *Secret of Secrets*—medicine. In working with medicine he began to realize that true diagnosis was impossible without astrology, which would inform us of the 'complexions' of unknown human beings, and thus the kind of medicine required for each different person. At the same time the *Secret of Secrets* had suggested alchemy, and this study was fully compatible with a parallel study of medicine. Later, in his most complete and Baconian medical treatise, he tells us how necessary both astrology[1] and alchemy[2] are for medicine. The study of metaphysics completes this science.

But in the process of his studies Bacon began to be drawn farther afield, as the relationship between the separate sciences began to dawn on him. Alchemy could be studied more or less as a separate science, but astronomy and astrology could not. They needed, above all, mathematics, and, indeed, in the *Opus Majus* astronomy and astrology are treated as part of this discipline. Mathematics and astronomy took him to *perspectiva* and the latter to the attempt to generalize his theories, culled from geometry and applicable especially to optics, in a theory of universal force. He had predecessors in all these particular fields, and there was no need in most of them to do more than understand and discuss with competent authorities[3] what they had said, and take note of the experiments they were performing. But he had had no predecessor as a synthesist since Aristotle himself,

[1] Steele, Fasc. IX, 154–55 (*De erroribus medicorum*).

[2] *Ibid.*, Fasc. IX, 155–58.

[3] 'I have sought out the friendship of all wise men among the Latins.' Brewer, *Op. Tert.*, p. 58.

a fact of which Bacon himself is very well aware.[1] Meanwhile he had never lost sight of his original purpose, to build up a theology on different lines from those of his contemporaries. His meditations on all the sciences, and his study of the Bible, continually reaffirmed the possibility of using his science both for theology and for the practical work of the Church.

When we consider the systematic classification of the sciences which Bacon produced in the works of his maturity,[2] we must not imagine that this was the way Bacon himself studied them. On the contrary, this idea of the interrelationship of the sciences, and the fact that science, to be worthy of the name, must include *all* sciences, though it must have been always with him since the days of the *Secret of Secrets*, never took on formal shape until he had progressed much further. This is the reason that he claims to be able to teach all he knows in far less time than it had taken him to acquire this knowledge, because it had now become possible to make a systematic compendium[3] and use the power of association for remembering facts that are related to each other.[4] So his students could avoid wasting the time that he himself had lost through unsystematic study.

The following diagram suggests a way in which Bacon himself may have proceeded. No new bibliographical material is given here, but the attempt is made to explain and account for the material provided by Little in his bibliography.[5] The numbers in parentheses refer to the separate items in this bibliography. Titles are only given when the book in question has been referred to in this study, and so will be familiar to the reader, or is of some special significance.

1. *Preliminary requirements*: Logic, grammar, languages. The first two were already acquired during his formal education. The languages were picked up during the next twenty years as opportunity offered.

[1] 'Hic facere non omittam, et sic fecit Aristoteles in scientia naturali.' Steele, Fasc. II, 3.

[2] The best of these is in the *Communia naturalium*, which shows the projected plan of his work, though he did not accomplish it all. His 'agriculture' and animal psychology, for instance, remain rudimentary; this, however, was less important, since Aristotle had already done this work from his own observations, which Bacon does not seem ever to have tried to duplicate.

[3] 'Tamen certus sum quod infra quartam anni, aut dimidium anni, ego docerem ore meo . . . quicquid scio de potestate scientiarum et linguarum dummodo composuissem primo quiddam scriptum sub compendio.' Brewer, *Op. Tert.*, p. 65.

[4] 'Si enim particularem scientiam et propriam cujuslibet primo petit, tunc de necessitate ingenium obruetur difficultate, memoria fragilis confundetur multitudine, et ejiciet sicut recipit lubrica et abominans evomet quodcumque receperit.' Brewer, *Op. Tert.*, p. 19. An admirable educational observation!

[5] Little, *Essays* . . . pp. 376–419.

2. *The works of preparation in science.* (Aliqua capitula, nunc de una scientia, nunc de alia.)

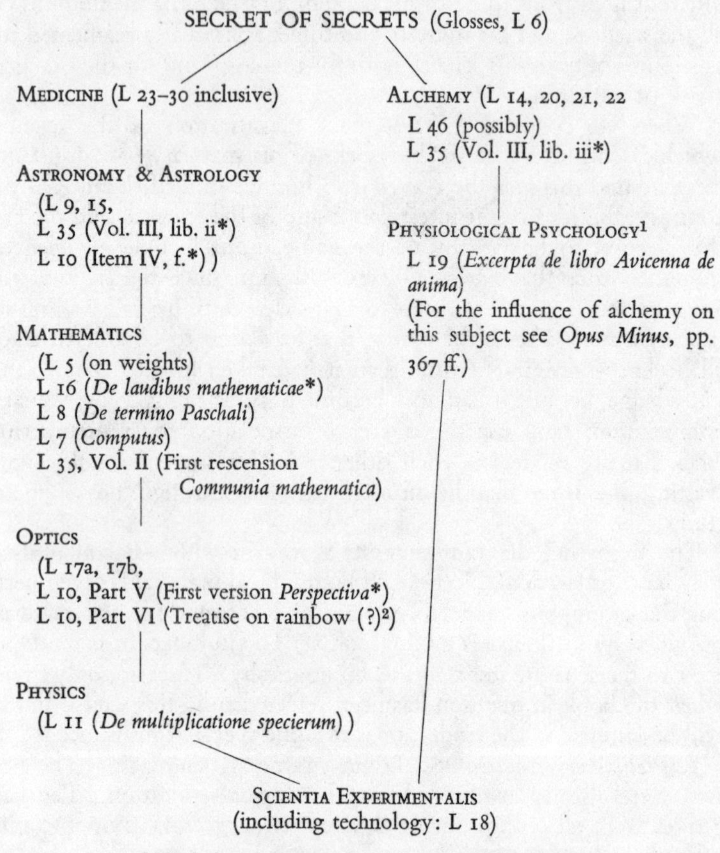

* Works later incorporated in full in one of the syntheses.

[1] D. W. Singer, 'The Alchemical Writings . . .' (1932), gives some information on the connection between this subject and alchemy. Avicenna's work, which interested Bacon enough to persuade him to make extracts, is primarily alchemical, though its official subject, the soul, has suggested to me that the classification of 'Physiological Psychology' would be appropriate. I have not, however, seen the MS.

[2] The first part of the section on *scientia experimentalis* in the *Opus Majus* (II, 166–202) forms a substantial treatise by itself, and is closely connected with optics, being a discussion of the rainbow. Although this was no doubt revised for the *Opus Majus*, as Bacon says that he had to make some observations before it could be completed (*Opus Minus*, p. 317), I suggest that the main body of the treatise may already have existed before the *Opus Majus* was written, and was incorporated into it. This will be further discussed when Bacon's *scientia experimentalis* is dealt with in more detail in Chapter IX below.

3. *Chronology of the works of preparation.*[1]

1.	*Liber de retardatione*	c. 1250
2.	Glosses on *Secret of Secrets*[2]	c. 1253
3.	Medical opuscula[3]	1250–60
4.	Alchemical works	1250–56
5.	Astrological works	c. 1252–56
6.	Excerpts from Avicenna (alchemical)	c. 1254
7.	*Metaphysica*	1255–60
8.	*De erroribus medicorum*	c. 1255
9.	*Reprobationes* on weights	c. 1256
10.	*De laudibus mathematicae*	c. 1257
11.	*Communia mathematica* (first rescension)	c. 1258
12.	*De secretis operibus naturae*	c. 1260
13.	*De termino Paschali*	c. 1260
14.	*Communia naturalium* (first part)	1260–67
15.	*De multiplicatione specierum*	c. 1262
16.	*Perspectiva*	c. 1263
17.	*De signis et causis ignorantiae*[4]	c. 1263
18.	*Computus*	1263–65
19.	Treatise on rainbow (?)	1263

4. *The works of synthesis.*

Opus Majus
Opus Minus
Opus Tertium
Introduction to *Secret of Secrets*
Communia naturalium (second part)
Compendium studii philosophiae
Compendium studii theologiae

II

One further point concerning Bacon's work in these years requires attention—the question of his friends and associates in his studies.

[1] These dates should be understood only as suggestions for a possible work programme. They take into account all noticed references to work as already written, and are therefore more likely to be relatively than absolutely correct. The more strictly scientific works are placed later than the 1260 censorship imposed by the Franciscans (see next chapter). Items 7, 14, and 17 might equally be regarded as the first attempts at synthesis and included in list no. 4.

[2] The *terminus post quem* for these glosses may be given as 1252, since there is a reference in them to a disease suffered by Alphonse of Poitiers in 1252, and to his subsequent recovery. (Steele, Fasc. V, 105; C. J. Webb, 'Roger Bacon on Alphonse . . .' (1927).)

[3] These medical opuscula can be partly dated relative to each other; but they may have been composed any time during the period, since they show no increasing knowledge. The *De erroribus medicorum* is the only one of these works which attempts to relate the sciences and should not therefore be dated before 1256.

[4] A. Pelzer discovered a special work entitled *Epistola de signis et causis ignorantiae modernorum* as long ago as 1919, and publication was promised. But the promise has not so far been fulfilled. From the title it would appear to be similar in content to the first part of the *Opus Majus*, and therefore probably incorporated in whole or in part in this work. Pelzer, 'Une source inconnue . . .' (1919), pp. 45 ff.

We hear of isolated workers such as Peter of Maricourt, a real experimenter and the author of a treatise on the magnet. And we have already noted how Bacon tells us that he 'sought the friendship of all wise men among the Latins', but comes eventually to admit that it is impossible for one man to have a really adequate knowledge of all the specialized fields of science, and that assistance should be requested by the Pope from other workers in the field.[1]

Though he makes no systematic effort to give us any account of these other workers, perhaps because he is anxious to exalt his own contribution, Bacon does give us many hints that he is not working alone, and that there are some people who agree with him in many of his criticisms. Perhaps the most definite statement occurs in the *Communia naturalium*, which work shows no signs of having been written for a Pope or anyone in authority, and is therefore more likely to be describing the true state of affairs in the study of natural science at the time. 'Some of these men', he says, 'seeing that they could not know natural philosophy through the help of Aristotle and his commentators, are turning themselves (present indicative) to the seven other natural sciences, to mathematics, and to the other authors of natural philosophy, as, for instance, to the books of Pliny and Seneca and many others, and so are coming to the knowledge of natural things, concerning which Aristotle, in his common books, and his expositor, cannot satisfy their interest in nature'.[2]

In his discussion of new inventions in the *De secretis operibus naturae*, Bacon does not claim to have invented flying-machines and self-propelling boats himself, nor the 'instrument, small in size, which can raise and lower things of almost infinite weight', which, although only 'of the length of three fingers, could lift a man and his companions out of prison, and raise and lower him'.[3] He has not read of these things only in books either, for he tells us that he knows a wise man who has explained them to him. Elsewhere he says: 'Let no one be astounded, for these things have been made in our days'.[4] He does not doubt that with the Pope's aid certain good and holy persons could be trained to work against Antichrist,[5] and a whole school

[1] Gasquet, pp. 501, 504, etc.

[2] Or, perhaps, 'satisfy their native diligence'. The words, 'non possunt satisfacere natura studio' could mean either. Steele, Fasc. II, 13. Cf. also *Opus Majus*, II, 215–16, 'via experimentalis . . . ad quam intendunt multi fidelium philosophorum'.

[3] 'Instrumentum, parvum in quantitate ad elevandum et deprimendum pondera quasi infinita.' Brewer, *De secretis operibus* . . . pp. 532–33.

[4] Steele, Fasc. XVI, 43–44 (*Communia mathematica*).

[5] Little, *Op. Tert.*, pp. 17–18.

of workers could be organized to give effect to his views on 'philosophy'.[1]

In other passages in his works Bacon describes himself as a kind of publicist for science. 'Wise Latins', he says, 'are experienced in these things (experiments), though they have not wished to compose writings about them'.[2] He hopes that 'others may go forward by the help of my works to greater things'.[3] Such passages as these suggest that Bacon knew well what his contemporaries were doing, but that he was not part of their inner circle. He appreciates their efforts, and tries to understand them and see their significance; but he himself is primarily a scholar and thinker. Neither in the section on *scientia experimentalis* in the *Opus Majus*, nor in his letter on the secret operations of nature where he goes into such details as the technical inventions that are to be expected in the future, does he say that he ever carried out a serious experiment himself. His knowledge displayed in the *Opus Majus* comes from books, and from information he has obtained orally. The exception is in the field of optics, where he has undoubtedly made numerous observations which could be called experiments, and which fulfil Webster's definition of an experiment as 'a trial made to confirm or disprove something doubtful'. It is perhaps unfair to expect him to have carried out what we should call to-day 'laboratory experiments' planned to discover some unknown principle or effect (Webster's second definition), although the contemporary alchemists were undoubtedly striving in this direction.

It is fairly clear that Bacon has observed the stars and paid special attention to the rainbow, with the aid of such simple 'experiments' as holding water in his mouth, then spitting it out (or blowing bubbles?—spargo is the word used), and noticing that the drops reflect different colours, and using hexagonal stones and crystals to watch the refraction of light.[4] From the way he writes of these it is quite clear that he has performed the experiments; elsewhere there seems to be no sign of personal observation at all, except when others perform the experiments, as in the case of the goat's blood and the diamond referred to earlier.[5] I cannot find that he had direct access even to an astrolabe, though he knows all about them, and suggests

[1] Brewer, *Op. Tert.*, pp. 54–56.

[2] Steele, Fasc. II, 10.

[3] Steele, Fasc. II, 10. An interesting reference to other experimenters may be found in Thorndike's book *Latin Treatises on Comets* (p. 140), where Aegidius of Lessines quotes the opinion of those 'skilled in the experimental art'. 'Hec est enim sententia maiorum in arte experimentali peritorum. . . .'

[4] *Opus Majus*, II, 174.

[5] *Ibid.*, II, 168.

improvements in them.[1] All his remarks seem to be from hearsay, or from books, and the little touches one would expect from actual observers and experimenters that reveal personal knowledge, touches that can so easily be detected in works of fiction and non-fiction alike by even the comparatively unskilled reader, are missing almost completely in Bacon's work. In one place he says that he 'sent across the sea to various other districts . . . (that he might) see natural things with his own eyes and prove the truth of the creature with his own sense of sight, touch, smell, and hearing *per certitudinem experientiae*',[2] but I am extremely sceptical of the truth of his statement. He may be telling the truth, but this invites the comment that he received singularly little value for his money and trouble, since he adds nothing in any of his works to the knowledge of his time of any natural creature—and there was surely room for improvement in the medieval knowledge of 'natural creatures!' This particular boast is addressed to the Pope and can be reasonably explained as an attempt to impress him. And I think he gives himself away completely in the next sentence by adding 'as Aristotle sent many thousands of men'. Aristotle sent men out scouring the earth during the expedition of Alexander. I fear Bacon is only up to his old habit of identifying himself with Aristotle. We have a long account of the information he gained from a returned traveller, Friar William Rubruck',[3] and no doubt he questioned other friends and acquaintances who returned from abroad. But I fear the picture of himself as the director of an army of far-ranging scientific investigators existed only in his imagination.

But he knows very well what it is that alchemists do, and he sends their most secret formula to the Pope in enigmas.[4] He may have been allowed to witness their experiments, but none of the extant passages suggests personal experiments of his own.[5] Bacon's great claim to fame as a scientist does not rest upon his technical work, but on his attempt to think through the implications of the work of others, and this is surely no less important. He has carried out this task in a masterful manner, as we shall try to show in a later chapter. But it remains the manner of an armchair scientist. I think he was always on the fringe of a circle of active workers, amongst whom was the solitary and disdainful Peter of Maricourt, and the *homo*

[1] *Opus Majus*, II, 202–3.
[2] Gasquet, 502.
[3] *Opus Majus*, I, 305 ff.
[4] Little, *Op. Tert.*, pp. 80–89.
[5] Patison Muir in his article on Bacon's relation to alchemy and chemistry comes to the same conclusion. 'He does not appear to have studied these events at first hand.' Little, *Essays . . .* p. 318.

sapientissimus, the famous critic of the biblical text, whom Bacon so much admired.[1] For these active workers Bacon acted as philosopher, synthesizer, and publicist, and there is every reason to believe he would be gladly welcomed in this capacity.[2] This would be in perfect conformity with his position as a poor friar who could not afford expensive alchemical experiments, unless his Order provided the means and the equipment and metals, often precious, that would be required for them.

In optics, however, he needed no raw materials and an absolute minimum of equipment; and it would be most suitable and simple for him to spend the long solitary hours gazing at the sun and moon, and at the rainbow, thinking out and checking the work of Ptolemy and Grosseteste, Al Hazen and Al Kindi on the reflection and refraction of light, and 'cosmic rays', theorizing on the 'multiplication of species' and meditating on the divine illumination of the *intellectus agens* which plays so important a part in his psychology.

He tells us that he spent more than two thousand pounds on his work, on 'secret books, different kinds of experiments, the acquisition of languages, instruments, tables, and other things'.[3] It has already been suggested that much of this money had to go for books, and for the services of copyists and the purchases of parchment when he was writing his own works. The *experientiae variae* and the instruments may have been nothing more than the optical experiments he mentions, and the stones and crystals from various countries, and magnifying glasses which were all that he needed for them. He says nothing of raw materials needed for the more expensive alchemical experiments. We know he spent sixty pounds on the writing of the *Opera* alone, and this needed no books other than what he already possessed, although he tells us that he did need tables. However, two thousand pounds was certainly an enormous sum of money in those days—though, of course, we have only Roger's own words for it that he spent it, and this, in a work to the Pope—and it may seem a large sum to lay out for a library, even of secret and expensive books. But this library of scientific works probably had to be built up from nothing, and, as we know, he did search for manuscripts of rare works. I do not think that it would be impossible for him to spend

[1] *Opus Minus*, p. 317.

[2] These would no doubt be the 'multi' who thought he was composing a *magnum opus* at a time when he claims to have been idle (Gasquet, p. 500). His presence at a kind of magical seance on one occasion is attested by the book of an anonymous writer who saw him there. Anon, *Liber exemplorum*, p. 22.

[3] *Opus Tertium*, ed. Brewer, p. 59.

such a sum on books, tables, services of copyists, and the purchase of writing materials, especially since he was very particular about having first-class copies and wasted much parchment. And he could have made monetary contributions to his alchemical friends, and he could have exaggerated the sum in order to impress his patron with the extent of his disinterested services to the cause of science. I am anxious to give Bacon all credit where it is due; but I am not greatly impressed with the evidences in his work of the detailed factual knowledge that should have been his if he had engaged in the extensive experimentation with which he has too often been credited.

I picture Bacon as an indefatigable reader and writer and thinker, perhaps teaching at the University of Oxford in the days of his earlier scientific interests, and later in Paris paying visits, listening to lectures, and sometimes publicly criticizing, as we have seen, and setting mathematical problems no one could solve. Then, returning to his study or, in later times, to his friar's cell, and thinking out the implications of what he had studied, seen, and heard that day; and finally after many years reaching the synthesis of knowledge to which he was to give such full expression in his *Opera*.

Meanwhile, as we shall see, his superiors made him do his regular work at the convent,[1] which he resented, as any thinker resents being taken away from his thoughts which he is striving so hard to put in order; and he also paid his debt to society and fulfilled one of the greatest needs in his nature by teaching. The prodigy John does not seem to have been his only pupil, at least not in earlier years; for Bacon tells us that he 'instructed young men in languages, figures, and numbers, tables, and instruments, and many necessary things'.[2] He had 'learned how to proceed, and what help he needed for his tasks'.

Amongst friends who were engaged in work he respected, from whom he learned, and from whom he had nothing to fear, he was no doubt a very different Roger Bacon from the jealous hater of authority and the somewhat sour moralist he shows himself to be in his relations with his superiors. There is no reason to disbelieve his numerous references to the very dear friends whom he loves; and though I have no doubt he was a hard taskmaster with John, and he both overpraises the lad, and congratulates himself unduly on the free

[1] 'Affuit enim instantia prelatorum meorum cotidiana ut aliis occupationibus obedirem et ideo non potui aggredi que volebam.' Gasquet, p. 500.

[2] Brewer, *Op. Tert.*, p. 58.

instruction and nourishment 'he' gives him (it was, after all, his job,[1] and the expenses were paid by the Order, as Bacon himself admits elsewhere),[2] he probably did not lack the domestic virtues in his private life, and unquestionably he was a man of great courage and independence. Martin Luther was also a very different person when urging the German princes to destroy the peasants from the peaceful figure he presents in the evening of his life with his wife and children around him.

[1] Bacon emphasizes the fact (to the Pope) that he had no obligations to John, and that he helped him *pro amore Dei* (Brewer, *Op. Tert.*, p. 59; Gasquet, p. 506) and on account of 'the goodness of the boy'. But it is interesting to see what the Constitutions of Narbonne (1260) have to say about the obligations of the friars to work. 'Since the rule says that the brothers to whom the Lord has given the grace of working must work faithfully and devotedly, we ordain that the brothers, both lay and clerical, be compelled by their superiors to write, study, and exercise themselves in the other labours for which they are competent, and if anyone shall be found to have been markedly idle he shall be set apart from the others *ad condignam satisfactionem*'. *Archiv. für Litteratur und Kirchengeschichte des Mittelalters*, VI, 104–5 (hereafter cited as *Archiv.*). Roger may have been aware of this rule when he makes the pointed remark that his superiors did not force him to write. Gasquet, p. 500.

[2] John, he says, 'servivit eis qui ipsi vitae necessaria exhibebant'. Gasquet p. 506.

CHAPTER VII

BACON AS FRIAR

I

BACON never tells us when or why he became a Franciscan when he was already in middle life, and there have been many speculations on the subject. It is not now believed that he professed on the very day that he entered the Order, though there is no reason why, in view of his maturity, he should not have done so. But the passage in Eccleston[1] which tells of an R. Bacon who did this is concerned with the Dominicans and not the Franciscans. The text, therefore, clearly refers to the Dominican Robert Bacon, who also entered his Order at a relatively late age, and who died in 1248.

In this study it will be suggested that there was a combination of many reasons for Bacon's decision; and though no certainty will be reached, a fairly brief discussion may reveal a few important traits in his character which have not yet been touched upon, and throw some light on the very limited area of choice available to the medieval scholar who wished to pursue his researches. As Charles suggests, if Bacon were unable, for financial or other reasons, to pursue individual unsupported research, he must obtain the patronage of either the King, the Pope, the Orders, or a University.[2] It is probable that Bacon examined all these possibilities, in addition to the alternative of continuing his studies unaided. But we shall try to show also that it may not have been only material advantages that determined his final decision. In spite of the unhappiness that he endured within the Order, its discipline and mode of life were not altogether alien to his character and temperament.

With or without a source of income, Bacon was not the kind of man who would have made a solitary experimenter, free, but without authority and influence in the world. His hero, Peter de Maricourt, was such a one. Bacon admires him, even envies him, and mentions with approval Peter's refusal to lecture to the Parisian crowd; but I cannot see Bacon emulating him. For all his contempt for the vulgus, he still needed its applause. He liked to teach, and he wanted to be an authority. These desires could not be fulfilled if he retired from the world.

[1] Eccleston, *De adventu* . . . p. 101. [2] Charles, pp. 19 ff.

We have no knowledge that Henry III of England ever patronized scientists, but Louis IX of France employed the distinguished Dominican encyclopædist, Vincent of Beauvais, as librarian and tutor to his children.[1] Bacon may have approached him, but if so, we know nothing of it. The only evidence of any notice extended to him by secular authorities is the fact that he appears to have edited a second edition of his book on the accidents of old age for the benefit of some *carissimus princeps*. This, however, may have been only an initiative on the part of Bacon, and not a mandate from the prince. Bacon may already have tried out the Papal Curia, as suggested earlier, and been rejected by the incumbent Pope. In any case, as the future was to show, popes hold office for too short a time for them to be effective as permanent supports for research. The University of Paris was engaged in other serious matters at this time, and Bacon's ideas had little relevance to them. Albert the Great was just laying the foundations of his enormous reputation; and Albert's approach to Aristotle, science, and theology was essentially different from Bacon's, although in some respects superficially similar; this particularly applies to his understanding of the relations between these subjects.[2] It is probable that Bacon knew of Albert's work, and it is doubtful if he would have cared to face the competition.

We may, I think, assume that Bacon hoped that his own University of Oxford, still under the influence of Grosseteste as it was, would give him some support, and that he made efforts to influence the authorities. But his ideas were not altogether those of his contemporaries, and especially his approach to theology was different and appealed to few of those who were in charge. And, as suggested earlier, he may already have made a powerful enemy, as well as an influential friend. This friend, however, was also a friend of Richard of Cornwall. Adam Marsh, in any case, ceased to lecture at Oxford in 1250, and in 1253 he had a serious quarrel with the university over the appointment of Thomas of York as regent master of the Franciscans without having a degree from the Faculty of Arts.[3] There can be little doubt that the jealousy of the influence of the Franciscans was already simmering at the university; and Adam, especially after the death of Grosseteste in 1253, may not have been the best kind of sponsor for an original investigator with a sharp temper.

[1] Thorndike, *History of Magic* . . . II, 458.

[2] Since this judgment may appear difficult to sustain, the reader is referred to Appendix B below, where a more complete account is given of the relations between Roger and Albert, and their differing ideas, especially on Aristotle and theology.

[3] Little, 'The Franciscan School . . .' (1926), pp. 823 ff.

So by eliminating the other possibilities it becomes clear that Bacon's area of choice was restricted to the two mendicant Orders, a monastery, or continuance in private life. The attractions offered by these Orders in the thirteenth century were so manifestly superior to those of the old monastic Orders that he probably never even considered the latter. I think also that, of the two, the Franciscans were the natural choice for an Englishman. The Dominicans in England, however strong they were in France, were not so rich in learned men as the Franciscans, nor did they enjoy the support of Grosseteste. Moreover, Bacon may have found it difficult to imagine himself in the same Order as his rival, Albertus Magnus, even though Albert was not working in England.

Assuming, then, that the Franciscan Order was a reasonable choice for him, there remains the impulse to join an Order at all to be accounted for. Edward Hutton, in his book on the Franciscans in England, has made an eloquent defence of Bacon's action, which might have been more convincing if he had had a greater knowledge of Bacon, and perhaps a little less sympathy with the 'persecuted' master. He comes to the interesting conclusion that Peter de Maricourt and Bacon's friendship for him were the deciding factors. For Peter, according to Hutton, was a Franciscan.[1]

Now Bacon never speaks of Peter as 'frater', but always 'magister', which would be most unusual if he were indeed a Franciscan. Neither Father Huber, Chevalier, nor Little acknowledge him as a Franciscan, nor Charles, who devotes several pages to Peter.[2] Wetzel, in the *Catholic Encyclopædia*, however, states it as a fact, and gives Schlund as authority. But the curious thing about Schlund's article[3] is that he himself comes to the conclusion that it was improbable! Schlund spends several pages trying to equate Peter with a certain Peter of Ardene, who was undoubtedly a Franciscan, but does not even succeed in convincing himself; and though he would like to retain his hypothesis he is forced to admit that there is little, if any, evidence in support of it. This has not prevented the latest biographer, Woodruff, from giving us an attractive picture of the lonely worker Roger Bacon in his convent at Paris, hard at work experimenting with Peter, and developing a deep friendship, with the kindly friars presumably smiling benignantly in the background![4] So on this evidence I am unable to support the suggestion that Bacon's friendship

[1] E. Hutton, *The Franciscans in England*... (1926), pp. 138–42.
[2] Charles, pp. 16–30.
[3] E. Schlund, 'Peter Peregrinus...' (1911), pp. 436–55.
[4] F. W. Woodruff, *Roger Bacon, a Biography* (1938), p. 58.

with Peter can have been a reason for his joining the Order. In any case it seems most probable that Bacon became a Franciscan when he was in England, and he was later transferred to France by his Order. And I have tried to show earlier that it is very unlikely that Bacon knew Peter at all before his days in the convent at Paris, or he would have included his name as an eminent mathematician at the time of the *Communia mathematica* (first rescension).[1] If reasons of personal friendship were influential in Bacon's decision, I think it far more probable that it was his friendship and reverence for Adam Marsh, who may also have been his teacher at a crucial period in his life.

Thorndike's reasons, though he only devotes a few lines to the matter, are on much sounder ground, when he says that both Orders were rich in learned men, including students of natural science.[2] Bartholomew of England was a Franciscan; Thomas of Cantimpré, Vincent of Beauvais, and Albert the Great were Dominicans.[3] Amongst the really important men of science, contemporary with Bacon and mentioned in Thorndike's work, only Peter of Spain did not join an Order. But Peter seems to have had a lucrative profession already, being a practising physician which Bacon never was, as well as being an authority on logic in the schools.[4] There is therefore no reason why Bacon should not have found himself a suitable niche within the Franciscan Order, had he not happened to be Roger Bacon, unable, like Servetus after him, to keep out of trouble with theologians. That Bacon never came up against a Calvin, and lived in a more enlightened age, was his good fortune rather than any superior endowment of tact and *savoir faire*.

I think that Bacon's material motives were mixed and various. He needed protection and leisure; and though he knew he would have to endure personal poverty, this will not have distressed him unduly. There is no sign in any of his work that he cared for personal possessions. His single-tracked mind was proof against worldly temptations, and he was certainly not indolent. He needed money for books, and for such experiments as he hoped to make; but if the Order had been interested in his work this need have caused no obstacle. Money could be found. His error of judgment seems to have been in his estimate of the Franciscans. He must have thought that they would be interested in his particular brand of theological and scientific inquiry, which consisted, not so much in a disinterested search for

[1] *Supra*, p. 88.
[2] Thorndike, *History of Magic* . . . II, 620.
[3] *Ibid.*, II, pp. 403, 374, 458.
[4] *Ibid.*, II, 488–89.

truth, as in the application of his scientific findings in the study of theology; and that they would appreciate and support what he was trying to do, and be content to put up with his rude independence and sharp tongue. It was a great deal to expect; but it might have been possible had anyone of importance believed in him, or had he already been a man of renown when he entered the Order as Alexander of Hales had been, and thus a glorious acquisition to it. The Franciscans could certainly have exalted him within the Order had they so desired it; and the fact that they evidently did not is to me the strongest proof that Bacon had no great public reputation when he entered it. Failing this, it would be much more natural for them to treat a man of his arrogance as a menial, as a pretentious person of no particular account, and lacking in Christian humility. 'They forced me with unspeakable violence to obey their will in other matters', he says.[1] And the death of Adam Marsh may have removed their sole impediment from treating him as they wished, especially if he had made an enemy also of Richard of Cornwall, the chief academic light in the Order in England after 1256.[2]

I do not think in Bacon's case that it is sufficient to consider only his material reasons for joining the Order. He was far from despising the ideal of holiness. He tells us himself that the Orders have a 'magnam speciem sanctitatis'; and so for this reason the world approves of them. Men in the Orders 'do not pretend to more than they can perform'.[3] And yet, he goes on, writing in 1272, we see that in these times all the Orders are corrupted—a fairly clear indication that, when still in the world, he believed them to be holy. Until now, he says later, the status of the religious has always been held superior to that of seculars, although the masters in Paris were now openly teaching the contrary, and supporting it with many arguments.[4] Although he admits their faults, Bacon nevertheless defends the religious against the seculars, by saying that perfection is twofold—one in the field of government, and the other in spiritual virtue. The Orders in the Western Church are vowed to chastity, as they are not anywhere else, in the East, or among the Greeks. They have a very far-reaching (largam) obedience. 'Bishops certainly have to obey archbishops and the Pope, but they can go where they want and do

[1] Reading 'in aliis' rejected by Brewer, but contained in the two best MSS. Brewer, *Op. Tert.*, p. 15,

[2] This attitude may not unfairly be compared with that of the traditional regular Army sergeant dealing with a conceited new private who has a Ph.D., but no other visible qualifications for a military career!

[3] *CSP*, p. 426.

[4] *Ibid.*, p. 430.

everything freely. But the religious cannot move a foot, or do anything without the express permission of his superiors. Pleasures and the pomp of the world are repugnant to the religious status, though they are tolerable or excusable in prelates'.[1] There, at least, speaks pride in his religious status.

Having once accepted the position of a religious it would, of course, be natural for Bacon to defend it. He does not necessarily accept its discipline gladly, but he recognizes its moral superiority; and this, for a man of Bacon's intense convictions, was important. He was certainly a moralist and a minder of other people's morals; and being a man of singular enthusiasm, I should expect him to have the courage of his convictions. The asceticism of his Order would not be without appeal for him. He never writes as if the delights of the world tempted him. We have seen that in his glosses to the *Secret of Secrets* he makes a special note of the fact that the possession of riches leads to great sorrow because of the fear of losing them,[2] and that courtiers are quickly depraved by riches and pleasures, even though they were good men when first chosen for their position;[3] of another pleasure he offers an earnest gloss that it may be useful as a medicine in old age, but not necessary![4] He could devote himself more wholeheartedly to the single love of his life, his work, if he were forbidden any source of temptation. Moreover, as Thorndike suggests, he could also be relieved of some of the burdens of teaching.

I do not think specially relevant the argument put forward nearly a century ago by the anonymous writer in the *Westminster Review* that 'the Franciscans were compelled to observe facts, devise remedies, and adopt measures which were not the methods of the schools', and so were of necessity experimentalists.[5] For, as the same writer says later, Bacon cared very little about the human race, or about anything that did not directly bear upon his philosophical system.[6] There may be more in the writer's suggestion that Bacon wrote his medical works for friends within the Order, and there is some evidence for this that he gives.[7] If Bacon had been a real experimentalist, and if the Franciscans had also been experimentalists, they might have found themselves in sympathy, and Bacon could

[1] *CSP*, pp. 428–29.
[2] Steele, Fasc. V, 95. *Supra*, p. 83.
[3] *Ibid.*, Fasc. V, 165–66. *Supra*, p. 84.
[4] 'Medicina necessaria tibi est amplecti puellam calidam et speciosam(!),' to which Bacon glosses, 'id est, utilis'. Steele, Fasc. V, 73, n. 4.
[5] *Westminster Review* (1864), p. 16.
[6] *Ibid.*, p. 29.
[7] *Ibid.*, p. 22 and note.

indeed have gained material support for his experiments. But I find the spiritual affinity between the 'experimental' methods of Bacon and the empirical work of the Franciscans an over-subtle idea, and very dubious in a man of Bacon's forthright and extremely unsubtle character.

Perhaps the key to his decision is to be found in Bacon's attitude to knowledge, and his belief that only the man of good morality could practise true philosophy and receive the illumination necessary for its understanding. Probably the most moral action that could occur to Bacon's mind would be to join a mendicant Order, and we shall see later in this chapter how he seems to favour the stricter 'spiritual' side of the Franciscan movement. We have seen how he approved of Grosseteste's sanctity of life. He also praises Aristotle and the ancients for the same thing. 'These philosophers', he says, 'had no divine grace bestowed on them, which makes man worthy of eternal life . . . yet beyond all comparison their life was better, both in the honesty of their living, and in their contempt for the world and all delights, riches, and honours, as anyone can read in the books of Aristotle, Seneca, Tullius, Avicenna, Alfarabi, Plato, Socrates (!), and others; and *propter hoc* they came to the secrets of wisdom, and found all sciences. But we Christians have found nothing worth while, nor can we understand the wisdom of the philosophers, for the reason that we do not have their morality. Because it is impossible that wisdom can exist at the same time as sin, but perfect virtue is required for this.'[1]

Bacon then tells us how these men lived, and the moral value of their lives. 'He (Aristotle) teaches men to aspire to future happiness and to despise transitory things. And this he taught not only in his public writings, but by deed and example, and he, as perfect teacher, together with his most noble and wise disciples, confirmed it. For, despising the world and riches, delights, and honours, he went into perpetual exile with his companions and they never returned to their own again. For he explained privately that this solitary life is more like the life of God and the angels than the common life of men, and in it he could more freely have time for wisdom and the contemplation of future happiness—as not only his books testify, but those of other philosophers, and not only Greeks but Latins.'[2]

Whether Bacon had, in fact, read any such thing in the apocryphal literature about Aristotle, or had invented it, or filled in a few casual references from his imagination, it is surely significant that he should

[1] *CSP*, pp. 401–2. [2] *Ibid.*, pp. 423–24.

assign such statements to his hero Aristotle. The passage may not tell us much about Aristotle, but it is revealing about Bacon. While at the time of writing this work he was acutely depressed by the disorders around him, and he may not have had a similar belief in the moral excellence of a withdrawal from the temptations and charms of the world at the time he entered the Franciscan Order, yet it seems significant that it should now come to the forefront of his mind. It was at least something of which he had persuaded himself during his fifteen or twenty years in the Order.

And on the value of sinlessness for cognition Bacon says: 'When therefore anyone from his youth falls into mortal sin, his soul is corrupted by a new corruption beyond what he has from original sin; and so he has in himself causes of many kinds of infinite depravity, so that he cannot behold the light of wisdom, nor does he wish to see it, nor could he if it were not for the grace of God. For this reason the Scripture says "Wisdom will not enter into the wicked soul, nor will it dwell in the body given over to sins". And this is not to be understood only of divine wisdom, but of wisdom of any kind. As Algazel says in his *Logic* that the soul is disordered by sins as a rusty mirror, old and dirty, in which the images of things cannot appear, and so no impression of anything can be made in such a soul. And he adds that a soul adorned by virtue is like a clean new mirror in which the species of wisdom shines, for which reason Socrates, the father of philosophers, when he was asked why he did not study the speculative rather than the moral sciences, said that he could not perceive the light of wisdom unless his soul had been cultivated with virtue—and then he would see God Himself and contemplate the causes and reasons for things, and sciences, truly in Him', and then Bacon follows with a discussion of how each specific sin, pride, envy, anger, and the like, clouds the vision.[1]

Though these were no doubt commonplaces at the time, they should not, therefore, necessarily be disregarded. If the medieval man had a very definite consciousness of sin, and the desire for holiness was fostered by his Church and society, Bacon belonged to this society, and was influenced by it to take a step approved by it, and for precisely those reasons that led others to take the same step. But Bacon had a supreme thirst for knowledge, and a belief in revealed knowledge, as we shall see when we come to study his science. He knew that if he were to be fit to receive such a revelation, then he must live the most moral life possible to him, and with his earnestness,

[1] *CSP*, pp. 407–8.

it might be, in medieval eyes, very moral indeed. And certainly in the thirteenth century any searcher after holiness would join an Order.

So, therefore, while the material advantages of his entry into the Order may have weighed seriously with him also, I do not think they can be said to have been necessarily predominant in his decision. At his best Bacon had some awareness of his faults, and at times he could be disarmingly humble; and at all times piety towards God was mixed with his arrogance towards men. So our only conclusion can be that many considerations, intelligent and emotional, entered into his decision, as into every decision made by human beings. And that even the bitter complaints that he voices against his poverty, ill-treatment, and the censorship exercised by his Order, were probably not a sign that he had regretted his decision and would have been happier anywhere else. He sought for happiness in a peculiar way, and it could not be expected that he would find it.

II

For Bacon's life within the Franciscan Order we have two sources of information—one first hand and direct, being Bacon's own remarks in 1267, and the other inferential, drawn from our knowledge of the Order taken from other sources. But even Bacon's remarks are not to be understood, and his actual life reconstructed by the historian, unless the effort is made to trace the relationship between Bacon and his Order. He himself, chafing against the restraints placed upon him and his work, is likely to be less than fair; and it is entirely possible that he was not aware of high matters of policy decided by his superiors, which are available for the consideration of the historian seven centuries later.

The hypothesis will be presented in this study that Bacon was a sympathizer with the 'left-wing' group in the Franciscan Order, those reformers who in the following century are known as 'Spirituals', and ultimately fall into heresy and are dealt with by the Inquisition. In Bacon's time these Spirituals are still only reformers, but they are very dangerous to the unity of the Franciscan Order, though not yet to the Church itself. It will be suggested that Bacon's sufferings were at least partly due to his sympathies with this group, for which he would be more likely to be disciplined, within the Order, than for any scientific views he may have held. It was not, therefore, any official attention by the Church or its instrument, the Inquisition, that affected him, but rather local antagonism by his fellow-friars and superiors among the Franciscans. In order to present the evidence for this hypothesis which, as far as I am aware, has not been suggested elsewhere, it is necessary to trace the development of the schism within the Franciscan Order at greater length than might seem justified in what purports to be a biography of Roger Bacon, and especially to say something about the prophesies of Joachim of Flora, which I believe to have been the determining influence in Bacon's attitude.

The mendicant Orders had arisen in response to certain definite needs in Christendom, and their potential value was clear to the ruling hierarchy in the Church which had consistently supported them since their foundation. From the end of the eleventh century the Church had taken an ever more active part in secular affairs, to the neglect of its spiritual duties, and members of the older Monastic Orders, as well as prelates and high officers in the Church, no longer could lay claim to any special sanctity of life. Many earnest Christians had become anti-clerical, some even falling away altogether into heresy. St. Dominic, believing that ignorance of Catholicism was at least partly responsible for this lapse, founded an Order which laid its emphasis upon preaching, while St. Francis, a man of greater feeling, but of perhaps lesser intellect, perceived the problem differently. By long meditation upon the life and passion of Christ he was able to see in a flash of intuition the immense power that Christ had wielded by His example; and he believed that Christendom could be regenerated by the power of the example of many lives lived after this pattern. By going amongst the lowest of the people, and especially those who had fallen away from the Church because of its hated wealth and ostentation, by preaching perhaps, but specially by acting, helping, curing, tending the sick and the poor, he believed that they would return to Mother Church. So he chose voluntarily, he, the son of a rich merchant, to embrace poverty as his bride.

So came into existence at almost the same time the two mendicant Orders, both pledged to poverty; the one, the Order of Preachers, to tell the people what it was they should believe; the other, the Order of Minorite Friars, to inspire them with a passion for living the lives of Christians, and showing them that the great, all-embracing Church really cared for them, low as they might be in the social scale, and neglected by the worldly prelates and ignorant parish priests whom alone they had hitherto seen as its representatives. Innocent III and his successors, while doubtful at first, soon accepted these Orders as a heaven-sent inspiration, and showered their favours upon them.

From this time onwards they were to be the active missionary movement within the Church, its good right arm—a task the Jesuits also assumed centuries later, when an even greater schism threatened and was partially successful.

Both the Orders were a menace to all the vested interests of the day. The ordinary clergy, not vowed to apostolic poverty, and content with the rewards that came to them from the holding of ecclesiastical office, objected to their mode of life and their dedication to their self-imposed aims, as we all dislike those who are obviously more saintly than ourselves; they objected still more later when the great power of the Inquisition, with all its tremendous possibilities, was thrust into their hands. They objected to the permission soon given to them to receive confessions, say masses, and administer the sacraments, for these had always been their own regular source of income. And it was natural that the ordinary Christian should prefer the services of the saintly friars to their own more tainted ministrations. The friars offered an unfair competition, against which they had no remedy unless the sources of their support could be undermined.

When the friars entered the universities, as they soon did, the secular masters, the students of law, and all who had been satisfied with things as they were, resented and feared them, and especially disliked the support given to them by the Papal Curia. They fought against every privilege granted to the friars by the Papacy, and they tried to restrict their advance, especially at the University of Paris; but always the Orders gained the initial victories. When the Parisian students dispersed to their homes in 1229, the Orders continued to teach and were granted chairs in theology at the university. All the privileged classes saw their security threatened; but while the Orders enjoyed the support of the Papacy and the respect of the people, they could do nothing serious against them. The only resource remaining to them was to try to undermine this support by attacking the whole way of life of both Orders, showing that they were not poor mendicant friars, but avaricious robbers, not supporters of the Church, but its most dangerous enemies, riddled with heretical tendencies; not holy saints, but licentious profligates.

This is the background of the tremendous polemic *De periculis novissimorum temporum* published by the distinguished and remarkably courageous theologian, William of St. Amour, in 1255, which was itself only the culmination of a fierce campaign carried on by secular masters and students against the friars. This campaign had a brief success in 1254 with the issuance of the bull *Etsi animarum* by Innocent IV a few weeks before his death, under which the privileges of the Orders were seriously curtailed. But the bull was repudiated by Innocent's successor, Alexander IV, and William of St. Amour published his polemic. Though the polemic was officially suppressed, the struggle continued, and every weapon that could be found was used against the Orders.[1] The distinguished leaders of both Orders replied to the attacks, and the seculars in turn pressed their arguments to the utmost. Every mistake made by the Orders, or any of their members, added more fuel to the controversy; and there is no doubt that the 219 errors condemned by Bishop Tempier in 1277 included some of the teachings of Thomas Aquinas because he was a Dominican, and condemnation of him would bring some more discredit upon his Order.[2] But long before this the Franciscan Order had been split from the top to the bottom by a controversy that had its roots in the teachings of the founder himself. And on this even the papal hierarchy was forced to take sides against the too strict application of the teachings of Francis.

For it was impossible that any established institution could support absolute poverty unless it were itself prepared to abdicate. A small band of apostles could manage to avoid holding property, and could rely on daily begging for their needs. But not an ecclesiastical body, dedicated to serve above all the interests of the Papacy. A strict Franciscan follower of St. Francis could not help but become anti-clerical if the Church failed to reform and divest itself of its wealth—which would, of course, mean the abdication of its necessary worldly responsibilities. And this anti-clericalism and the emphasis laid on leading a good life here on earth could hardly fail to lead to certain forms of heresy—Pelagianism or semi-Pelagianism at the least, or Donatism, which claims that grace cannot be transmitted through an unworthy priest. The Poor Men of Lyons, the Waldensian heretics, were not far from the Franciscan ideal; yet these were proscribed and punished, as were the later followers of Wyclif, the Lollards.

[1] For the history of this quarrel between the seculars and regulars, or religious, in its early stages, see H. Bierbaum, 'Bettelorden und Weltgeistlichkeit . . .' (1920). Extracts from the text of the *De periculis* are given in Bierbaum's study, together with a selection of the replies of the friars, and counter-charges by the seculars. Bacon's own account of the quarrel, which he tells us in 1272 had been going on for twenty years, is to be found in *CSP.*, pp. 429–32. For the bull *Etsi animarum* (November, 1254), see Huber, *A Documented History . . .* (1944), p. 134, and a lively and accurate story in the old work of H. C. Lea, *A History of the Inquisition* (1887), I, 283–84. Huber is at a loss to account for the severity of the bull; Lea attributes it, as does Bierbaum, to the influence of William of St. Amour and the gradual loss of patience with the whole controversy, and a doubt whether the friars were worth what they were costing.

[2] *Chartularium* . . . I, 544–55.

The Franciscan Order, then, can be considered as always potentially anti-clerical, if it lived up to its ideals. But there was a possibility that it could remain as an example in itself of the ideal of poverty, and thus draw to itself those Christians who longed for a life of self-abnegation, and felt this was the best way to express their religious ideals. This might have been possible if the Order had not had duties to perform on behalf of the Church which were only possible for an organized institution, administering, if it did not own, property, and with a secure source of income. The leaders of the Order were divided from the beginning into those who wanted to perform the tasks of the Papacy, as an institution, and those who had joined it because of the ideals of poverty and self-abnegation. The division is seen even among the generals of the Order from the very time of St. Francis. Brother Elias was an 'institutionalist', the first of those who were later to be called 'conventuals', while John of Parma, who was probably General at the time of Bacon's entry into the Order, belonged to the opposite, or 'spiritual' party. And though Brother Elias was deposed by his fellow-friars, having been premature in his desire to retreat from the stricter Franciscan ideal, it was, on the whole, his outlook that prevailed within the movement in later years.

It is possible that the views of St. Francis, which were, in any case, not always clear to his followers, would have been satisfactorily modified by his successors as soon as his personal companions, who had known what stress he laid on poverty, had disappeared from the scene. Without a renewal of the message of St. Francis, his teachings might have been conveniently forgotten, for there were other aspects of the Rule that could have been kept by 'conventuals' and 'spirituals' alike. But probably more important than even the memory of St. Francis was the influence exercised by a work of peculiar evangelical appeal especially to Franciscans. This was the series of books which came later to be known as the 'Everlasting Gospel', ascribed to Joachim of Flora, a Calabrian monk who had died around the turn of the century. The seductive appeal of these books, which utilize to the full the method of allegory and personal exegesis of the sacred words of the scriptures, tempted the spiritually gifted friars to try their own powers at prophesying, and Joachim became the posthumous foster-parent of great numbers of activist heresies which persisted for many centuries, and created the profoundest disorder, especially within the Franciscan Order. In all ages of history human insecurity has led to the belief in prophetic visions which purport to reveal the future, preferably a future in which the individual believer is persuaded that he will be on the right side, while his enemies will perish. Such beliefs are food for martyrs and the very stuff of heresy, from the tiny persecuted group of Christians at the time of Nero to the adherents of British Israel and Jehovah's Witnesses in our own day.[1]

Joachim of Flora proclaimed that there would be three ages in the history of mankind, corresponding to the three persons of the Trinity. The first was the age of the Father, who ruled through power and fear (the period of the Old Testament), the second the age of the Son, when the wisdom of the Father would be revealed through the Son (the period of the New Testament and the Catholic Church). Finally there would come the age of the Holy Spirit, a new dispensation of universal love in which there would be no further need of disciplinary institutions. Latins and Greeks would be united in the new spiritual kingdom, and the Church would be freed from everything carnal and worldly, and the 'eternal gospel' would abide until the end of the world.[2]

It need hardly be added that the age of the new dispensation was in the near future, specifically in 1260. Life would go out of the first

[1] The fundamental research on the whole Joachite (following Lea, I am adopting this form of the word in preference to the more awkward Joachimite, favoured by Webster) movement is to be found scattered through the first six volumes of the *Archiv für Kirchengeschichte des Mittelalters* (1885–92), edited by H. Denifle and F. Ehrle. Probably the fullest, and even the fairest, account (certainly the best in English to this day) of the social and religious implications of the movement and its history through several centuries is still to be found in the old work of H. C. Lea, *A History of the Inquisition* . . . (1887), even though he could only base his research on the recently completed studies by Denifle and Ehrle. Nothing of much importance has been contributed to the picture in this century, and the carefully slanted and selected recent work of Father Huber makes one wonder sometimes whether he and Lea are writing about the same subject. The problem of the 'spirituals' and their attitude towards ecclesiastical corruption is not to be dismissed simply with such words as: 'In reality they were nothing more than proud recalcitrant religious who tried to force their own whims on an Order that already had its mode of living clearly defined by the Holy See' (*A Documented History* . . . p. 186). However factually accurate this may be, it would surely be more judicious in the twentieth century to face some of the questions the author so consistently begs. Obedience to the superiors in the Order *may* be the supreme Christian virtue; but must it be exercised to the exclusion of all others?

[2] It is still not known how much of the Joachite literature belongs to Joachim himself, and how much to the numerous pseudo-Joachims who followed him. On this subject there is an extensive monographic literature, especially in Italian; but it is of no great importance for this study, in which we are interested in the prophesies themselves and not their authors. I have consulted the sumptuous edition of the Istituto Storico Italiano of the *Tractatus super quatuor evangelia*, edited by Ernesto Buonaiuti (Rome, 1930), and shall have occasion to refer to it again. The minor works of Joachim and his condemned book against Peter Lombard were also printed by the same institute, but are of no importance for us. These books are generally conceded to be genuine works of Joachim. For our purpose the most important thing is that Joachim was one of the first and certainly the most influential of a long line of prophets who interpreted the scriptures in the Middle Ages according to their own private revelations. The process, once initiated, was extremely infectious. The Spiritual Franciscans, and later the Fraticelli, could always make use of some of this literature to support their views, and call down thunder on the Church, as the Hebrew prophets had thundered against the kings of Israel in their day, and for the same reason.

two gospels in 1200 'ut fieret evangelium eternum'.[1] The forces of Antichrist, who was to come first, would be arrayed against the forces of Christ and would suffer defeat. But the children of the Holy Spirit must prepare themselves for this glorious era, and be ready to do battle with Antichrist, or he would conquer. And the signs of the coming of Antichrist, who had already been prophesied in the clearest terms in the Bible, were dissensions and feuds.[2]

Now the Franciscans, by virtue of their whole history, as members of a movement founded by one whom even his greatest opponents would admit was a saint, could be expected to regard themselves as the spearhead in the fight against Antichrist. And Joachim had been indiscreet enough to suggest that just such a movement as this would arise, even though he called it an order of 'monks', since friars had not yet been thought of.[3] And if one of the weapons of Antichrist was the power to offer the delights of this world to those who were ready to worship him, then it was clear that only by retaining the pristine purity of the Order could the spears of the defenders of Christianity be kept sharpened. In his lifetime the Emperor Frederic II was widely regarded as the Antichrist, others believed that Genghiz Khan was more fitted for the rôle. Salimbene, the Italian Franciscan chronicler, only abandoned his belief that Frederic was the Antichrist when Frederic died before the great year of 1260.[4] Cardinal Regnier accused Frederic in violent language of being the 'precursor of Antichrist',[5] in a letter which was published throughout Europe. But whoever was to be the great protagonist of the forces of evil, these forces at least could be recognized by the faithful, and they must make ready for the day when they would appear.

In 1254, as the year 1260 approached, a certain Franciscan brother, Gerard of San Borgo, wrote a book which he called the *Introduction to the Eternal Gospel*. This made far more specific and pointed the more vague and general prophesies of Joachim, and set up the three most important books of Joachim as constituting in themselves the 'Everlasting Gospel', by which name they came to be known thereafter.[6] Gerard's work also related the prophesies of Joachim directly to St. Francis, who was the 'angel of light', and the 'order of the sign

[1] *Archiv* . . . I, 99.
[2] Joachim, *Tractatus* . . . pp. 99, 164–65, etc.
[3] *Archiv* . . . I, 103, 115–16, etc.
[4] 'Sed postquam mortuus est Fredericus . . . et annus ducentesimus sexagesimus elapsus, dimisi totaliter istam doctrinam et dispono non credere nisi quae video.' Salimbene, *Cronica* . . . pp. 302–3.
[5] 'Praenuntius Antichristi.' Matthew Paris, *Chronica* . . . V, 61.
[6] *Archiv* . . . I, 100.

of the living God'. The 'monks' of Joachim now became specifically the Franciscan Order, which, according to the protocol of Anagni which condemned the *Introduction*, he had 'incredibly exalted'.[1] The book created a furore, and was condemned in a special meeting called by the Pope at Anagni, the proceedings of which have been printed, and which give us the official reasons for the condemnation.[2]

At another time the book might have escaped the attention of the authorities, or been quietly suppressed by the Order itself. The Franciscan general at this time was John of Parma, a man of pronounced 'Spiritual' leanings, who would never have condemned it on his own initiative, and was, indeed, suspected of having written the *Introduction* himself.[3] But it was pounced upon by William of St. Amour as evidence for his charges against the mendicant Orders, and he went specially to Rome to attack it. Though it was written by one of their number, the Franciscans did not dare to defend it since it was obviously heretical; and its exaltation of the Franciscan Order would naturally arouse the enmity, not only of the seculars, but of the Dominicans who were otherwise their natural allies against the seculars. Under attack already for their way of life, the Franciscans now had an even more serious charge against them; and if William of St. Amour had not overplayed his hand by publishing his *De periculis* the following year, and if the Orders had not been so badly needed by the Papacy and found in Alexander IV a Pope who was especially favourable to them, William might have convinced the Holy See. The bull *Etsi animarum* of Innocent IV, already referred to, was probably issued in revulsion against the excessive pretensions of the Orders as shown by Gerard's book.[4]

The learned and famous leaders of the Orders were also far from impotent in the battle of words. Thomas of Cantimpré, a Dominican, gives credit to the eloquence and learning of Albertus Magnus for the defeat of William and the condemnation of the *De periculis* with greater publicity than the relatively quiet suppression of the *Introduction* at Anagni.[5] William was forced into exile, where he continued his polemics, until his peaceful death some years later. But Gerard, being a friar, was disciplined by his own Order, being thrown into a dungeon from which he was never to emerge in the eighteen years of life remaining to him.

[1] *Archiv* . . . I, 101, 116. [2] *Ibid.*, I, 99–142.

[3] Huber, *A Documented History* . . . p. 141; Lea, *History of the Inquisition* . . . I, 285; III, 22.

[4] *Supra*, pp. 128–29.

[5] Thomas of Cantimpré, *Bonum universale*, II, ix, quoted by Lea, *History of the Inquisition* . . . III, 23.

Now it seems evident that in the struggle between the two groups in the Franciscan Order, Roger Bacon was on the side of the 'Spirituals'.[1] There is, in my view, enough evidence in his work to show a very considerable sympathy with Joachite ideas and methods, and on one occasion he actually tells the Pope that the prophesies of Joachim ought to be taken seriously.[2]

If our reasons for Bacon's joining the Franciscan Order are correct, one of the attractions it had for him was its ideal of holiness. And though, as a scholar, he chafes against the restrictions placed upon him in the Order, he never suggests they should be relaxed. As we have seen, he vigorously defends the Franciscan ideal against the attacks of the seculars in 1272.[3] In this he would only be following what was probably the majority opinion in his Order at the time, and would be in line with the policies and views of Bonaventura, the current Minister-General. None of this would in any way render him suspect to his superiors. But in his attitude towards prophesies, and his constant stressing of the immediate expectation of Antichrist, he goes much further than the majority of his contemporaries, and seems to range himself by the side of the heterodox Spirituals, and could have laid himself open to the reprisals which accompanied the forced resignation of the previous Minister-General, John of Parma, and the publication of the *Introduction to the Everlasting Gospel*.

We know that in 1267 Bacon was in Paris, and that he had 'for ten years been exiled from his former University fame', and that he had regarded this exile as distasteful, that he suffered from the 'unspeakable violence' of his superiors, that he therefore did not feel like writing at all, and that he was weary and languid.[4] In Wood's life of Bacon, printed by Brewer, there is also reference to a curious passage in the *Opus Minus* which has not come down to us in the so-far-published fragments, but which there is no reason to doubt that Wood in his time was able to consult. He gives the actual passage as follows: 'For my superiors and brothers, disciplining me with hunger, kept me under close guard and would not permit anyone to come to me, fearing that my writings would be divulged to others than to the chief pontiff and themselves'.[5] While this, as will be shown later, only has reference to the period when Bacon was composing his

[1] The use of the word 'Spiritual' to describe the group that was interested in Joachim and the stricter interpretation of the Rule is an anachronism in the second half of the thirteenth century and does not properly apply until the fourteenth. The word as it will be used in this study, hereafter without quotes, should be taken to apply to these 'left-wing' groups.

[2] *Opus Majus*, I, 269.

[3] *CSP*, pp. 431–2.

[4] Gasquet, p. 500; Brewer, *Op. Tert.*, p. 15.

[5] Brewer, *Op. Tert.* (introduction), p. xciv.

works for the Pope, strictly contrary to the regulations of the Franciscan Order,[1] the totality of the references do seem to show that he was under some kind of restraint in the Paris house, even if it never amounted to as much as imprisonment. His transfer from Oxford to Paris also requires some explanation, as it would not seem to have been voluntary on Bacon's part. I suggest that this may have been due to his local reputation as a Joachite, rather than to any suspicion that his works contained magic, astrology, or any of the other supposedly dangerous ideas which Charles and others have thought were responsible for his persecution.[2]

In the *Opus Majus*, as we have seen, he reminds the Pope of the prophesies of Merlin, the Sybil, Sesto, and Joachim, and tells him that these are to be taken seriously. Curiously enough, when he refers to the same prophesies five years later, the name of Joachim is omitted.[3] This may have some significance, since the closing years of the 1260's were full of more polemics than at any other period, and the name of Joachim might have increased in disrepute. The important thing about these prophesies is that they do not date from biblical or classical times. Even the Sybil is not taken from the distant Roman past, but refers to recent apocalyptic literature, which took the form of utterances of a cryptic nature in the ancient 'Sibylline' manner, though, as Matthew Paris informed us, there had always been great interest in the original Sibylline books, and conjectures as to their contents.[4] Merlin does not come from some mythical Arthurian legend, but is supposed to be the 'author' of a number of modern prophesies. They were, of course, collected under his name because of his fame as a wizard.[5] We have no information on Sesto, but he also probably belonged to the current crop. In fact, Bacon tells us of one prophet who is still alive and expecting to see his prophesies fulfilled within his own lifetime.

'Forty years ago', Bacon tells us, 'it was prophesied, and many have had visions on the subject, that there would be a pope in these times who would purge the canon law and the Church of God . . . and there would be justice universally without the noise of litigation (strepitu litis) . . . and it will happen that the Greeks will return to the obedience of the Roman Church, and the Tartars for the most

[1] *Archiv* . . . VI, 103.
[2] Charles, pp. 45 ff.
[3] *Opus Majus*, I, 269; *CSP*, p. 402.
[4] Matthew Paris, *Chronica* . . . I, 50–52.
[5] L. A. Paton, *Les prophecies de Merlin* (1927). The prophesies are printed in Vol. I, and interpreted in Vol. II. For the Sibylline utterances see II, 8–10, 154, and for the general connection of the prophesies with those of Joachim, chapter VI, pp. 157–268.

part will be converted to the Faith and the Saracens will be destroyed.[1] Again, later, he says: 'One most blessed pope will arise who will take away all corruption... and the world will be renewed and the fulness of the nations (plenitudo gentium) will enter and the remnants of Israel will be converted to the faith'.[2]

These passages should be compared with the account of the commission of Anagni which dealt with the book of Gerard of San Borgo and condemned it. The quotations are derived from Joachim's book of the concordance between the Old and New Testaments. 'The people will fall from their pride and become one people with the Gentiles, and there will be rule by the saints over the people called Joseph. And at that time the succession of the Roman pontiff will be from sea to sea and from the river to the ends of the earth.'[3] Joachim makes use himself elsewhere of the same passage from the Epistle to the Romans as Bacon, speaking three times in his *Tractatus* with the same fervour of the *plenitudo gentium*, which is at hand.[4]

Bacon, it will be noted, insists that his Pope will do the things which he personally favoured, reform the canon law, etc. It is one of the manifest advantages of apocalyptic prophesies that they can be changed to suit the visionaries' own views. And, in fact, as we have seen, Bacon does not attribute the prophesy to Joachim at all, but to some prophet who lived only forty years ago, while Joachim had died in 1202. Bacon's prophet is still saying it. 'Per revelationem dixit et dicit', Bacon tells us; and, moreover, he has prophesied that he himself will live to see the day.[5] And if this should be thought to be merely a piece of polite flattery for his exalted reader, this suggestion can be discounted, for the prophesy is again repeated by Bacon five years later, when Clement IV is dead and there has been an interregnum in the Papacy.

The whole tone of the early pages of the *Compendium studii philosophiae*, published by Brewer, belongs to the apocalyptic literature of the time. Morals are decaying, the Papacy has been vacant for years, dissensions are rife, and there seems to be no cure except a divine intervention. All this heralds the immediate approach of Antichrist. The work of Joachim and the pseudo-Joachims is of the same

[1] Brewer, *Op. Tert.*, p. 86. Salimbene quotes some verses which evidently refer to Pope Gregory X (1272–76) as this 'papa sacer', and their use by Merlin shows that this particular prophesy was composed after Gregory's elevation to the Papacy, and thus after Bacon's appeal in the *Opus Tertium*. So Bacon cannot be relying on 'Merlin' for his prophesy. Paton, *Les Prophecies*... II, 177–78. Salimbene, *Cronaca*... p. 492.

[2] *CSP*, p. 402.

[3] *Archiv*... I, 108.

[4] Joachim, *Tractatus*... pp. 80, 99, 116 (Romans xi. 25).

[5] Brewer, *Op. Tert.*, p. 86.

nature. Antichrist is coming, as the Scriptures foretold; and his time is near. Joachim uses the geography of the Bible in the same way as Bacon, he quotes Scripture to the same purpose, and he is full of allegory.[1] And one of his most popular books, the first part of the *Everlasting Gospel* concerns the concordance of the Old Testament and the New, from which Gerard draws inferences for the third age which is now being ushered in in the thirteenth century.[2] And Bacon, as we have seen, is continually referring to the 144,000 of the elect, and makes use of the idea even in his classes in philosophy in his Parisian days.[3]

I think it therefore clear that Bacon is steeped in the Joachitic and apocalyptic literature of his time, and is greatly influenced by it in his own work and his attitude to life, and he is especially impressed by the idea of the imminent approach of Antichrist. This, however, was far from peculiar to him. The important thing is what result his beliefs had upon his overt acts and whether these could lead him into any trouble within the Order. We have seen how he tells his fellow-friars that the signs show that Antichrist is at hand, and they retort to him that he is himself a disciple of Antichrist and a heretic.[4] This, however, may not have any more significance than when we call a man who has presumed to vote for the current President of the United States a 'communist'. A heretic was no doubt a usual term of mild reproach in the Middle Ages. But at least the passage shows that Bacon could not keep his mouth shut about his views. The extreme urgency of Bacon's appeal to the Pope is stressed by saying that Antichrist when he comes will know science and be able to make some use of it (the 'Bolshevik bogey'). So Christians must themselves learn how to counteract this science with better science of their own. This is Bacon's personal contribution to the prophetic literature, and, of course, bears the imprint of his own interests and desires upon it.[5]

As Professor Thorndike has pointed out,[6] it is unlikely that Bacon was punished for views on astrology and science that were common at the time, and approved by respectable theologians and authorities such as Albertus Magnus. He finds no evidence that even magic, which Bacon did not practise and, indeed, condemned, was the object of criticism by the authorities; and he has pointed out in many other places how widespread the interest in astrology was in Bacon's

[1] Joachim, *Tractatus* . . . 42, 146, and *passim*.
[2] Huber, *A Documented History* . . . p. 139; *Archiv* . . . I, 99–100, 116–17.
[3] Steele, Fasc. XIII, 384.
[4] *CSP*, p. 430.
[5] *Opus Majus*, II, 221; Little, *Op. Tert.*, p. 17.
[6] Thorndike, *History of Magic* . . . II, 674–77.

time. Indeed, Thorndike's whole work shows how unlikely it was that these were the 'suspected novelties' for which Bacon, according to a late fourteenth-century chronicler, was later condemned.[1]

But theological novelties were a different matter, and Bacon was undoubtedly to some degree guilty of introducing these. But I doubt if these would have been even understood by most of his contemporaries, so different were they from the usual scholastic subtleties which did not interest him, as aids for theology. He was merely an extreme conservative in theology in so far as he wanted to return to exclusive scriptural exegesis; the only innovations he wanted were improved interpretations resulting from an increased knowledge of the natural sciences and geography. But his criticisms of theologians were a different matter, and they could certainly have been partly responsible both in 1257 and 1278 for measures of restraint placed upon his writings, and perhaps his person. But the offence which was considered most dangerous of all by his superiors, for which the stiffest penalties were imposed, was the attempt to provoke schism within the Order.[2] And the Joachites and Spirituals were above all accused of just this crime. If Bacon was a Joachite, or of Joachitic sympathies, with or without committing any overt acts of conspiracy, this would have been known to his immediate superiors; and knowing also that he was an accomplished writer, they may have feared that he would use his talents to promote Joachitic views. And these could easily have been reconciled with his science, and not only reconciled, but actually used to emphasize the importance of his scientific knowledge. This suspicion might have been enough for the authorities to suggest a removal in or around 1257 to Paris, where he might be kept under closer supervision than in England. In England he had friends and a family, and possibly means for publishing his work without the formal sanction of his Order would have been more easily available. It is certainly not suggested that he was actually imprisoned in his French convent, nor prevented from carrying on his legitimate studies; but he may have been to some extent quarantined from the outside world. This is consistent with

[1] *Chronicle of the Twenty-Four Generals*, p. 360. Crowley (*Roger Bacon* . . . pp. 55–67) disagrees. His arguments carry considerable weight and are worthy of close study; but they do not seem to take sufficient note of the universality of astrological beliefs in Bacon's day, though there might have been opposition to them within the Franciscan Order. Crowley emphasizes, as is emphasized equally in this study, the fact that it was his own Order that disciplined him.

[2] 'We lay under a perpetual curse anyone who presumes either by word or deed in any way to work for the division of our Order. If anyone contravenes this prohibition he shall be considered as an excommunicate and schismatic and destroyer of our Order. . . . Brothers incorrigible in this shall be imprisoned or expelled from the Order.' Extract from the Constitutions of Narbonne, *Archiv* . . . VI, 116.

what he relates of this period, and the attitude of the friars towards his work.

The trouble within the Order came to a head in 1257 with the forced resignation of John of Parma, and this is the period when Bacon himself says he went into exile, either from the university or from his native land or both. The hypothesis is therefore offered that Bacon entered the Franciscan Order in England some time before the publication of Gerard's book, say about 1252. He would be less likely to have entered it afterwards, as he might have realized the potential danger to himself of his Joachitic views. He was relieved of some of his teaching duties, but allowed to continue his studies in the natural sciences and make such experiments as he wished, and to continue to observe and perhaps take part in the experiments made by his associates. This life was satisfactory to him, and he made much progress. But it was interrupted by the troubles consequent upon the publication of Gerard's book, and the *De periculis* the following year (1255), and perhaps by the return of Richard of Cornwall to England in 1256. At all events, during the years 1254 to 1257 he became suspect, and was unable, as usual, to keep his views to himself. He believed that he was supported by the well-known views of the Minister-General. But when John's enemies were able to force him to resign, Bacon also paid the penalty of his indiscretions, and, as a preventive measure, was transferred by his superiors to Paris.

Bacon reacts to this by weariness and languor and unwillingness to do any further work.[1] Moreover, as his superiors have sent him there for disciplinary purposes, they are no longer willing to let him spend all his time in scientific pursuits, but insist on his doing his regular work in the convent, from which he may have been excused before. It may be worth noting that his new Minister-General, Bonaventura, was not apparently very favourably impressed with the science of astrology,[2] at all events at the time he was studying in Paris, only a few years before his appointment as Minister-General. And though I should not expect him to be even aware, at this time, of Bacon's existence, the latter could not expect much sympathy for at least this part of his work from his General. Bonaventura certainly has his own synthesis of knowledge, which takes little account of natural science, and is thus poles removed from Bacon's.

[1] Gasquet, p. 500.

[2] In dealing with the question: 'Utrum ex impressionibus luminarium causetur in hominibus diversitas morum', Bonaventura condemns the idea that the stars actually cause anything in human beings, saying that this is contrary to Christian faith and the evidence of the senses. *Opera* . . . II, 361 (Comm. in Sent. Dist. XIV). See also Crowley, *Roger Bacon* . . . pp. 55–58.

Finally in 1260 comes the official censorship announced by the decrees of the Chapter of Narbonne, and thereafter Bacon knows that he cannot have anything further published without permission from his Order. The only way to avoid this censorship is to obtain the support and patronage of one even higher than Bonaventura, and this opportunity is not presented until the arrival of the mandate from the Pope in 1266. The same Pope, when only a Cardinal, had sent Roger a mandate, but even this was not a high enough authority, unless he also tried to use his influence with the Franciscans. And though he may have set to work at once, as Thorndike suggests,[1] or at least tried to raise the funds necessary for it, as I shall suggest in the next chapter, he cannot do anything with the work until his patron finally becomes Pope.

If it is asked why Bacon never refers to his part in the Joachitic controversy, we can only reply that it is characteristic of him, and quite natural for him to believe, that it is the neglect of natural science by all authorities that is at the root of the evils of the day, and presumably his own troubles too. He tells us that no one since Robert Grosseteste and Adam Marsh has understood mathematics and optics, his own fields of activity, that no one experiments except the obscure Peter of Maricourt, that doctors do not use astrology as they should, that languages are little studied, and so on. This exalts his own contributions and makes them unique and himself more interesting and important as a lone investigator in possession of the truth. This is a piece of psychological self-defence; yet, as we have seen, it is by no means true, as he admits elsewhere. But one can justly feel oneself to be a martyr if one is persecuted for the truth's sake. Few convictions are more comforting to us than the certainty that we are right and the rest of the world is wrong; and if we suffer for it, that is a part of the painful pleasure involved. But if we are merely one of a crowd, punished for an indiscreet tongue or a petty infraction of discipline, there is little enough romantic in that, and we prefer to convince ourselves, and inform the world as publicly as possible that we are persecuted for righteousness' sake. We could not have been wrong, or perverse or misguided, oh no!

There is no reason to suppose that any of Bacon's associates had Bacon's vision of the way in which the facts of natural science could be used for the greater understanding of theological truth, nor for its supreme value and practical importance in the coming conflict with Antichrist. There is no reason why, even in the thirteenth century,

[1] Thorndike, *History of Magic* . . . II, 622–24.

any ordinary scientific worker should place special emphasis on prophesies. It is these prophesies and Bacon's evident belief in them that would seem more suspicious to Bacon's superiors in the Order than experiments, astrology, alchemy, or any of his mathematical or optical studies. But his transfer to France, and the subsequent censorship, would hit all his writings equally, and increase his feeling that he was a lone struggler against the darkness of ignorance, waiting to be rescued by a magnanimous and enlightened patron—the feeling that suffuses the great *Opera* (especially the early pages of the *Opus Tertium*) and has been the inspiration of romantic historians and biographers ever since.

The new General, St. Bonaventura, was himself a supporter of apostolic poverty, and had defended it already before his appointment in a tract in reply to the polemics of the seculars. In his last years he defended it again from further attacks that followed the death of Clement IV.[1] In the disturbances of 1255 he had himself been forced for a time to give up his teaching at the University of Paris, and his doctoral degree was held up until he had been in office as General for a few years.[2] So his personal experience of the dangers of schism would tend to make him take the division in the Franciscan Order itself seriously. He realized the hopelessness of apostolic poverty for the Order as a whole, while he desired to move as little as possible from the ideal of St. Francis, as far as the individual members of the Order were concerned. Recognizing the moral power of self-sacrifice, he did not want to abandon it; and he knew also that if the Franciscans became only one more Order within the Church, without any pretensions to sanctity, they would command even less respect from the people than the already far decayed monastic Orders which had been the butt of satirists for generations. For, living by daily alms as they did, the public would be constantly aware of their exactions. So Bonaventura's policy was one of compromise, giving strict instructions to the friars that they were to exercise discretion in their begging, and in no circumstances to lend colour to the accusation of the seculars that they were robbers.[3] But at the same time the Order itself was permitted by arrangements with the Holy See to hold property, but not in its own name, and administered by papal procurators.[4]

[1] St. Bonaventura, *Opera* . . . V, 124–65 (*Quaestiones disputatae de paupertate*); VIII, 233–330 (*Apologia pauperum*).

[2] Huber, *A Documented History* . . . pp. 147–48.

[3] Bonaventura, *Opera* . . . VIII, 468.

[4] Huber, *A Documented History* . . . pp. 173–76.

Being forced to tread this delicate path, and give offence to as few as possible, it was absolutely essential that no friars should wantonly give any handle to the enemies of the Order as Brother Gerard had done in 1254, and Bonaventura was determined to prevent this if possible.

It seems that in these circumstances a prohibition against publishing writings without the permission of the Order was an essential step, and one that the most ardent proponents of free speech would find it difficult in the thirteenth century to discredit. It had, at the time it was imposed, all the features of a modern wartime censorship, for the very existence of the Order itself was at stake. It should not, I think, be held against the Franciscans and Bonaventura that it was inaugurated; and the wording of the decree itself shows how repugnant it was to the superiors in the Order.

'Let no one glory', the preamble states, 'in the possession of virtue in his heart if he puts no guard on his conversation. If anyone thinks that he is religious and does not curb his tongue, but only allows his heart to lead him astray, then his religion is vain. It is therefore necessary that an honourable fence should surround the mouth and other senses and acts, deeds and morals, that the statutes of the regulars may not be destroyed by perfect men, but kept intact, lest they should be bitten by a snake when they let down the barrier. . . . If anyone think that the penalty for the breach of statutes of this kind is severe, let him reflect that, according to the Apostle, all discipline in the present life is not a matter for rejoicing but for sorrow; yet through it, it will bear for the future the most peaceful fruit of justice for those who have endured it'.[1]

It was unfortunate for Bacon that this censorship prevented the free exercise of his talents, and that he was not permitted to write and publish whatever he desired. But there is no reason to believe that permission for publication would have been refused for any genuine work of science. Indeed, as his *Computus* was certainly written during the censorship, and presumably copied and published, it is shown that he was not completely reduced to silence.[2] But it was a different matter for the works written to the Pope, and a study of the decrees of Narbonne are interesting as showing to what extent Bacon offended both in letter and spirit against these decrees. It could, indeed, be

[1] *Archiv* . . . VI, 87 ff.

[2] Steele, Fasc. VI. The editor points out (p. xxv) that the work is unexceptionable in tone except for a few pages (pp. 146 ff.), and, curiously enough, the original hand in the MS. breaks off at this point. Steele suggests that this was due to fear of the altered tone on the part of the copyist.

argued that he was treated very leniently rather than made a 'martyr of science'.

In the fifth rubric occur the words: 'Let the brothers carry nothing in words or in writing which could conduce to the scandal of any-one. . . . Let no brother go to the Court of the Lord Pope or send a brother without the permission of the Minister-General. Let them, if they have gone otherwise, be at once expelled from the Curia by the procurators of the Order. And let no one apply to the Minister-General for permission unless serious cause or urgent necessity demand it'.[1]

In the sixth rubric is the decree that particularly applied to Bacon: 'We prohibit any new writing from being published outside the Order, unless it shall first have been examined carefully by the Minister-General or provincial, and the visitants in the provincial chapter . . . anyone who contravenes this shall be kept at least three days on bread and water, and lose his writing'.[2]

'Let no brother write books, or cause them to be written for sale, and let the Provincial Minister not dare to have or keep any books without the license of the Minister-General, or let any brothers have or keep them without the permission of the Provincial Ministers'.[3]

Finally there is the general provision against anyone who 'by word or deed presumes to work for the division of our Order',[4] which has been referred to earlier. Though Bacon's works for the Pope may not offend against this decree, his *Compendium studii philosophiae* certainly does, though I am doubtful, as will appear in the last chapter of this study, whether this work was ever published. But it could also be argued that the attack on Alexander of Hales, the Franciscan authority, in the *Opus Minus* might also make for division within the Order. And the general Joachitic and apocalyptic tone of all the later works show where his sympathies lay. If these opinions were accompanied by orally given pronouncements to his friends and companions, and to superiors in the Order, they may well have been sufficient to account for his troubles. It is, on the other hand, quite possible that Bacon himself may not have been aware of the true reasons for his treatment, as the private in an army is not always aware of the decisions of high policy that affect him, and that he may attribute to quite other motives than the true ones.

[1] *Archiv* . . . VI, 103.

[2] *Ibid.*, VI, 110. The regulation is made more severe and prison prescribed as the penalty in 1279 and 1282. *Ibid.*, pp. 110–11.

[3] *Ibid.*, VI, 116.

[4] *Supra*, p. 138, n. 2.

CHAPTER VIII

THE WORKS FOR THE POPE

IN this study of the life of Roger Bacon it will be clear that we have been minimizing his importance in the history of his time. The picture we have presented of a brilliant and unstable personality, prevented, partly by his own faults, from making a name for himself consistent with his undoubted talents, is not a specially appealing one. We do not think that he was persecuted for his freethinking, or for his advanced and unpopular scientific views, but rather that he was neglected as a relatively unimportant 'crank' until his persistent outspokenness, especially on matters outside his professional work, annoyed his fellow-friars enough to persuade them to have him disciplined. Bacon might have sunk into a complete obscurity, as other cranks before and since, if he had been willing to give up, and if he had not happened to have a circle of friends who believed in him. And it is their assistance and Roger's continued self-confidence and initiative that finally bring him out into the full light of history. This is indeed an appealing and romantic episode, that this obscure writer and research worker should suddenly have received a request for his opinions and suggestions on what ailed society from the reigning Pope, the highest authority in Christendom. And when Bacon in most extravagant terms describes the honour that the Pope has done to him, 'the unworthy sole of your foot',[1] he was not expressing only the mock humility of the courtier. For it was indeed a surprising honour, and an immensely welcome one. We see him contrasting in his mind the position he had lately held as an obscure scientist within his Order, and made to do menial tasks, with the new estimate he can have of himself as the chosen adviser of the Pope. It is rare, indeed, that such an opportunity ever comes the way of the neglected cranks and writers of the world, who dream of the great success that will come to them some day, the recognition that the public will one day accord them—'you'll see, when I have my book published; you'll see when *they* will come to me and beg for my invention!'

But to Roger Bacon the miracle did happen; and all his local

[1] Brewer, *Op. Tert.*, p. 7.

enemies had to admit that their despised brother was of some account after all. The triumph must have been very sweet!

It was not, however, a miracle in the sense of a pure 'act of God'. Human agents were behind it, though the story is not systematically recounted in the works themselves, but must be carefully extracted from scattered information which is, fortunately, fairly copious for this period. By far the most complete account is to be found in the 'Gasquet' fragment, which is either the prefatory letter to the final draft of the *Opus Majus* as sent to the Pope, or perhaps a part of the *Opus Minus* which also accompanied the *Opus Majus* to the Pope. The early pages of the *Opus Tertium*, as printed by Brewer, were, in my view, originally written as a second preface to go with the major work, and also contain much biographical material. The circumstances preceding the receipt of the Pope's mandates, and what Bacon did to fulfil them will therefore be taken from these two accounts. I think they are entirely consistent with each other if one recognizes that they are alternative prefaces, written at an interval of several months, and in slightly different circumstances.

I have been sceptical of many of Bacon's statements about his researches, and to some extent discounted them as attempts to impress his patron. I see, however, no need to regard these pieces of biographical information with the same scepticism because they are not likely to impress, nor are they capable of impressing, anyone. They are different, but not contradictory, sets of excuses for a definite failure on his part. Bacon had spent several years in preparing a work which his patron believed had already been written when he first requested it, and he was not entirely happy even with the final result. He believed it could have been much better if he had had a longer time and greater resources at his disposal. And in the course of preparing the work he had become aware of some of his own deficiencies. These facts made an apology and excuses necessary; but there must be real reasons behind the excuses. Bacon was not lazy or incompetent; in such circumstances, with such a chance offered him, he would undoubtedly do the very best of which he was capable. If he did not succeed as well as he had hoped, if he had to delay for several years before sending a completed work, there was a real reason for it—and these are the genuine reasons which we must try to extract from his excuses. And what he says on this subject seems to me extremely probable, and exactly what I should expect in view of the circumstances in which he found himself, as a friar in a convent where he was under close supervision, with a censorship to combat, without access to funds, and above all with an injunction of secrecy imposed by his patron which he had to do his best to honour. Only such obstacles would have prevented him from doing what he would have considered a better job of work, and in a shorter time.

The following are the bare facts in chronological order. Some time before Guy de Foulquois (or Foulques) became Pope Clement IV, while he was still papal legate and Cardinal-Bishop of Sabina, Roger Bacon sent him a proposal through a clerk in the Cardinal's suite.[1] We do not possess this letter, and, indeed, it may have been only a verbal message conveyed through the clerk, whose name was Raymond of Laon. But we know that the initiative came from Bacon because he speaks of it later as 'my proposal', and complains that it had not been properly understood by Raymond, and so had been incorrectly transmitted to the Cardinal. Apparently Raymond told his master that Bacon had a writing that he would like the Cardinal to see. Bacon tells us that his message really concerned 'writings which he was ready to compose but which were not then written'.[2]

The Cardinal replied with what Bacon calls 'your first mandate', but aware of the fact that the Order prohibited such unauthorized writing, and knowing that he had no authority as a Cardinal to claim any dispensation in Bacon's favour, he told him to proceed with secrecy.[3] No doubt he failed to realize the difficulty that this would provide for Bacon, but the latter must have been aware when he took the original initiative that some provision would have to be made to circumvent the censorship which no mere Cardinal could overrule and which Foulquois, even when Pope, still had to take seriously.[4] It is probable also that even such a headstrong character as

[1] 'Raymundus . . . meum propositum nullatenus intellexit.' Gasquet, p. 500.

[2] 'Scripturis faciendis, non tunc factis.' Gasquet, p. 501.

[3] 'Pretendit utrumque mandatum quod fui obligatus . . . ne communicarem.' Gasquet, p. 501.

[4] I cannot agree with Thorndike (*History of Magic* . . . II, 627) that Bacon implies that he was 'exempted from this restriction in the earlier request from the Cardinal as well as in the later papal mandate'. The relevant sentence says: 'It was known to Your Magnificence, as both mandates show, that I was obligated by a most strict order not to communicate any writing made by me in this condition, as indeed our whole congregation is known to be obligated, and so I was disgusted at the idea of writing anything at all. . . . I have often seen the most secret writings divulged through the deceit of scribes, and so I might have had a bad conscience through transgressing the precept'. The whole passage runs in the Latin: 'Magnificentie quidem vestre innotuit ut utrumque mandatum pretendit quod precepto fui obligatus artissimo ne scriptum in hoc statu a me factum communicarem, sicut et nostra tota congregatio firmiter noscitur obligari, et ideo componere penitus abhorrebam. Nam componi nichil potuit nisi scriptoribus traderetur, qui vellem nollem transcriberent pro se ipsis vel amicis, et sic communicarent omnibus ut pluries vidi scripta secretissima per fraudem divulgari scriptorum et inciderem in conscientiam de transgressione precepti.' (Gasquet, p. 500.)

Now, this passage, it is true, refers to the earlier years and is intended to explain why no

Bacon would have had some idea where he was to get the funds. There was only one possible source for a friar in his position—his brother and family. He tells us that he wrote off to England, but received no reply, since 'exiles and enemies of the King occupied the land of my birth'.[1] As Thorndike reminds us, this occupation came to an end with the victory of the King and the death of Simon de Montfort in 1265, so that the appeal may be placed definitely before this time. News from England would not travel so slowly that Roger would be still unaware of the King's victory by June, 1266, when the second mandate arrived. It is therefore clear that the attempt to get money from England was in response to the first mandate, and not the second. Unfortunately for Bacon, even though the occupation was over by 1266–7, his family had been ruined, and he had not 'heard from his brother until this day'.[2]

In the early part of the year 1265 Guy de Foulquois was elected Pope, and some time in this year or the early part of the next Bacon again took the initiative, sending a request this time through Sir William Bonecor, an English envoy who was carrying messages from King Henry III to the Pope. We know that Bacon sent a 'letter with

writings were ready when Raymond took his first message. But has the situation changed after receipt of the mandates? Bacon goes on to tell us that his superiors were insistent that he perform his daily occupations, and he 'neglected to write his scientific work until he received the Cardinal's mandate (magnifica sapientie spectacula . . . neglexi antequam primum vestre dominationis recepi mandatum). Then: 'After I received the papal letters I deliberated *sensu secretissimo* what could be done', and he tells us how he sent to England for money without success. 'And besides all these things I suffered a special difficulty from my superiors because they make demands of me and I could not excuse myself fully because your Lordship had commanded me to take care of this business secretly nor did your Glory ask anything of them'. (Et preter hec omnia habui speciale impedimentum ab eis qui mihi presunt eo quod alia a me petunt et me excusare ad plenum non potui quia jusserat vestra dominatio ut secrete istud negocium tractarem, nec aliquid eis vestra gloria demandavit. Gasquet, p. 502). Bacon makes the same complaint again in almost the same words in Brewer, *Op. Tert.*, p. 15. Bacon, however, in this passage makes the matter even more clear when he says: 'Primum impedimentum fuit per eos qui mihi praefuerant quibus cum nihil scripsistis in excusationem meam, *et eis non potui revelare vestrum secretum*. (Italics mine.) If this had not been the case—and Bacon certainly implies this when he complains that the Pope had not asked anything from the Order—then there would have been no need to hire copyists outside the Order and incur his heavy expenses. Or, if he had merely gone outside the Order because he wanted to, he could hardly have expected the Pope to reimburse him. What he is saying is that the unfortunate injunction to secrecy forced him to go outside the Order for copyists; but that even this was dangerous because the copyists were unreliable. I do not see how the passages quoted can bear any other interpretation. It seems to me quite clear from these passages that the work was to be kept secret from the Order, as much as from everyone else, and that both mandates had enjoined secrecy upon him.

[1] Thorndike, *History of Magic* . . . II, 623, n. 4.

[2] The Gasquet fragment must be read very carefully to see how the early sentences apply to the arrival of the first mandate from the Cardinal, and the latter to the arrival of the second mandate from the same Cardinal who had now become Pope. The early chapters of the *Opus Tertium* are not so systematic and refer almost entirely to the second mandate which Bacon obeyed, and are primarily concerned with the difficulties which he successfully overcame.

verbal explanations', but again this letter is not extant.[1] It may, however, be considered certain that he will have referred to the first mandate and explained the difficulties he had experienced in carrying it out, and I think if he had already started the *Opus Majus* he will have said so. From the tone of the reply it would appear that he also insisted on the urgency of the matter. Bacon, in referring to this message, later tells the Pope that the messengers were careless, since they had not fully explained his financial difficulties.[2] From which it would seem that in the letters he had referred to the difficulties within the Order that prevented him from writing freely, and the financial difficulties were reserved, as was natural, for verbal explanation. At all events the Pope replied to this communication with a letter which is extant and dated June, 1266. In this he asks Bacon to send him his writings and his remedies for current evil conditions; but he is to do this with as much secrecy as possible, and notwithstanding any prohibitions of his Order.[3] We know that Bacon, in spite of the difficulties, was ultimately able to do this; but it is still uncertain in what order and what years he wrote the works, what was his original intention, and how much of it he carried out, and how much he abandoned as unfeasible.

Professor Thorndike[4] thinks that Bacon started to work at once on the receipt of the first mandate, and that the *Opus Majus* was nearly finished if not sent by the time of the arrival of the second; but that Bacon had had no news of it and so prepared the *Opus Minus* and presumably also the *Opus Tertium* to take its place in case it had not arrived or the Pope had found it too long to read. Thorndike shows that the *Opus Majus* could have been sent to a cardinal and not a pope, since in this work the epithets suitable only for a pope are not so common as in his other works, and could, for the most part, apply equally to a cardinal. Chapters obviously addressed to a pope, such as the last chapter of the first part of the *Opus Majus*, occur in other works in almost the same form and could have been transferred later. Father Mandonnet, on the other hand, thinks that the *Opus Minus* and the *Opus Tertium* were composed at the same time as the *Opus Majus* or before,[5] and that they were eventually not sent at all, being incorporated in the major work as far as was necessary, and then

[1] 'Tuae devotionis litteras gratanter recepimus, sed et verba notavimus diligenter quae ad explanationem . . . Bonecor . . . viva voce nobis proposuit.' *Opus Majus*, I, 1–2 and note.

[2] Brewer, *Op. Tert.*, p. 16.

[3] *Opus Majus*, I, 1–2 and note; Brewer, *Op. Tert.*, p. 1. (The version of this letter provided by Bridges I have used since it appears to be the better text.)

[4] Thorndike, *History of Magic* . . . II, 624 ff.

[5] Mandonnet, 'Roger Bacon et la composition . . .' (1913).

abandoned. He does not think the *Opus Majus* was sent until 1268, thus explaining Bacon's numerous excuses for delay in obeying the mandates.

Both of these hypotheses require consideration in some detail, but the truth, in my view, lies somewhere between the two. I think that Roger did begin to compose a work for the Pope on the receipt of the first mandate, that he assembled much scattered material, and did what preliminary work he could without finances. The years 1264 to 1265 were largely spent in trying to procure funds for his work from his family; but on his hearing the news that nothing was to be obtained from this source, he temporarily abandoned the enterprise until his patron became Pope, when a new opportunity offered. But I cannot accept the suggestion that this work Bacon was engaged on in response to the first mandate was the *Opus Majus* or that it was largely finished at the time of the arrival of the second, and certainly not sent. I believe Mandonnet's evidence to show that there is a fair possibility that the *Opus Majus*, as sent finally to the Pope, contained much that had originally been in the other works, but I do not think these other works were abandoned when the *Opus Majus* was despatched. I do not think the *Opus Tertium* was sent, but I think the *Opus Minus* accompanied the larger work. My reasons for these conclusions and my hypothesis as to exactly what Bacon was doing in the years from 1264 to 1268 will follow in due course.

I cannot accept Professor Thorndike's hypothesis for the following reasons:

1. He fails to attach sufficient importance to Bacon's second initiative, the letter sent by Sir William Bonecor. He says: 'When Roger learned that Foulques as Pope was still interested in his work, visions of what the apostolic see might do for his programme of learning and himself flashed before his mind, and after a fresh but vain effort at a *scriptum principale* which kept him busy until Epiphany, he composed the supplementary treatise the *Opus Minus*—with its analysis of the preceding work for the benefit of the busy pope'.[1]

Now how did the friar learn that the Pope was still interested in his work? He learnt it because he himself had sent a letter via Bonecor. Although this letter has not been preserved, we know from the reply that it was a suggestion as to how the evils of the time could be remedied. It cannot have been the *Opus Majus* itself. If the *Opus Majus* were already composed, or even in the process of being composed, wouldn't Bacon have mentioned it, and elicited some kind of

[1] Thorndike, *History of Magic* . . . II, 624.

reply from the Pope, instead of merely sending a verbal explanation and a letter? If, on the other hand, it had been temporarily abandoned and the first mandate had therefore not been obeyed, Bacon might well have taken another initiative as he did, apologized for not obeying it, and pleaded his insuperable difficulties, and asked his patron if he were still interested. From the point of view of Bacon's position within the Franciscan Order, a cardinal would have no power over his superiors, whereas Bacon would think a pope had only to command and be obeyed. Support of this kind would warrant his resumption of his abandoned task. The project was therefore more practicable, from Bacon's point of view, than earlier, if he could obtain papal support. The second initiative and mandate are thus fully accounted for by this hypothesis, as I do not find they are in Thorndike's.

2. In all three of the *Opera* and in the Gasquet fragment the emissary is spoken of as Bacon's favourite pupil, John,[1] and in the Gasquet fragment and in the *Opus Tertium* Bacon gives him an elaborate introduction. He also goes into some detail on John's capabilities in the *Opus Majus*. Now if John had already taken the *Opus Majus* to Rome, and he was still available to take the *Opus Minus* at a later time, then he must have returned from the Curia, in which case Bacon would have known of its reception. There would, therefore, be no point in speaking of sending a digest because of the perils of the road. However, Bacon may have been sitting at home waiting for news, and in the interval he could have started work on the other *Opera*. But in this case, why make another elaborate introduction for John who, if he returned in time to take them, would already be known to the Pope? If he did not return, then he would not be the emissary, and again, there would be no need for an introduction. I am unable to account for the two separate introductions for the lad except on the supposition that they are alternates, and that one replaces the other. But that there was only one journey taken by John and only one intended, I believe to be certain.

There are several discrepancies in the account of John given in the various passages in the *Opus Tertium* where he is mentioned. But only in the first passage is the present tense used, and only there is there an introduction to him. All these other passages are consistent with John's presence in Rome, and the last instance I shall give seems

[1] Gasquet, p. 506; *Opus Majus*, III, 23–24; *Opus Minus*, p. 315; Brewer, *Op. Tert.*, pp. 61–63.

to be consistent only with the fact that he is already there. The following are the passages in question:

(*a*) 'The lad John has taken the crystal . . . and I have instructed him in how to demonstrate it.'[1]
(*b*) 'If you have no time to examine these difficulties, John is more capable than anyone.'[2]
(*c*) 'John, whom I sent, will be able to prove this before your eyes.'[3]
(*d*) 'If you want to see (this) more fully, bid John write out the more complete treatise in good letters.'[4]
(*e*) 'As I proved in the treatise *De radiis*, which John took with him in addition to the principal works.'[5]
(*f*) 'But the third writing (on alchemy) I sent from my hand by John that it might be transcribed for your glory.'[6]
(*g*) 'So now I am sending a corrected exemplar so that John and his companions may correct what had remained uncorrected.'[7]

I am therefore entirely in agreement with Professor Thorndike that most of the *Opus Tertium* was indeed composed after the *Opus Majus* had been sent, but not that part of it which contains the introduction for John, the biographical information about his own difficulties in composing the work which is duplicated in the Gasquet fragment, nor various other parts which are incorporated more or less completely into the *Opus Majus*. But I agree that much of the *Opus Tertium* does indeed consist of afterthoughts of which Bacon thought the Pope should be informed. It was not, however, to be sent by the hand of John, but by some other emissary, who was to communicate with John when he reached Rome. As we shall see, I do not believe that this part of the work was ever sent, nor probably ever completed, for the Pope had died in the interval.

3. If the *Opus Majus* was partly composed I find it difficult to explain what it was that Bacon was writing and abandoned 'before

[1] 'Puer vero Johannes portavit crystallum . . . et instruxi eum in demonstratione.' Brewer, *Op. Tert.*, p. 111.

[2] 'Si tempus non habueritis examinandi has difficultates, Johannes potens est in his plusquam omnes.' Brewer, *Op. Tert.*, p. 135.

[3] 'Et hoc poterit Johannes quem misi probare ante oculos vestros.' Brewer, *Op. Tert.*, pp. 225–26.

[4] 'Si vultis copiosius videre jubeatis Johanni ut faciat scribi de bona littera tractatum pleniorem.' Brewer, *Op. Tert.*, p. 270.

[5] 'Ut probavi in tractatu De Radiis quem Johannes extra principalia opera deportavit.' Brewer, *Op. Tert.*, p. 230.

[6] 'Tertium autem scriptum misi de manu mea per Johannem ut Vestre Glorie transcriberetur.' Little, *Op. Tert.*, p. 82.

[7] 'Et ideo nunc mitto exemplar correctum ut Johannes cum suis sociis corrigat ea que remanserant incorrecta.' Little, *Op. Tert.*, p. 61.

Epiphany', after the arrival of the second mandate.[1] We are told that with all his strength he tried to obey the Pope's request, but he could not complete it, and therefore started another different project. If he had started already, and made considerable progress with, the *Opus Majus* after he received the first mandate, and then, on the arrival of the second mandate, instead of continuing this he set to work on another opus altogether, what he calls his *scriptum principale*, and then abandoned it also, this would seem an extraordinary thing to do. Thorndike calls it a 'fresh, but vain, effort'.[2] But why should he undertake it just then?

We do know that Bacon had always wanted to produce a real *scriptum principale*, and this is what he would have liked most of all to produce for the Pope. I believe, with Thorndike, that he did in fact try to compose it after the arrival of the second mandate, but I find it difficult to believe that he would do so if he had a nearly completed *persuasio*, the *Opus Majus*, at his disposal. If, on the other hand, he had already sent the *Opus Majus* and he feared it had been unsuccessful, then he might try his hand at a more inclusive work. But what were his reasons for writing the minor works we know he did produce? Why in these works does he give digests of the major work, and point out in some detail the parts he considered most important and interesting? He tells us himself. The Pope is a very busy man, and might not have time to read even the *Opus Majus*. So it would be most unlikely that, with this thought in his mind, he should start to compose an even more difficult and comprehensive work after he had finished and sent the *Opus Majus*. I think that the order of composition, or at least the order of undertaking his works, must have been in decreasing order of difficulty. 1. The *scriptum principale* (abandoned). 2. The *Opus Majus* (composed). 3. The *Opus Minus* (a digest of 2, plus supplementary information). 4. The *Opus Tertium* (a digest of 3 and 4, composed, for the most part, after the despatch of these, when he had leisure to think over their omissions). Then, with more leisure in the years that followed, and after the death of his patron, he set to work again on the abandoned *scriptum principale*, no longer for a pope, but as a compendium of all his knowledge.

In one respect, however, both Thorndike and Mandonnet have helped to draw attention to an outstanding difficulty, though they

[1] 'Omni virtute conabar usque post Epiphaniam . . . sed non potui . . . perficere concupita.' Gasquet, p. 501.

[2] Thorndike, *History of Magic* . . . II, 624.

propose to solve it in different ways. The second mandate was only received in 1266, and both the *Opus Majus* and the *Opus Tertium* from internal evidence were apparently written in 1267,[1] and the *Opus Minus* is clearly written before the *Opus Tertium*. This is a tremendous body of work. And yet Bacon explains the enormous difficulties he experienced in producing it, and apologizes profusely for the delay. This can only be accounted for by counting the years from the first mandate and not the second (Thorndike) or by putting the despatch of the first work well on into 1268 (Mandonnet). I do not think Thorndike satisfactorily accounts for Bacon's apologies on his hypothesis that the *Opus Majus* was already sent by the time of the arrival of the second mandate. But if it was only in the process of composition, and it was not finally ready until 1267, then the apologies were warranted if we consider that it was in answer to the first mandate. It is my own view that much of the preliminary work for either a *scriptum principale* or a *persuasio* like the *Opus Majus* had been carried out after the receipt of the first mandate. Chapters of various separate works had been assembled which are incorporated later into the *Opus Majus*—hence the absence of references to the Pope in these parts—but could equally have been put into a *scriptum principale*. I think that Bacon attempted the latter and abandoned it after Epiphany, 1267. What was needed to make these separate parts into a *persuasio* was not so very much in total quantity, and this was accomplished in the early part of 1267. And I shall try to show that those parts of the *Opus Majus* that are really new and written specially for it, are the worst and least digested part of the work.

Mandonnet's hypothesis has already been briefly stated, and several points in it have been touched upon in the course of the foregoing discussion. The following are his main contentions.

(*a*) Bacon did not start work until the second mandate. The first mandate, in my view, and evidently Professor Thorndike's, has been unaccountably neglected.

(*b*) Bacon then started work on a large *persuasio* (the *Opus Majus*) and a small *persuasio* at the same time, the latter because of the dangers of the road, and Bacon's fear that the Pope was too busy to read a large work.

(*c*) A first edition of the *Opus Majus* was completed in 1267, but Bacon was dissatisfied with it, and did not send it.

(*d*) In the course of 1267 the *Opus Minus* was abandoned in favour of the *Opus Tertium*.

[1] The passage on the reform of the calendar, referred to later, appears in *Opus Majus*, I, 281, 'sicut hoc anno 1267 accedit'.

(*e*) Before Epiphany 1268 both minor works were abandoned, and various passages in them incorporated into a new and revised edition of the *Opus Majus*.

(*f*) A new introduction was written in early 1268 (the Gasquet fragment), containing the biographical information from the *Opus Tertium*. This was attached to the revised edition of the *Opus Majus*, and both were sent.

Vanderwalle has dealt in considerable detail with what Mandonnet has been able to put forward as evidence for his hypothesis.[1] He has certainly succeeded in showing how unsatisfactory most of it is, but to some extent he has himself neglected the real difficulties in the traditional view. And he makes clear how much of Mandonnet's hypothesis rests on the assumption (for it is little more) that the Gasquet fragment is the prefatory letter to the *Opus Majus*. I also believe the fragment belongs with the *Opus Majus*, but since I think the *Opus Minus* was also sent, it is not of the first importance to which work it was attached. I think in any case it was the only biographical information sent, and the only introduction for John. Gasquet's own arguments for his contention that it was a prefatory letter for the *Opus Majus* have never been refuted, as far as I am aware, and they still carry much weight.[2]

Stripped of the assumptions and conjectures, Mandonnet's evidence amounts to the following.

(*a*) The Gasquet fragment can be placed as subsequent to the biographical information in the *Opus Tertium*, because John's age is given as at least a year less in the latter work.

(*b*) Bridges, in his edition of the *Opus Majus*, used two groups of MSS. which are substantially different, particularly in the first part of the work, and, above all, with a different opening paragraph.

(*c*) The numerous duplications in the works, especially between the *Opus Majus* and the *Opus Tertium*.

Vanderwalle dismisses the first point as either an error in detail on the part of Bacon or a copyist, or a loose way of speaking, and instances other cases of Bacon's use of round numbers. I agree that this is too slender a thread to build a whole hypothesis upon; but I

[1] Vanderwalle, 'Roger Bacon dans l'histoire . . .' (1929), pp. 177–95.

[2] Gasquet's arguments are as follows: 1. The fragment appears to be complete in itself. 2. Another summary of the *Opus Majus*, longer than the one in this fragment, is contained in the *Opus Minus*. Two summaries of the same kind were not necessary in the same work. Therefore the fragment does not belong to the *Opus Minus*. 3. The account given of the *Opus Minus* in the *Opus Tertium* contains nothing which could be taken as referring to this fragment. 4. The document itself is described as a letter. 5. The *Opus Majus*, to judge from its opening paragraph, had such a prefatory letter. In 1897, when Gasquet wrote, Bridges had not published his revised version of the *Opus Majus*; but the letter in the new edition is referred to in unmistakable terms 'secundum tenorem epistolae precedentis' (*Opus Majus*, III, 1).

cannot dismiss it quite so peremptorily, since the years are stated in definite terms by Bacon, and there is no question of round numbers when one is dealing with the difference between six and seven.

In the Gasquet fragment Bacon says of John: 'Nec vidi eum nisi Parisius a 7 annis', and: 'Hic adolescens meo consilio instructus est a 7 annis'.[1] In the *Opus Tertium* he says: 'Propter hoc consideravi unum adolescentem quem a quinque vel sex annis feci instrui'.[2]

We might legitimately say that 'five or six' years is a loose expression, though Mandonnet insists that Bacon uses it, not because he did not know how long John had been with him, but because it was between five and six years. The passage could therefore be disregarded if it were not that Bacon makes a further reference to the lad in the next two pages.

He says: 'Quamvis juvenis sit viginti annorum aut viginti et unius ad plus',[3] and 'Cum enim hic juvenculus quindecim annorum venit ad me'.[4] This surely means, and can only mean, that John had been with him between five and six years.

Mandonnet's second argument that there was a second edition of the *Opus Majus* is dismissed by Vanderwalle on the grounds that most of the known revisions apply only to the early pages of the work, and do not justify us in calling it a really new edition.[5] Only a very careful examination of the MSS. of the *Opus Majus* can support or refute Mandonnet's contentions. While this, of course, is true, as I shall point out formally later, the purpose of putting forward hypotheses is not so much to establish, at this stage, the truth, but to show where the probabilities lie, and to indicate lines that might be taken in research with the MSS. Two important differences between the two 'editions' may be pointed out here. In the opening paragraph of the first version published by Bridges the words 'secundum tenorem epistolae' occur. In the revised version the word 'precedentis' is added, as well as other matter.[6] Bridges himself did not see the significance of the change, but continued to think that the word referred to the *Opus Minus* which was originally conceived of as a letter, and was, indeed, probably meant in the first version. But it is difficult to see how the *Opus Minus* could be called an 'epistola

[1] Gasquet, p. 506. [2] Brewer, *Op. Tert.*, p. 61.

[3] *Ibid.*, p. 62.

[4] *Ibid.*, p. 63. Mandonnet's arguments on this subject appear on pp. 60 ff. of his monograph.

[5] Vanderwalle, 'Roger Bacon dans l'histoire . . .' pp. 180 ff.

[6] The words 'donec certius scriptum et plenius compleatur' are also inserted, showing that Bacon still had the intention of writing a longer work at his leisure, an intention he also expresses in the Gasquet fragment. Mandonnet, p. 169.

precedens'.[1] The second important difference is the exclusion of a whole chapter from the *Opus Majus* in the revised version. But it has not disappeared altogether; on the contrary, it turns up in its entirety in the Gasquet fragment. As this chapter contains a request for a minimum support for scientific activity, and emphasizes that the author is demanding no radical changes, it is easy to see why Bacon would want to call it especially to the Pope's attention by inserting it in his final preface.[2]

Mandonnet's third argument on the duplications in the different works is important. The duplications must be explained, but no certainty can be arrived at by these means alone as it is rarely possible to decide in which directions the transfers, if any, were made, or if Bacon used the same passages in different works, quite intentionally in case the Pope should only read one of them. Only when we have decided which works were sent can we decide whether the duplications could have served any purpose.

Taking Mandonnet's hypothesis as a whole, I find myself unable to accept it, though in framing my own hypothesis it will appear how much I am indebted to him for certain suggestions. Above all I find it impossible to ignore the really considerable evidence there is for Bacon's intention to send more than one work, his reasons for sending them, and his actual descriptions in the *Opus Tertium* of what was contained in the others. In the *Opus Minus* he says that in case the work he is describing (obviously the *Opus Majus*) should be lost owing to the uncertainties of the road, he has made a summary of the whole tract in a compendium.[3] In the *Opus Tertium* (early pages) he says: 'It was necessary (past tense) on account of the very great dangers of the road to compose another opusculum in which I might make clear the gist (intentio) of the *scriptura principalis*'.[4] Again: 'If by any chance it should happen on account of the perils of the road that the *Opus Majus* should be lost, you would have its gist here . . . so that my work may be known to Your Wisdom, and so that some things may be treated better and more clearly, and other things changed and others added'.[5]

In the fragment of the *Opus Tertium* edited by Little, Bacon is quite specific. 'I touched on these matters concerning places of the world

[1] Bridges expresses this view in *Opus Majus*, III, 159. The two different versions he prints in *Opus Majus*, I, 1–2, and III, 1.

[2] *Opus Majus*, I, 31–2; III, 34–35 (Part I, chap. xvi). In Vol. III Bridges prints the chapter in parentheses.

[3] *Opus Minus*, p. 322.

[4] Brewer, *Op. Tert.*, p. 5.

[5] *Ibid.*, p. 67.

and the alteration of places and things through the heavenly bodies, and concerning judgments and secret works, but I did not put them all in the *Opus Majus*, but only what concerned places. Other things I put in the *Opus Minus* when I came to declare the gist of that part of the *Opus Majus*. For I did not then propose to treat more things in the *Opus Majus*, as I wished to hurry on account of the mandate of your Holiness.'[1] Again: 'Because these things are very difficult (discussion of the vacuum) I thought that I would take note of them in one of the works. But in the first and the second I did not give much thought to them, not enough to excite me to write about them, or I omitted them purposely because of the length of the work and because of my great haste.'[2] This last passage comes from the later pages of the *Opus Tertium* as edited by Brewer. I believe both passages quoted in this paragraph were written by Bacon at leisure, after the other works had been despatched, and suggest that they can bear no other interpretation. Since Little, in his examination of the MSS. of the *Opus Tertium*, found clear evidence that the work was written in sections at different times,[3] this will be taken as a fact, requiring explanation in my hypothesis.

To sum up again briefly, the following points need to be covered by any hypothesis:

(*a*) What was Bacon doing between the first and second mandates?
(*b*) Did he reply to the Cardinal by sending a work, and if not, why not?
(*c*) When he received the second mandate, what did he do?
(*d*) Why did he compose the *Opus Minus* and the *Opus Tertium*?
(*e*) Why are there two variants of the *Opus Majus* and numerous duplications between this and the other works?
(*f*) Why was the *Opus Tertium* composed in sections?
(*g*) What works did Bacon ultimately send and when?

Let it be said at once that no certainty can be arrived at without a very complete investigation of the Baconian MSS. to see how far really separate editions of his work can be traced. And, even if this is done, it is quite possible that not enough MSS. are known for anyone to be able to do more than frame yet another hypothesis. The purpose of presenting one here, which, like Professor Thorndike's,[4] is only made on the basis of the printed texts, is only that it may be able to suggest certain lines of investigation for anyone who,

[1] Little, *Op. Tert.*, p. 18.
[2] Brewer, *Op. Tert.*, p. 199.
[3] Little, *Op. Tert.*, pp. xv, xxi. Cf. also the passages which suggest John's presence in Rome, pp. 150–51, above.
[4] Thorndike, *History of Magic . . .* II, 625, n. 1.

unlike myself, is competent to undertake the formidable task of scrutinizing the MSS. What I have tried to do is to suggest a way in which the works may have been composed, which, as far as I can see, both takes care of all the known evidence, and appears psychologically possible, if not probable. If my scheme is complicated, this, I hope, is the reflection of Bacon's own unsystematic manner of working, and not of any personal preference for the obscure.

If we take the date of the receipt of the first mandate from the Cardinal as 1263 or 1264, it is first necessary to consider the state of Bacon's work at this time, and the chronological chart given on p. 111 above may be consulted, even though this too is conjectural. If the *Communia naturalium* of Bacon, as appears from internal evidence, had already been begun several years before the *Opera*, then Bacon had already outlined a scheme for a compendium of the sciences.[1] In the Gasquet fragment he also tells us that he had had the intention of committing to writing what he knew, and this fact was known to many.[2] But he had not made much progress, partly owing to the censorship and his own weariness and languor. He had, however, composed 'some chapters, now on one science and now on another'.[3] But, as these were imperfect, he had taken no care of them, and he no longer had them in his hands.[4] It is clear that Bacon needed some encouragement to proceed with his labours, some belief that someone of importance would read his works if he composed them. This, therefore, in Bacon's own words, is the background for the first initiative taken through Raymond of Laon.

His hopes realized, and the first mandate in his hands he must first decide what to write for the Cardinal; and the relatively clear and systematic account given in the Gasquet fragment gives no indication that he had ever anything in mind but the compendium of the sciences, which had been planned and partly executed. This work was an ideal that Bacon had set himself, and even when he finally sends the *persuasiones* to the Pope he still has it in mind, as we have seen.

The first necessity, however, was money. And to obtain this he sent off to his family in England. There was no hope of obtaining anything from his Order, because he could not even tell his superiors

[1] Steele, Fasc. II, 3–9.

[2] 'Verum enim est quod a multis retroactis temporibus proposui litteris mandare que nosco, et hoc pluribus innotuit.' Gasquet, p. 500.

[3] 'Proculdubio nihil composui nisi quod aliqua capitula, nunc de una scientia, nunc de alia. Gasquet, p. 500.

[4] 'Illa que conscripsi non habeo, nam propter imperfectionem eorum de ipsis non curavi.' Gasquet, p. 500.

about the project since he had been told to observe secrecy. The second necessity was to assemble all the chapters he had already written, the *De signis et causis*, the *De laude mathematicae*, the *Perspectiva* and probably other works that could not ultimately be used in the *Opus Majus*, but which could have formed part of a *scriptum principale*. And we know he made progress from 1263 to 1265 on the *Computus*, though this was extremely technical.

His hopes, however, must have received a disastrous check when he heard of the rebellion in England and knew he could expect no funds from there. But there was one new thing in his favour. The Cardinal, whom he had disappointed so far, had now become Pope. A mandate from him would be an altogether different affair from a mandate from a cardinal. He could, perhaps, obtain money from the Curia, and at all events the Pope's commands would weigh heavily with the Franciscans and perhaps win him some official support from his superiors. So he composes a careful letter to the Pope, hinting that he has 'remedies' for the evils of the time, and mentioning briefly his difficulties resulting from the censorship of the Franciscans, and explaining why he had so far been unable to produce anything for his patron. At the same time, as we have seen, he sent a verbal message by Sir William Bonecor, probably a friend of his own or of his family from English days, delicately mentioning the matter of money.

The reply that he receives from the Pope in due course both raises his hopes and dashes them. There is, indeed, a mandate from the head of Christendom; but there is no money and no instructions to the Franciscans to support him. On the contrary, there are the same instructions to keep the whole matter secret. This put Bacon in an impossible situation. He had now the chance of his life, but no way of taking advantage of it. I have tried to show that he was already suspect to his superiors. If now he tried to raise funds he must explain why he wanted them. He had technically broken a regulation of the Order when he approached the Pope,[1] and though this might be a venial offence since the regulation was primarily intended to prevent the brothers from making personal petitions, it could not be expected to endear him to them.

Bacon tells us what he did. He 'solicited many great men'; he said 'that some business of yours had to be transacted in France', though he did not 'say what it was that needed so much money'. But he was continually repulsed so that he knew he could not proceed in this

[1] See above, p. 143.

manner. So in dire straits he forced his friends and poor men to expend their all, and sell many things and mortgage the rest, even going to the usurers and promising them that he would send an expense account to the Pope. But he finally decided that he would not send an expense account until he had been able to send him a writing which would please him as evidence for his expenditures.[1]

Now I do not think Bacon could have done all this without telling the friars at least something of his venture. They could not fail to know that he had a writing in progress, and that he was trying to raise money for it. If the work was carried out under their auspices, Bacon could have used copyists within the Order, and the use of outside copyists, for whom he was trying to raise money, would at once have aroused suspicion. I think it probable, therefore, that Bacon did show his superiors his letter from the Pope, which was in itself fairly harmless, and let them know that he was replying. But the letter gave them the reason for the secrecy and for the use of outside copyists. The friars would then only know enough to make them jealous and suspicious, and extremely inquisitive; but Bacon would have technically complied with the Pope's injunctions. What follows, then, becomes explicable. In view of the source of the mandate the friars would not dare to forbid the enterprise altogether; but they would make it difficult for him, by refusing to relax their regulations and making him do his usual work.[2]

At last Bacon succeeds in raising sixty pounds. But meanwhile he could not afford to remain idle, and he tells us that he worked with all his power until after Epiphany to finish his intended work, and he collected many things, but he found he could not complete what he had desired.[3] I think there can be little doubt that this work, which he abandoned after Epiphany, 1267, was the *scriptum principale*. In the same Gasquet fragment in which he gives us this information he tells us why he abandoned it. For a real compendium of science it

[1] 'Considerans igitur vestram reverentiam et praeceptum, sollicitavi multos et magnos . . . et dixi quod negotium quoddam vestrum debuit tractari in Francia per me, licet illud non expressi, cujus executio indiget pecunia magna. Sed quotiens reputatus improbus, quotiens repulsus, quotiens dilatus spe vana . . . Etiam mihi non credebant amici, quia non potui eis negotium explicare; unde per hanc viam non potui procedere. Angustiatus igitur . . . coegi familiares homines et pauperes expendere omnia. . . . Et etiam propter vestram reverentiam decrevi quod non facerem rationem de expensis antequam aliqua mitterem quae vobis placerent, et quae oculata fide darent testimonium expensarum.' Brewer, *Op. Tert.*, pp. 16–17.

[2] 'Et primum impedimentum fuit per eos, qui mihi praefuerunt, quibus cum nihil scripsistis in excusationem meam, et . . . instabant ineffabili violentia ut in aliis eorum voluntati obedirem.' Brewer, *Op. Tert.*, p. 15.

[3] 'Omni virtute conabar usque post Epiphaniam Domini quatenus opus postulatum destinarem et multa collegi talia, sed . . . non potui propter impedimenta que occurrebant perficere concupita.' Gasquet, p. 501.

was necessary that one man should write on one subject, and another on another.[1] It was necessary also to consult other workers in the field and obtain advice.[2] Bacon, after having made the attempt, came to the conclusion that he himself was not competent to prove the details of the sciences. He was apt to become confused unless talking about the truth which he personally knew.[3] But it was possible for one man to *explain the possibilities* of science. So he determined on a second-best, a *persuasio*, which would whet the appetite of the Pope, and perhaps persuade him to subsidize and give his support for a real co-operative effort, details of which will be given in the next chapter. This *persuasio*, of course, was the *Opus Majus*.

Bacon tells us a little about his method of composition, which will no doubt apply to all his works to the Pope. Evidently he was one of those writers who write first and think afterwards, revising their first copy rather than planning the whole in advance. He tells us that he never writes anything difficult without reaching the fourth or fifth exemplar before he has what he wants.[4] In this case also he needed to complete experiments or observations, taken not only in the daytime, but at night, as he had to wait for a lunar rainbow to observe its colours.[5] But in spite of the difficulties he did succeed in producing the *Opus Majus*.

The reason that it was not an impossible task for him to produce the *Opus Majus*, and even in a fairly short time, was that much of the preliminary work had been done, and he had been able to assemble the separate parts already written. He already had his synthesis fairly clear in his own mind on nearly all the separate parts of his universal science. What was required was the unification of the whole, and the infusing into it of a spirit that would persuade his exalted reader to action. The causes of error were familiar to him from long brooding on the subject, his knowledge of languages was sufficient for him to be able to turn out the short part concerned with these. He had long ago thought out the way in which the sciences could be used for theology. Much of the mathematical work was already done in the

[1] 'Non tamen quod unus sciat singula nec majorem partem, sed aliquis unum, alius alterum.' Gasquet, p. 502.

[2] 'Necessarium igitur est in tantis rebus quod consilium alterius habeatur . . . sicut artifex . . . indiget variis cesoribus ac sculpentibus et componentibus ea que faciliora sunt.' Gasquet, p. 501.

[3] 'Me non obligo ad singularium probationem nec sufficio solus . . . non sum confusus loquens de veritate quam scio.' Gasquet, p. 504.

[4] 'Nihil scribo difficile quod non transeat usque ad quartum vel quintum exemplar antequam habeam quod intendo.' Gasquet, p. 501. 'Nam quantumcumque bene sciret eam . . . exemplaria quinque vel sex multiplicari oporteret, antequam unum haberet electum et fideliter consummatum.' Brewer, *Op. Tert.*, p. 14.

[5] *Opus Minus*, p. 317.

form of the *De laude mathematicae*, and *Perspectiva* was complete. The first part of *scientia experimentalis* may have been already prepared in the form of the treatise on the rainbow. This left him with what should have been the crown of his whole work, moral philosophy. And this he has neither thought out, nor prepared anything for, except the inferior *Metaphysica*, which he uses all the same, poor as it is. The bulk of this part is occupied with a quite undigested report on Seneca's *De ira* which he has recently found. But the whole of the moral philosophy reads as if Bacon was writing quickly and without much thought, and mostly the platitudes and commonplaces that would be the stock-in-trade of any medieval friar, who had listened to his required number of mediocre sermons. It is with reason that Mandonnet wonders how any Master of Arts who had studied the ethics of Aristotle 'a été reduit à traiter si improprement et confusément de la philosophie morale'.[1] Nevertheless, the *Opus Majus* as a whole, in spite of its piecemeal character and unevenness of style, was a masterpiece of persuasion and enthusiasm. Bacon's guiding thought of the unity of science and its value for theology was enough to give the whole work unity and direction.

So far our account has been reasonably straightforward, and I believe the foregoing pages are an approximately true account of Bacon's labours up to the production of a first edition of the *Opus Majus*. What follows will be more hypothetical, an attempt to deal with the discrepancies and difficulties set forth in the early part of this chapter.

We have suggested that Bacon wrote the *Opus Majus* at considerable speed, and we have mentioned the fact that he was not satisfied with the part on moral philosophy. This he tells us himself in three passages in the *Opus Tertium*, the first in one of the early pages, and the other two in the part that I believe was never sent. In the earliest passage he says that he only 'touched upon' the sixth part of moral philosophy.[2] In another he does not say how many parts he wrote, but he tells us that all the parts which follow the excursus on Seneca were not corrected or signed, and he is sending now a corrected copy.[3] In the third passage he tells us that he excused himself from the sixth part altogether.[4] In the account of the *Opus Majus* contained in the Gasquet fragment there is no mention of a sixth part either, though

[1] Mandonnet, 'Roger Bacon et la composition . . .' p. 166.
[2] 'Hanc solam tango propter causas quas assigno.' Brewer, *Op. Tert.*, p. 52.
[3] 'Alia vero quae sequuntur . . . non sunt correcta nec signata; propter quod modo mitto exemplar correctum.' Brewer, *Op. Tert.*, p. 305.
[4] 'Excusavi me ab expositione istius partis.' Little, *Op. Tert.*, p. 76.

this is not conclusive, as the digest in this fragment is very short, though otherwise it appears to be complete.[1] I think this evidence is enough to show that Bacon at least made some changes in the part on moral philosophy and that he was dissatisfied with it.

I think, however, that he sent off the *Opus Majus* to the copyists to be put into 'bonae litterae' as the Pope had desired. This would take some time, as the work was of a considerable length. But it was already three years since the first mandate, at the least, and he dared not delay much longer. Now as soon as the work was at the copyists Bacon, left with nothing to do, begins to think of all the things he has omitted from the great work. He is afraid also, or at least he tells himself, that there is a danger of the work being lost on the way. So he starts to work at once on another writing, intending at first to use it only as an introductory letter to the *Opus Majus*. It may even have been started before the *Opus Majus* went to the copyists and was the work referred to in the opening paragraph of the first edition.[2] In order that this new work would be still of some use if the major work were lost, Bacon gives in it a digest of the most important material in the *Opus Majus*; this would also be useful if the Pope were too busy to read the greater work. This new work is the *Opus Minus*.

This work could, indeed, have served as an introduction to the *Opus Majus* if Bacon had been content to let well alone. But it is apparent that more and more things occurred to him that he ought to have inserted in the *Opus Majus*. Supposing the Pope should think he didn't know anything about alchemy, or astrology, because they had been handled so briefly in the *Opus Majus*. And he had not been specific enough about the sins committed by theologians, the seven sins of theology. So these inexcusable omissions are put into the *Opus Minus*, which now becomes a formidable opus in its own right. But, having written it, Bacon cannot bear not to send it. So off it goes, too, to the copyists to be put into good letters. But time is running short, and the work, being much longer than he had bargained for, is also going to be more expensive. And the *Opus Majus* still needs an introduction, of which it has just been robbed. Both works, it may be imagined, are now at the copyists and there is going to be a large bill to pay when they come back, or before.

With money on his mind he begins what should have been the introduction to both works. And in this *Opus Tertium* we have the long and moving account of his 'impediments'. But, strangely enough, in addition to this we have also the remark that he has been

[1] Gasquet, p. 510. [2] *Supra*, p. 155.

relieved of some of his impediments. And there is an air for a few pages of a new freedom, when he compares himself with Cicero recalled from exile. Specifically, he states that he has 'gained the remedies for his former impediments', and is now able to add some necessary things which he could not put in before.[1]

I should like to suggest that at this time, when he had sent nothing to the Pope, and when financial troubles were threatening to overwhelm him, he finally gave up the attempt to produce and despatch the works in secrecy, and turned to his superiors for support. This necessitated his showing them a copy of the *Opus Majus*, so that they could see it was in no way harmful to them or discreditable to the Order. The *Opus Majus*, in fact, is reasonably restrained, and in it Bacon refrains from personal attack on his enemies. The friars may even have given the work and its author their grudging admiration. But it is surely true that, if Bacon had been relieved of any of his difficulties, this could only have been through action taken by the friars. He needed money and he needed assistance; and above all, perhaps, he wanted to be relieved of his menial duties. I cannot see who else could have helped him unless he had received some gifts of money. And, as we shall see in the final chapter of this study, this hypothesis is consistent with what we know of Bacon's later life.

We know that he did not tell the Pope of this minor defection. But in reading the early pages of the *Opus Tertium* one is continually struck by Bacon's emphasis upon his troubles; this might well be a way of explaining his defection to his own conscience. 'What tremendous efforts I did make, and you, sitting on top of the world, were, of course, unaware of them. How could I help myself?'[2] Moreover, since it seems almost certain that the Pope had not received any work by the time Bacon began the chapters of the *Opus Tertium* that contained the introduction for John and the long account of his own troubles, he could expect no new initiative from the Curia. Bacon himself, as we have seen, had already decided that he would not ask for any subsidy until he had sent the Pope something that would please him. If he had already despatched even a part of his work he would have mentioned the fact, and might well have now found himself able to request financial assistance.

So he starts to work on the *Opus Tertium*, still, I think, originally

[1] 'Et impedimentorum remedia priorum nactus, potui aliqua addere necessaria, quae prius ponere non valebam.' Brewer, *Op. Tert.*, p. 5.

[2] 'Non miror vero si non cogitastis de expensis his, quia sedentes in culmine mundi habetis de tot et tantis cogitare, quod nullus potest mentis vestrae sollicitudines aestimare.' Brewer, *Op. Tert.* p. 15.

intended as an introduction to the *Opus Majus*. But the temptation is too much for him, and he begins to make this into a major work too. Perhaps the passage on the calendar, of great importance for the Church, but expressed too technically in the *Computus*, occurred originally in the *Opus Tertium*.[1] At all events, the same passage occurs word for word in the *Opus Majus*. In the *Opus Tertium*, also, is the account of John, and the mention of his age which we have discussed earlier in this chapter.

While the *Opus Tertium* was approaching a formidable size, with much new and much that had been better thought out, I suggest the first edition of the *Opus Majus* returned from the copyists, and Bacon was greatly distressed, for it no longer represented his best thought, and in the cold light of the morning the part on moral philosophy offended him. His best thought was now also to be found in the *Opus Minus*, where it could stay since it would be sent. But the *Opus Tertium* could not be sent as it was, nor could the *Opus Majus* without revision. There is only one thing to do—revise parts of the moral philosophy, and cut out the rest. This, he tells us, in the latest version of the *Opus Tertium*, he accomplished. And here I accept Mandonnet's suggestion that he proceeded to extract the parts of the *Opus Tertium* that he wanted to put in the major work, and sent the revised version to the copyists, or perhaps now gave them to brothers in the Order to copy. But by now it must have been the end of 1267, a busy year, indeed, for Roger! He had sent no word to the Pope because all this time he had been expecting to have a completed work ready for John and his companions.

If we consider the state of his work at this time, we shall see that he would have a more or less complete *Opus Minus*, a revised *Opus Majus*, and a seriously mutilated *Opus Tertium*. In addition he had a number of separate works that he planned to send to the Pope, that were never incorporated in the *Opera*.[2] There is no point in preparing a further version of the *Opus Tertium* at this stage, for what is wanted is an introduction only, including a recommendation for John. John, however, is a year older than when Bacon first wrote an introduction for him in the *Opus Tertium*. So Roger prepares a new, brief, and systematic introduction, in the form of a letter, with an entirely accurate account of the *Opus Majus* as it was finally sent, and, as we have mentioned earlier, he takes a whole chapter which sums up his needs and his suggestions for the study of science, and incorporates

[1] Brewer, *Op. Tert.*, pp. 272–91.
[2] *Ibid.*, pp. 199, 227, 230; Little, *Op. Tert.*, pp. 61, 82.

this into the introductory letter. This, of course, is the Gasquet fragment. John and his companions take everything except the mutilated *Opus Tertium.* And it may be some confirmation of the hypothesis here set forth that the Gasquet fragment, Bacon's original copy of a part of the *Opus Majus* with his own notes in the margin, and a more or less complete *Opus Minus* have all been found in the Vatican library, while no MS. of the *Opus Tertium* has yet been found there, in spite of a lengthy search.[1]

So the works are at last on their way, and Bacon is left alone, and, as usual, more things occur to him that he has not said, and he is still worried that John and his companions may not arrive safely. And he is still not happy with the part on moral philosophy, and especially those that he has not corrected and signed.[2] So he starts to work once more on the *Opus Tertium*, though it is really substantially a new work. Many passages in it are superior to the similar parts of the *Opus Majus*, and there are many new discussions altogether, such as the analysis of the vacuum.[3] But I do not think the work was either finished or sent, since Pope Clement IV died towards the end of 1268, and there was no longer a patron of authority ready to listen to him. In fact there was now an interregnum in the Papacy, Bacon's reaction to which will be discussed in the final chapter of this study.

It is possible that Clement read the books that Bacon sent to him, but if so, there is no record of the fact. There is no further mention of John in any extant writing of his master. The only reference that Bacon makes to his own labours of these years and the great works he had sent to the Pope is to be found in the *Compendium studii philosophiae*, where he merely says that he sent an account of the opinions of the ancient philosophers about the truths of Christianity to the lord Clement in the form of a compendium.[4] Presumably this refers to the part on moral philosophy in the *Opus Majus*. Of his works on science and their reception there is never a word.

[1] A. Pelzer, 'Une source inconnue . . .' (1919), p. 47. Only the marginal notes are in Bacon's hand.

[2] Brewer, *Op. Tert.*, p. 305.

[3] *Ibid.*, pp. 149 ff.

[4] *CSP*, p. 424.

CHAPTER IX

THE UNIVERSAL SCIENCE OF ROGER BACON

IT has sometimes been supposed that the science of Roger Bacon is full of contradictions. He believed in revealed and experimental knowledge at the same time; he thought of theology as the queen of sciences and the crown of all knowledge. Even George Sarton, who has understood Bacon in many ways so well, seems to think that his 'fundamentalism' was somehow at variance with his scientific vision, a kind of atavism that he had not yet thrown off in spite of his 'modern' approach.[1]

H. O. Taylor, in the chapter on Bacon in his *Medieval Mind*, gives his considered judgment as follows:

> His writings remain, such of them as are known, astounding in their originality and insight and almost as remarkable for their inconsistency. They are marked by a confusion of method and a distortion of purpose, which spring from the contradictions between Bacon's genius and the current views he adopted.[2]

While in some respects this is a fair criticism, I think it can only be fully justified if we look upon Bacon as a modern born out of due time, which, indeed, is to some extent Taylor's view. I do not find the writings inconsistent to the same degree when they are considered in relation to his knowledge and outlook. Medieval scientists make assumptions different from our own, but they are not altogether unreasonable in view of the meagreness of the material at their disposal.

On the other hand, Raoul Carton has made a tremendous attempt to establish Bacon as a philosopher in his own right. His three long monographs, based only upon the work of Bacon's maturity, and without benefit of his earlier Parisian lectures, seem to me to form a superstructure too heavy for the foundations. Carton, in my view, takes too seriously the few passages in Bacon which are relevant to his scheme. While the result may be of interest to students of medieval philosophy in general, I find it comparatively little value for an understanding of Bacon himself.[3] Of the seven hundred pages that Carton devotes to Bacon I have found it impossible to make much

[1] Sarton, *Introduction to the History of Science*, II, 960.

[2] Taylor, *Medieval Mind*, II, 516. (4th edit., 1925.)

[3] For Carton's monographs see complete bibliography.

use. And it seems to me that the modest attempt at constructing the philosophy of science which is implicit but never stated in Bacon's work, is as much as is necessary for the understanding of the scientific synthesis which he himself projected.

I do not believe that it is necessary to make excuses for Bacon. His science, including his 'fundamentalism', seems to me remarkably consistent, and in accordance with the best knowledge of his time. He is not, however, a good apologist for himself because his gift for systematic analysis is greatly inferior to his imagination and vision. He does not clearly state his assumptions and postulates, which he largely took for granted, and are those of his time. He has not yet found it necessary to keep his religious beliefs and his natural knowledge in separate compartments; he is far, indeed, from the doctrine of the double truth, associated with the name of Averroes, that what is true in philosophy may contradict the revealed truths of religion and vice versa. Bacon's belief in revealed knowledge in no way vitiates his claim to be a scientific thinker. It may be alien to the modern viewpoint, but it is consistent with his own, and his theory of psychology supports it. The active intellect is God, or, in Adam Marsh's phrase, the 'raven of Elias', and the human soul is capable of receiving knowledge from this source through its own highest faculty, the *intellectus possiblis*.[1]

In this chapter, therefore, rather than state the scheme adopted by Bacon in his work for the Pope—which has in any case been effectively done by Bridges in his introduction to his edition of the *Opus Majus*—we shall endeavour to sketch the philosophy of science which Bacon took for granted as his intellectual framework, but himself never stated in formal terms. Bacon was primarily a thinker (if not a systematic one) and his contribution to the details of scientific knowledge is meagre; it seems, therefore, fairer to make any judgment of his work dependent on our understanding of his achievements as a scientific thinker and philosopher. This intellectual scheme has been drawn entirely from Bacon's own statements, though in some details I have drawn out to their logical conclusions various remarks which are only suggestions. And I have used his illustrations, which are of so much interest to himself, as indications of the thought behind them, even when his thought is not explicitly stated. Since the whole of his work has been utilized for this purpose, specific notes and references will not usually be made unless there is some passage where

[1] Brewer, *Op. Tert.*, pp. 73–75.

Bacon himself states his theories in unequivocal terms, and consultation of this particular passage will be of value to the reader.

1. *How can nature be known?*

Before ever he starts to investigate, the scientist, faced with all the varied phenomena of nature, must, above everything else, have some form of belief. He must believe that knowledge of at least some part of nature is attainable; as a human being he will probably also have a belief in the potential usefulness of his endeavour. What he considers useful will likewise depend upon prior beliefs. If he thinks that the life of every man upon earth is of great value, then he may hope that his work will serve to prolong this life upon earth. If he believes that life should be pleasurable, then he will guide his research in such a way as to make the lives of his fellows more pleasurable. If, like Bacon, he accepts a goal of salvation in the next world through faith in a certain religion, he will order his scientific work in such a way that the number of believers, candidates for salvation, will be increased, that the understanding of existing believers will be deepened and their faith strengthened. No scientific worker can be without a belief, whether it is stated explicitly or taken for granted without question.

But he must also have a belief that there is a possibility of finding out the *truth* about a certain range of phenomena. Again, this need not be explicitly stated, even to one's self. We may reasonably deny the possibility of absolute truth, and say that truth is only what is perceived to work in practice. We may hold the theory that we can only perceive the appearances of things, but never the things-in-themselves. In this case we shall only investigate the appearances, and the relations between them. At least, then, the relationships are true, and the fact that the knowledge works is true.

Modern science in general has been based upon the realization that, in the natural world, we can never know either the 'what' or the 'why', but only the 'how'. By the examination of the successive stages of a process, and learning how to repeat them at will, we can in fact learn *how* the second stage follows the first. And we say glibly that the second is *caused* by it, though we have known ever since Hume that this is not really so. But we have ceased altogether to try to discover the other why, the 'for the sake of which', the final cause in Aristotle's metaphysical scheme. And though we have been able to disintegrate matter into electrical charges, we still hesitate to say that this is what matter *is*, because the principle of organization cannot be simply disregarded. Yet this limited knowledge of modern times is of immense practical value because we can repeat the 'cause' and 'effect' at will. And we can erect a theoretical science of causes and effects throughout the whole of nature. This is always subject to checking, and is entirely effective for practical purposes within the limited area to which it is applicable.

Now the medieval man had the use of a most remarkable aphorism, which does not seem to modern scientists to be true. But, even if true, it was not originally based on verifiable empirical facts; nor can it conceivably be proved. It is, in short, an entirely illegitimate and unscientific assumption. Yet this cardinal tenet of medieval science was regarded in the thirteenth century not as a pleasing moral aphorism, but as a scientific axiom, as true as any geometrical axiom from the system of Euclid, and as useful for deducing further data by the syllogistic method. 'Natura nihil facit *frustra*', said the medieval. Nature does nothing *in vain*.

If this beautiful and sublimely simple axiom can be accepted as true, at once the whole of natural knowledge becomes potentially available for man. It supplies the synthetic principle that can never be inferred empirically from the data. Nature, instead of being a collection of disordered and chaotic phenomena, only to be investigated in its separate parts, becomes an ordered whole, bound together by *purposes*; and these, being analogous to human purposes, are comprehensible to the human understanding. A parasite growing on a tree does not just happen to grow there because the seed took root in a favourable spot, which is all that can be verified by empirical methods. To a believer in purposes the parasite could be there because it did something for the tree, because it benefited the plants in the neighbourhood, because it fed the animals and birds that ate it, or conceivably for the purpose of decorating the baronial hall for Christmas festivities, or even to act as a symbol for man of mutual aid in the kingdoms of nature. It could, for the medieval, be any or all of these things. The doctrine allowed scope for the human imagination, and it really did explain natural phenomena in a way which was satisfying to human aspirations. To understand these phenomena it was only necessary to transfer our own knowledge of human purposes to the field of nature; if one went far enough and had enough knowledge, it was possible to know the whole of nature, even without personally examining every phenomenon. Universal science was not beyond the possibility of man. When Bacon was asked in the course of his Parisian lectures whether plants had a sense of touch, he could and did confidently reply in the negative. The sense of touch, he said, is useful for animals and human beings because they have the power of locomotion. What would be the use of a plant's ability to feel if it could not do anything about it, if it could not escape from its enemy? Nature would not give it this power *in vain*. Therefore the plant has no sense of touch.[1]

Now to our science this question is insoluble. We cannot identify ourselves with a plant, and therefore cannot know subjectively whether it feels. We know that it lacks a central nervous system, and therefore does not feel through the same mechanism as man or animal. On the other hand, we have observed plants that react in a specialized way to the near presence of certain animals. We call this an 'automatic reaction'; but this is only a verbal explanation, giving no positive information. We smile at the medievals for thinking that the question was even legitimate and could have an answer.

The modern ecologist, one of the few synthetic scientists of our day, has set himself the task of observing the behaviour of living creatures in relation to their environment. His fundamental hypothesis is that nature does preserve a balance amongst living creatures; from which it follows that much can be learned from this natural economy. He has discovered that if we change any important factor, there will be a chain reaction of events, any one of which may cause serious disturbance in fields far remote from the one in which the first change was made. Nature, as he puts it, seems to 'hang together'. He speaks of the various activities in nature as having a relation to others; his science is descriptive and normative, or practical. But it cannot really be speculative in the sense in which Baconian and medieval science was speculative, because there can be no verifiable laws in this modern science, no universals to which the ecologist can relate his particulars. If he speaks of the *function* of an animal or plant in nature, he is careful to explain that this implies no anthropomorphism; he is only stating what the plant or animal actually does in nature.

The medievals, in the absence of the tedious observation and inquiry that show how each part of nature is in fact dependent on another, contented themselves with simplifying science—and we may excuse them on the grounds of their ignorance. And if we ask them ironically how they are going to inform us of the purposes of natural phenomena which appear to have no connection whatsoever with

[1] Steele, Fasc. XI, 186–87.

man or with any living creature, they would reply that it is quite true that such purposes can never be determined by observation and inquiry. But this does not mean that they are unknowable, and that men may resign themselves to their ignorance. On the contrary, *this* information has been given by God in the form of revelation.

It should be understood that revelation was not to the medieval an alternative form of knowledge to empirically acquired data. It was an absolutely essential part of it if there were to be any final understanding of a phenomenon which included its purposes. It was one of the primary tasks of the scientific investigator to complete, and, as Bacon emphasized, to confirm, the knowledge given in summary or occult form in the Scriptures, and in the writings of the Saints and Fathers of the Church, and of anyone who had had direct access to the revealed knowledge.[1]

The knowledge least accessible to man, the purpose of those heavenly bodies that seem at first sight to have nothing to do with man, was, according to Bacon, the first of all to be revealed, to the sons of Seth, the grandsons of Adam. The reason we cannot believe in astrology to-day is that we cannot conceive of any possible *mechanism* by which the stars, which our instruments may tell us are millions of light years away, could affect humble man. Billions of stars, galaxies, and nebulæ, which can only be seen at all by the aid of the most powerful telescope, according to our way of thinking can have no relation to man. In our search for efficient causes in the universe, cosmic rays have been discovered, and these make sense to us; and we proceed to investigate the means of their transmission. Our 'why' is answered by the statement that such or such a body gives off these rays by a recognizable process which we can even duplicate in the laboratory on a small scale. When the only stars that could be seen were those visible to the naked eye, it did not seem so impossible that there was a relationship between their movements and the vital processes of the human being, or even his path of life. Each planet, according to its position at a given moment in the sky, would have its effects on earth. For nature was one. Superiors ruled inferiors, and rays from the planets converged on the central earth.

This was the kind of knowledge that could only come originally

[1] Cf. p. 73 above and note 3, on how Bacon changes the sense of Josephus who had claimed that the patriarchs had lived for such long periods in order to be able to make astronomical discoveries. Bacon explains their longevity by the necessity to understand what had been revealed to them.

from revelation. However far back into the past the observations went, they could not make astrology into an empirical science, whatever might be said of true astronomy. For the relations of the observed movements to man must necessarily be hidden. We see a star in the sky and observe its movements; but the correlation with man's activities or with parts of his body is a theoretical one and cannot be based solely on observation. But once the knowledge had been revealed, as long as it was not lost but preserved through the generations, it could be *checked* empirically. Bacon suggests that this should be done, and it is the heart of his *scientia experimentalis.* If the revealed knowledge (hypothesis) could be confirmed by observations in the world of sense, this would help to confirm faith in *all* revelation, including the truths of religion. It was not enough to accept the revelation on authority alone; since, as Bacon realized, we can never be really certain until a thing is demonstrated to be true by the evidence of our senses. But at the same time everything that had been revealed could not at once be demonstrated to be true by experience. It was necessary to accept certain kinds of statements on the basis of authority, on the presumption that they were true; this acceptance depended upon the nature of the authority. As we have seen, Bacon had no objections to prophesy if the source were satisfactory to him. He might have even accepted scientific revelations if they had come from Joachim or St. Francis, since they had lived the kind of lives which make revelation possible. It is not unlikely that Bacon himself hoped for a personal revelation. But in the absence of any sign that moderns were fit to receive them, it was safer to believe that all scientific knowledge had been revealed long ago, and there was no need to repeat the revelations. However, these original revelations had become distorted by translation from one language to another, and by being transmitted through unbelievers. The truly scientific method was surely to try to discover in all their pristine purity the revelations first given to the sons of Seth, to Solomon, to the Hebrew prophets, and so on down to Aristotle and Avicenna, each being a lesser authority than his predecessors.

Now in most scientific fields revelation of this kind was a necessity. The medieval man could only hope to learn a little from empirical inquiry in comparison with the enormous amount that he could never know; and heavenly purposes were completely hidden from him. If a man were suffering from a stomach ailment, the medieval scientist had not yet the technique to determine the interrelationships between the stomach and the rest of the body. Even to-day these relationships are very imperfectly understood. But a medieval would have thought it ridiculous to say that these relationships were confined to the body as we see it before us; for the body itself was composed of matter and form, of soul and body. And the soul-element could not be observed by means of the five senses. Though the soul separated from the body at death, it could not be seen escaping; it was a non-physical entity. Moreover, there were other non-physical entities existing in the world which could also be neither seen nor touched—angels and demons. And it was quite possible that these entities might have taken possession of the soul, being of similar substance. A demon could, like electricity, only be perceived in its outward manifestations, and, being evil in nature, it could cause all kinds of diseases if it were united with the soul. Furthermore, man himself was also part of the universe, a *minor mundus*, or lesser world, in himself. His temperament or *complexio* was ruled not only by the elements and humours within his bodily organism, but by his relationship with the heavenly bodies. Finally, these same heavenly bodies which ruled the temperament and the bodily organization of man were themselves intimately connected with the rest of the universe, and especially with the plants and minerals that might be used for his cure. A plant that was especially subject to the influence of the planet Venus might be the required remedy for a disease of the kidneys ruled likewise by Venus; or perhaps an extract of copper, the mineral under the influence of Venus, might be indicated. But again, this would depend upon the man's own make-up. If he were especially choleric, the remedy might be contra-indicated for him, while it might work for others. The time of the year the disease occurred, and the climate of the country, would also have their effects.

It can, therefore, be seen at once that medieval medicine would be far from simple, and an enormous amount of 'knowledge' would be needed, both for diagnosis and prescription. But it did not rest on nothing but ignorance. It was based upon the appreciation of the relation between man and the universe which had been revealed as a necessary supplement to our feeble empirical knowledge. A medieval man would have considered it wildly unscientific to treat man as an organism in isolation, analyse a few mechanisms, and call it knowledge or science. Where medieval medicine would no doubt break down would be in its real ability to predict, or effect apparent cures. And it is one of Bacon's more lasting titles to fame that he suggested empirical verification of the data of revelation. It was not due to any scepticism on his part of the fact of revelation. But he wanted to separate folk-lore and magic from the genuine data of revelation. The testing by experiment of the old wives' tale of the ability of goats' blood to crack diamonds is a case in point.[1] Bacon's reverence for the text of Aristotle, and his irritation with the bad translations that were in circulation among the Latins, and his own consequent studies in philology, are a result of this belief. How could a corrupt text be used as deductive material for science, any more than an incorrect equation in mathematics? Ultimately the best experimental proof for the correctness of our mathematics is the verifiable fact that the George Washington Bridge has so far withstood the theoretically calculated strains put upon it in practice. The experiments in Bacon's time probably failed to confirm the deductions from the 'hypotheses' provided by revelation. But it was truly scientific of him to see the need for such experiments.

When Bacon stated that the first stage of knowledge was credulity, the second experience, and the third reason,[2] he was not recommending credulity; he was merely stating the obvious fact in medieval, and, indeed, in all science. We must first believe those who claim to have made an experiment, or those who have received or heard of a revelation. This is not the belief of certitude, but the equivalent of what we should call a hypothesis, a provisional belief. As Bacon says, we only finally believe it after proving it by experience, and then the soul can rest in the light of truth. Bacon himself instanced the fact that a magnet attracts iron, an improbable fact, but nevertheless true. We first hear of it through an experimenter. When later he makes the famous statement that he will believe anything, however apparently incredible, as long as it comes from a good authority, this does not mean that he denies the necessity for proving it by experiment. But as an attitude towards the phenomena of the world, it is a more probable prelude to discovery than a severe scepticism which refuses to believe in anything until it *has* been proved. The importance of the method, of course, lies in the insistence of the scientist on the provisional nature of the belief. As we shall see later, Bacon does not deny the possibility of attaining provisional truth also through reasoning, the mathematical method; but again, even in this sphere, certitude only comes from experience.

[1] *Opus Majus*, II, 168.

[2] 'Non oportet hominem inexpertum quaerere rationem ut primo intelligat hanc enim nunquam habebit nisi post experientiam: unde oportet primo credulitatem fieri donec secundo sequatur experientia ut tertio ratio comitetur.' *Opus Majus*, II, 202.

This means that experience is fundamental for both forms of knowledge:

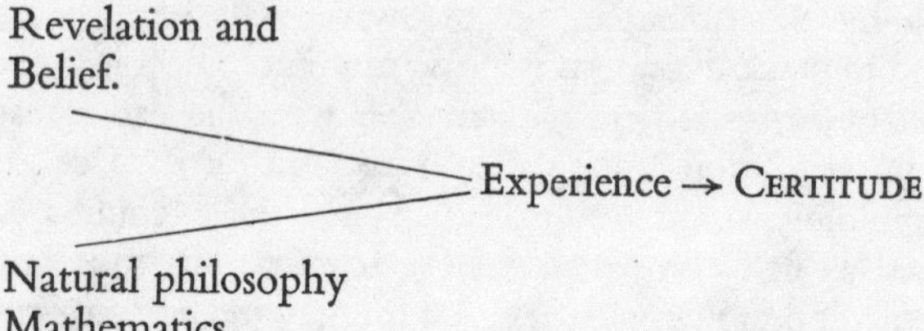

Nature, as we have seen, can be known by revealed knowledge and certified by experience. Is this the only knowledge of nature? Can it be known, and is the knowledge trustworthy, by experience alone?

Bacon seems to take the knowledge obtained through the senses, as far as it goes, for granted. He is worried by no epistemological problem. It might, therefore, be considered surprising that he seems to have no conception at all of the so-called 'natural history method of inquiry', the inductive method favoured by his later namesake, the attempt to find 'laws' of nature from a series of planned experiments and observations.

The reason that I think Bacon would give to justify his omission would be that experimental knowledge by itself is worthless, but only gains philosophical validity from its position within a theoretical framework. This is the point of view we should expect from a man who was primarily a thinker in search of universal knowledge. But even modern science would admit this. There is no limit whatever to the number of experiments one could make. But it is useless to make them unless there is some way of either interpreting them or using them. And this is precisely what Bacon suggests.

'The science of experience', he says, 'verifies all natural and artificial things . . . not by arguments as the purely speculative sciences do, nor by feeble and imperfect experiences as the operative sciences'.[1] Then he goes on to describe the activities of Peter de Maricourt, and explains that Peter knows the natural sciences by experience—medicine, alchemy, astronomy, and astrology—and he makes inquiries even from old women, soldiers and farmers, and would be ashamed if he did not know as much as they. But lest all this should be construed as experiment for its own sake, Bacon adds that without this kind of work it would be impossible for *philosophy* to be completed.[2]

[1] Brewer, *Op. Tert.*, p. 46. [2] *Ibid.*, p. 47.

It would, therefore, seem that the operative sciences by themselves have no great value for philosophy. But Bacon has great respect for those who make these experiments, since they will verify the speculative scheme. Moreover, they are of great practical use when controlled by a Christian ethical system.

2. *The philosophy and ethics of the study of nature.*

Bacon's conception of the origin of scientific knowledge might have led him to advocate only a return to the ancients to see what they had said, check it by experience, and call this a universal science. In the *Opus Majus*, indeed, he urges as strongly as he can the full study of the ancients and the more recent Arabs, and the establishment of a definitive Latin text of their works. But this is by no means the whole of his message. He might have been content if the science of the ancients had been complete, if the knowledge possessed by Solomon had been recovered in its entirety. Then all that was necessary would have been a checking with experience.

But Bacon's ambition was far greater than this. He wanted to create a theoretical framework which would take care of *all* branches of science, even those which had not been dealt with by the ancients in any of the books available to the Latins. And, above all, he wanted to make use of this knowledge. It has already been pointed out how Bacon viewed himself as another Aristotle, trying to do for his own time what Aristotle had done in his. Such a work was, in fact, necessary. Aristotle had done a gigantic work, nothing less than the founding of a systematic science out of a heterogeneous mass of philosophic speculations and a limited quantity of sense data, most of it observed personally by himself and his associates. Aristotle had had to formulate methods of describing and classifying these phenomena, he had even to show how to think about them—how, in short, to direct the human mind purposefully in its thinking so that concentration upon a limited set of data was possible. In this he had much help from his predecessors, especially from Plato, who had shown the possibilities of pure thought, untrammelled in the world of ideas, but without the limitations of form that are necessary to the practical scientist.

So Aristotle had to start from the very beginning and say: 'What do we mean when we say that a thing *is*?'—the categories of being—and take the principles of description he then formulates over into all the fields he can investigate. As a true Greek he searched for understanding and knowledge, and at his death he left a methodical body of knowledge, drawn up according to systematic and logical principles, capable of being understood by students in the ages that followed, once they had mastered the logic that informed it.

But in the fabric of this colossal theoretical work, surely unequalled in the history of mankind, two things were faulty—a metaphysics of being which does not account for man, and, as a consequence of this, a failure to unite the sciences of nature and the sciences of man. It is the sign of Bacon's genius that he saw both of these clearly and tried to remedy them.

The Christian Fathers had already seen that a metaphysics of being was insufficient to carry the scientific structure; it gave the principles that underlie all sciences, but it did not place man within the structure, and did not give him a purpose commensurate with all the works of the universe which he was capable of understanding. Since they believed that these very purposes had been revealed to them in their religion, they chose another metaphysics more in keeping with these high purposes. Then, since Neo-Platonism laid little stress on the sciences, and, indeed, to some degree emphasized the worthlessness of human knowledge, science was neglected as unimportant. It fell into the hands of practical men who used it, but were not capable of giving it its due place in a total view of the universe.

Bacon, as a Christian and a student of science, refused to accept this neglect of science by the Church as the proper policy for Christians. He explains at considerable length the reasons the Father neglected it, and tries to point out that this was due to the abuses of science or philosophy rather than to any inherent evil in it,[1] or to their ignorance of it because translations were not available to them.[2] But Bacon knows that the burden of proof is upon himself, and it is therefore essential that both the theoretical structure of his science and his precepts for its use be welded into a grand whole that is altogether Christian in its foundations.

It was necessary, then, that the two inadequacies of Aristotle should be repaired, and a different emphasis laid upon the whole. The underlying thought must no longer be: 'All men by nature desire to know', though Bacon had always admitted this desire. In his Parisian *Quaestiones* on the *Metaphysics* he had said that any orderly and discreet person would naturally desire to know, but not a disorderly and confused person. Moreover, the corporeal complexion of the

[1] 'Non igitur propter aliquod malum philosophiae . . . sed propter abusores eius.' *Opus Majus*, III, 32.

[2] 'Non fuerunt in eorum temporibus translatae nec in usu Latinorum et ideo neglexerunt eas.' *Opus Majus*, III, 33.

person might prevent the natural appetite of the soul from expressing itself.[1] Elsewhere he defends the natural desire against the argument that it is acquired for the sake of gain.[2] It is interesting how little Bacon stresses the Greek ideal of knowledge for its own sake in his later work. He had been entirely won over to the idea of the beauty and usefulness of knowledge. The beauty is seen by the student because even a little knowledge is part of the great whole, the wonderful works of God; the usefulness lies in its contribution to the last end of man. The Christian influence is unmistakable. Knowledge cannot be an end in itself, but must be a means to an end; intellect must ultimately be subordinated to the will. The acquisition of knowledge ceases to be a natural instinct, of no ethical value; or all knowledge would be given by nature, as Bacon had argued even when he was still only a philosopher.[3] It becomes a moral virtue to seek for knowledge now that he has become a scientist. But now also the merit lies not in the mere search but in the application of the knowledge in accordance with ethical principles. Man must search for knowledge and apply it. Completed knowledge which is of surpassing beauty will incidentally benefit the soul; but its value is not exhausted thereby.

Now when Aristotle analyses the relationship between the sciences[4] it is primarily a logical analysis. He sees the way in which each contributes to the other, and he recognizes that the relationship is one of subalternation. He even sees the hierarchy of higher and lower sciences. But the emphasis Bacon gives to this is subtly different. He knows the subalternational relationship, but he does not state it in logical terms. He emphasizes rather the manner in which each helps the other, providing its tools so that it may progress further. And the whole picture is changed by the insistence upon the supremacy of moral philosophy or ethics. The whole structure of universal science, beautiful as it is, might not be worth struggling for if it were not to be used.

Now this again is different in Aristotle. His *Ethics*, wonderful as it is, is not based on his knowledge of science, but upon his knowledge of the nature of man and his ordinary life as a citizen. Coming from a man who, as Mandonnet points out, must have studied in the

[1] Steele, Fasc. X, 2–3.

[2] *Ibid.*, Fasc. XI, 1.

[3] 'Finis intentus hominis est felicitas quam acquirit per meritum et non mereretur per scientias et virtutes si haberet a natura; acquiritur ergo scientia homini per laborem doctrine et virtutis ut possit magis acquirere finem intentum.' Steele, Fasc. X, 5.

[4] Aristotle, *Post. anal.*, 87*a* ff.

Faculty of Arts, it is remarkable that Bacon could produce no better moral philosophy than he gives us in the last part of the *Opus Majus*. The reason for this is simple. Aristotle's *Ethics* cannot tell us what we are to *do* with our knowledge; it is in no sense the crown of his scientific achievements, but only another empirical inquiry, this time into the nature of man and his place in society. Like his work in biology and physics, it is primarily an inquiry into principles, derived mainly from experience by the inductive method. To tell us in detail on what principles science should be used would have required an entirely new system of ethics, and this, perhaps, never occurred to Aristotle; and Bacon had not the time, and probably had not the ability, to produce it. He knew that science must in some way be brought into relation with the Christian scheme of salvation. But as he had not done this thinking except in very general terms—it is, after all, possibly the most difficult question in modern ethics, and we have certainly not solved it to-day, though the need is far more urgent—all Bacon does in the *Opus Majus* is give us a few details on how science could benefit organized Christianity, and how it would help to a fuller understanding of the Scriptures. In doing this he neglects Aristotle, since Aristotle's ethics can only be properly understood within the framework of his philosophy and psychology. He prefers the moral platitudes of Seneca which are *ex parte* utterances derived from his own experience of life in the Roman Empire and the ethical philosophy of Stoicism. But it cannot be denied that Bacon saw the need for a system of ethics which was the culmination of his science, even if he did not produce it.

It is to be understood, therefore, that theoretical and practical knowledge, or what we should call pure and applied science, were no more separable for Bacon than they are for us. But he did not make the mistake of thinking that the practical application of pure science was an end in itself, nor did he assume without argument that its end was the greatest comfort and pleasure to be obtained by it for human beings. He gave thought to the problem of the ends of both forms of science. The pursuit of pure science resulted in, first, the perception of its beauty, and thus was good for the soul; but at the same time it resulted in practical inventions which would be good for the Church, and ultimately able to help in the conversion of more Christians, all able to share in the hope of salvation. The pursuit of practical science, as well as helping the Church, served again to confirm the faith by proving the truths of revelation, even such esoteric matters as the Holy Trinity, the Blessed Virgin, and the resurrection of the body—which truths could not be discovered by these means, but, having been revealed, could be confirmed.

Nevertheless, for purposes of analysis it may be well to distinguish between Bacon's ideas on the increasing of knowledge, or speculative science, and practical science, as he understood it. The key to his scientific system is, of course, to be found in his special science that he calls 'scientia experimentalis', which, as suggested in the introduction to this study, should probably be translated as the 'science of experience' rather than experimental science, which suggests some kind of experiments in our modern sense. In the Romance languages the derivatives of the Latin *experimentalis* retain this meaning to-day.

We have discussed already the mediating position experience holds between revealed and natural knowledge, as giving certitude to both. But this is only one of its functions. It must also add knowledge, and guide its application. Indeed, Bacon distinguishes clearly between the three 'dignities' or 'prerogatives' of this science. Only the first is concerned with what we should call to-day the 'experimental method', and is the function we have described already. When Bacon says that this science is the ruler of the separate sciences, and compares it with the navigator who gives orders to the carpenter, or the soldier who gives orders to the smith, he is describing the rôle of the third 'dignity', the principles which should guide the application and use of the special sciences.

The second dignity of the science of experience is concerned with the relating of the knowledge of one field of science with the others. It is one of the outstanding deficiencies of our modern scientific system that we lack precisely such a science as Bacon is here suggesting, though in the twentieth century steps have already been taken in the direction of providing one. In view of the enormous content of our special sciences to-day and the way in which each overlaps the other, we have a very great need for it. But on the other hand this knowledge is now so specialized within each particular field that it may be for ever impossible to provide it. Already it was impossible in Bacon's day for one man to understand all fields, and Bacon himself ultimately saw this. When he appealed to the Pope to patronize a corps of scientists, each working in special fields but contributing his knowledge to the whole, he was suggesting the only possible measure that could be taken to provide the basis for this second dignity.[1]

Since Bacon did not give it a name, but only called it the second

[1] 'Omnia enim magnifica ad usum hujus scientiae pertinent, licet preparetur operatio multorum per alias scientias.' Brewer, *Op. Tert.*, p. 45.

dignity of the science of experience, let us call it simply 'synthetic science'. It could be a science within its own right, and perhaps some day it will be. Its function, according to Bacon, was to concern itself with those great truths which, though they belong to other sciences, lie outside the scope of their investigation.[1] As an example of what he means he suggests that the behaviour of animals in the light of nature may have value in determining the medicines to be used by human beings who have forgotten these secrets of nature. If the animal eats a plant that will prolong his life, and the human being has forgotten the use of it, could he not be reminded of it, and profit from the example of the animals? Here we have a direct connection between the separate sciences of biology, medicine, and psychology which is very much used to-day, though in practice the specialist in one science will have to think out the application for himself, and may be in complete ignorance of the findings of his fellow specialist in his own different field of inquiry.

These particular sciences are recognized to-day as being closely connected, and even the specialist will be expected to know something of the work going on in at least these allied fields. Theoretical physics and agronomy are not so closely connected that they will be equally studied by the experts in the biological sciences. But it is at least possible that the remarkable visible effects in the soil of fantastically small quantities of such elements as boron, may be worth studying by physicians who may have insufficiently considered whether small doses may not have as important effects within the human body as large doses, even if they do not work in the same manner. And the fact that valuable minerals may be present in the soil in huge quantities but unavailable to the plant until certain agricultural practices have been carried out, might suggest certain useful experiments to dieticians and doctors on the conditions necessary for the proper intake of minerals and vitamins in the human body. It is even possible that the 'revealed' Christian Science of Mary Baker Eddy or ascetic practices recommended by the Hindu scriptures may have something to offer to the specialized studies of physiological and psychological therapy.

It was the ability of all the separate sciences (revealed, speculative, and practical) to contribute knowledge to the others that Bacon so continuously stressed. If he had foreseen our age of specialization he might have been even more emphatic. Was it so unscientific of him to suggest a special synthetic science, whose business it would

[1] 'Quod in terminis aliarum scientiarum explicat veritates quas tamen nulla earum potest intelligere nec investigare.' Little, *Op. Tert.*, p. 44. Gasquet, p. 510.

be to examine the findings of the special sciences and co-ordinate them?

His plan for a compendium of scientific knowledge produced by co-operative effort under the patronage of prelates and princes, which would explain the state of each science in tabloid form for the benefit of non-specialists was a truly remarkable idea for his age, and is an excellent example of his practical thinking. He states concisely the seven conditions required for such a compendium as: (1) true, (2) well-chosen, (3) systematic, avoiding confusion, for instance, between natural things and metaphysics, (4) moderately short, (5) clear, though he admits the difficulty of combining clarity with brevity, (6) proved by trustworthy experience, (7) as perfect as possible.[1]

It would be difficult indeed to produce such a work in our day without excessive oversimplification; but many undergraduate schools in the United States have adopted something not unlike it. And the whole effort of President Hutchins and his associates at the University of Chicago has been infused with ideas not far different from Bacon's, and with the same purpose in view.

The third 'dignity' of the science of experience is to Bacon the supreme one. We cannot call it by the name of any of our separate sciences, since one part of it concerns the uses to which the results of all the sciences are to be put. And this brings it at once within the sphere of the higher science of moral philosophy. But in so far as it belongs to what we call science, it is concerned with the practical application of all the other separate sciences. To-day this is the function of the engineer and technician in the widest sense of these terms. It is true that the engineer does command the services of all the pure scientists. The geometrician, to use Bacon's example, does not make a burning glass, though he studies the principles on which it must be built. The technician asks the geometrician only for the practical results of his findings, and then makes his mirror.[2] Or the physician asks the astronomer for the results of his findings when he compounds a medicine.

But in Bacon's view the practical scientist or technician has yet a further task. This makes him, in Bacon's scheme, superior even to the mathematician, or to the synthesizer who takes the results of one science and applies them in another. The technician must see the *possibilities* in the work of each of these separate sciences. He must visualize from the work of the mathematicians the theoretical

[1] Brewer, *Op. Tert.*, p. 57.

[2] Little, *Op. Tert.*, p. 51.

possibility of building a flying-machine; he must draw out to their conclusions their ideas which may have been applied only on a small scale. On seeing a burning glass he must realize that if one were built that were large enough, a mirror could be constructed on the same principles, which would burn up everything combustible at a great distance and annihilate armies.[1] He must see that with a combination of mirrors it would be possible to see to the other side of the English Channel as Julius Caesar is said to have done.[2] Since saltpetre in small quantities can make a shocking noise, it must be possible to use it in such a way that the noise would be greater than the human being could bear.[3] The Palomar telescope and the block-buster bomb would not be surprising to Bacon because they are only applications on a large scale of principles valid on a small. This ability of the engineer to see the possibilities both of existing discoveries and the theoretical principles on which they are based is to Bacon the highest achievement of a scientist.

So the total of Bacon's science of experience is seen to make a great deal of sense if it is split up into its separate parts; and his theoretical scheme, with its hierarchy of sciences graded according to their contribution to practical life, seems valid within its own framework. Schematically it would appear as follows:

MORAL PHILOSOPHY
↗ ↖
Third dignity—Use
↗ ↖
Second dignity—Synthesis
↗ ↖
First dignity—Verification
(Separate sciences) ↗ ↑ ↖ ↖ ↖
Revealed science. Alchemy. Astronomy. Astrology. Agriculture, etc.

A modern pope might also agree that moral philosophy should be in the same position at the top to supply direction to the separate sciences. When Pius XII made a public statement regretting the necessity for the hydrogen bomb but supported research looking

[1] Little, *Op. Tert.*, p. 52.

[2] *Opus Majus*, II, 165.

[3] 'Per igneam coruscationem et combustionem ac per sonorem horrorem possunt miri fieri, et in distantia qua volumus ut homo mortalis sibi cavere non posset nec sustinere.' Little, *Op. Tert.*, p. 51.

towards its production, Bacon would have approved his utterance. The engineers and technicians were lords in their own domain, but even they must bow to the superior wisdom of spiritual advisers who could state authoritatively whether their endeavours were directed to the ultimate good of mankind. Only those trained in moral philosophy could answer this question, not the scientists themselves.

CHAPTER X

THE LAST YEARS

AT least twenty-four years of life remained to Roger Bacon after the death of his patron, Pope Clement IV. For his last work, the *Compendium studii theologiae*, mentions the current year as 1292.[1] Tradition has it that after the completion of the *Opera* he returned to his native land, and a statement of a fourteenth-century chronicler says that he was imprisoned by the Minister-General of his Order, Jerome of Ascoli, for 'suspected novelties'; otherwise we have no evidence for his activities during these twenty-four years beyond the internal evidence of his writings. This chapter will, therefore, again discuss the probabilities, attempt to make a critical estimate of the evidence for his supposed imprisonment, and produce a final hypothesis on what may have actually happened and why.

We have seen that in the *Opus Tertium* there is an indication that some of Bacon's difficulties with his superiors had been resolved, and there were fewer impediments to his writing. We have suggested that this was due to the fact that the friars had been permitted to read the *Opus Majus* and found nothing dangerous in it. All through this study we have tried to show that Bacon, previous to his work for the Pope, was neglected within his Order and comparatively unknown outside a small circle. Whether this is true or not, his prestige proportionately increased on account of his mandates, and the works that resulted from them; and he ceased to be a man of so little importance. At all events, during the next few years he was able to continue his writing, though, for the most part, he spent his time making revisions and completing work that he had undertaken earlier. The introduction to the *Secret of Secrets*, as has already been pointed out,[2] was almost certainly subsequent to the *Opus Majus*, as were also the second recension of the *Communia mathematica* and the greater part of the *Communia naturalium*. There are also the Greek and Hebrew grammars, which are known to be subsequent to the *Opus Tertium*.[3] But in 1272 there is also the *Compendium studii philosophiae*, which shows anything but a calmly scientific frame of mind at the time of writing.

Where did he write these works? There is no definite evidence

[1] *CST*, p. 34. [2] *Supra*, p. 82. [3] *Supra*, p. 106, and note 2.

that he returned to England. Little wants to use the fact that the glosses to the *Secret of Secrets* were written in England as evidence that Bacon returned there now.[1] But since it has been claimed earlier in this study that the glosses long antedate the introduction to this work, and only the latter is subsequent to the *Opus Majus*, this cannot be used as indisputable evidence. On the other hand, I do not think that tradition in this case can be altogether disregarded.

If Bacon had been away from his native land all the time from 1257 to 1290 or 1292, and had earlier studied and taught in Paris, as we know he did, this would mean that the greater part of his life was spent in France. The bulk of his MSS. in the centuries since his death have been found scattered through English libraries, and far fewer are known in continental collections, except in the case of works definitely associated with his French period. His memory was so highly esteemed in England that stories and legends soon sprung up around his name. In particular there is one which associates him with one Friar Thomas Bungay, with whose assistance Bacon is supposed to have made by magical means a brazen head![2]

This appears a rather surprising activity for Bacon, who was an opponent of magic (though a brazen head might be considered rather a 'secret work of art and nature', of which he did approve); and for Thomas Bungay, who was the Provincial Minister of the Franciscan Order in England from 1271 to 1275, and at other times reader in theology both at Oxford and Cambridge. The bibliographer, Pits, certainly attributes a book on magic to Thomas, but this is not otherwise known;[3] it would seem more probable that Pits knew the legend and provided Thomas with a bibliography to suit it. At all events, only a series of questions on the *De coelo et mundo* are known to be from his hand, and a few Aristotelian commentaries and questions which occur in the same MS. as the questions on the *De coelo* may also have been his.[4] The Elizabethans who used his name may have been looking for some pleasant comic alliteration with the better known Bacon, and have chosen Thomas Bungay as a suitable figure and a fellow Franciscan. But it is also possible that Roger did, in fact, know Thomas in the years after the *Opus Majus*, in which case this association no doubt occurred in England. Bacon could have

[1] Little, *Essays* . . . p. 20.

[2] See especially the essay by J. E. Sandys, 'Roger Bacon in English Literature', in Little, *Essays* . . . pp. 359–72.

[3] *Dictionary of National Biography*, art. Roger Bacon.

[4] Little, *Franciscan Papers* . . . (1943), pp. 136, 191; Little and Pelzer, *Oxford Theology and Theologians* (1934), p. 75.

interested the head of the Franciscan Order in England in his scientific work, and perhaps they made some experiments in England together. Outside the legend, however, there is no evidence for any association between them.

If, however, Bacon had been sent to France in 1257 as a disciplinary measure and to have him in a place where he could be kept under more supervision than in England, and if he had in 1267 or 1268 made his peace with his superiors and shown them that he was not writing anything subversive, and if, as a result of his mandates and the increased prestige resulting from them he became a somewhat more important man in his Order, I think the reasons for keeping him in France would be at an end; and I think the friars would be more likely now to listen to any appeal he made to them for return to England. In the absence, therefore, of any evidence to the contrary, and in view of the tradition which associates him with England, I think he probably did, in fact, return there soon after the *Opus Majus*, and began to revise his scientific work. In this new leisure much of the *Communia naturalium* was written, which contains some of the best work of his entire career. Most of it is very carefully thought out, though it is more difficult to read, being far more scholastic than the *persuasiones* to the Pope. But in the midst of this peaceful activity we find that Bacon also wrote the most violent and unrestrained polemic of his entire career. How is this to be explained?

I think in spite of the 'peaceful activity' just spoken of, Bacon found it difficult to concentrate on it. Just below the surface was seething the indignation against society that had always been present. The failure of the great effort of his life could not be accepted with equanimity; and in the disorders that followed the death of Clement IV he really did see the tribulations that were to precede the coming of Antichrist. He could no longer hope for the reforms he had proposed to the Pope. In fact, there was no longer a pope at all. The work he was now doing was severe and required little imagination and enthusiasm, and he probably did not have his heart in it, since he could no longer hope to *achieve* anything with it in his lifetime. It would be natural for him to pay more attention than ever to what was entertaining and marvellous, and I suspect the foundation for the later Baconian legend was laid at this time. This, however, is merely conjecture, while the state of his emotions in 1272 was expressed clearly in his polemic. And the polemic itself is in the form of an introduction to his *scriptum principale*, which, though it was not complete, may have been as complete as he thought it was ever likely to be. Now was the time when I should expect him to return to his Joachism if it had ever existed; and it is from the *Compendium*, as evidence of a long-continuing state of mind, that most of our material was drawn for the earlier period in Bacon's life reconstructed in chapter VII. It is in this work that he tells us how he tried to prove by logic to his fellow friars that the time of Antichrist was at hand.

For, indeed, the times were disordered. During the interregnum following the death of Clement, the struggle between the seculars and the Orders had broken out afresh, and rivalry between the two Orders made the confusion worse.[1] Twenty-nine known polemics were issued by the seculars and religious against each other in Paris alone during the years from 1269 to 1271; these were attacks on the poverty and spiritual pride of the Franciscans and Dominicans, and counter-attacks and defences by the leading lights of the Orders. William of St. Amour, from his safe haven, already in 1266 had reaffirmed his previous attack on Joachim, and the status of the religious in a long and heavily documented work, with copious quotations from the Scriptures. Though Clement IV refused to accept this work as any improvement on the banned *De periculis*, William was undismayed, and his disciples in Paris, Gérard of Abbéville, an archdeacon, and Nicolas of Lisieux, a lay theologian, were in constant touch with him. And once Clement was dead they probably thought there was some real chance of humbling the Orders while there was no pope to stop them. An old polemic of Gérard, attacking the Franciscans in particular, was reissued in 1269, and was replied to by St. Bonaventura, the Franciscan General. Nicolas of Lisieux concentrated on the Dominicans and was replied to by St. Thomas Aquinas. The moving spirit, William of St. Amour himself, died in 1272, and the round of polemics ceased. But it had been violent while it lasted.[2]

There were external wars. Italy was overrun by Charles of Anjou, the succession to the Empire was disputed, and civil war between the factions still raged. And though Bacon does not refer to it, at the University of Paris the quarrel between the Faculty of Arts and the Faculty of Theology was coming to a head, with Siger of Brabant leading the Faculty of Arts in its opposition to the new teachings of

[1] A public dispute on poverty between the Dominicans and Franciscans at Oxford before the Faculty in 1269 is recorded by Little, and an eyewitness account by a Franciscan is printed by him. Little, *Grey Friars in Oxford*, pp. 320–35.

[2] For these troubles see the full account based on original sources and examination of the documents by P. Glorieux, 'Contra Geraldinos, l'enchaînement des polemiques' (1935), pp. 129–55.

St. Thomas and the more orthodox theologians, which finally resulted in the condemnation of the 219 errors in 1277.[1]

When Gregory X was chosen Pope in early 1272, Bacon does not seem to have held the high hopes that others did. But there was a tremendous outpouring of prophesy from other quarters. It seems almost certain that the main body of the prophesies of 'Merlin' belong to his reign. The 'holy Pope' is referred to by name as 'Gregory the Cardinal', who, when he comes to the throne, will establish a reign of peace and confound the enemies of Christianity.[2] He will even perform miracles not seen before. Salimbene states that Gregory was actually influenced in his dealings with erring prelates by certain prophetic verses known to him before he became Pope; and he gives a high estimate of his saintly character, quoting a poem that antedated the prophesies, and no doubt helped to influence the form they took.[3] The prophesies of Merlin announce the miracles of Antichrist, and set forth the evil works of the clerics under whom the world has degenerated. Like Joachim, he 'predicts' the rise of the two Orders, but, unlike Joachim, Merlin says that they too will become a prey to worldliness.[4] And this was exactly what the stricter Franciscans within the Order were saying themselves.

It is against this setting that the *Compendium* of Roger Bacon must be judged. It is related to Bacon's other work by the fact that it is an introduction to his scientific scheme, and it ends by a discussion of grammar which, as Vanderwalle has shown, was almost certainly replaced by a later, more complete treatment in his strictly grammatical works.[5] But it is primarily a polemic of precisely the same kind that was being put out by seculars and friars at the time. It shows clearly Bacon's state of mind at the time of writing it. He is almost in despair at the condition of society, though he attributes it to the kind of reasons we should expect of him. In addition to the largely political complaint of the prevalence of Italian trained lawyers, and the supremacy of the civil over the religious and ecclesiastical codes, he adduces the neglect of the *integritas sapientiae*, ignorance of true learning, failure to follow the good old practices of the time of Grosseteste, and feeble theology based on the *Sentences*. As an

[1] *Chartularium* . . . I, 544–55.

[2] L. A. Paton, *Les Prophécies* . . . II, 175–78. Many prophesies had been attributed to Merlin earlier, and, as we have seen, Bacon calls the attention of the Pope to them (*Opus Majus*, I, 269). The series of the 1270's was, however, the fullest and most influential.

[3] Salimbene, *Cronica* . . . pp. 488–92.

[4] Paton, *Les Prophécies* . . . II, 188–90.

[5] Vanderwalle, *Roger Bacon dans l'histoire* . . . pp. 104–106.

educational theorist, it is the defects in education that he holds primarily responsible.

But in the *Compendium* Bacon has no longer anything constructive to offer. The attack is almost entirely destructive, an emotional outburst. But the work is valuable as a detailed, if one-sided, account of the studies of the time. There is no indication as to where it was written. The studies dealt with are Parisian; but this was natural since, as Bacon himself tells us, Paris is still the leader of the world in theological studies. Bacon in any case was probably more familiar with conditions in Paris, having spent so many recent years there. It is, perhaps, more likely that it would be written away from Paris, in view of the fierce attacks he makes upon conditions and personalities there.[1]

The work is only known as a fragment, and in only one MS., and we cannot tell whether it was ever published.[2] Such a fragment, unfinished as it is, and its later part replaced by a more systematic and complete work, could have little value except as a polemic. Since it seems certain that the *scriptum principale* was never finished, there was no need for the publication of an introduction, though Bacon might well have composed one, or the beginnings of one, at a time when his feelings had become unbearable. Then, having said what he must, he abandoned it, and set more calmly to work on a separate grammar which he did complete, and which replaced the later pages of the *Compendium* as we have it. I am hesitant to suggest, as Charles and others have done,[3] that the attacks made in this work were responsible in themselves for any suppression or persecution that followed later in the decade. I think it more probable that Bacon permitted himself the luxury of letting off some of his despair and anger on paper, while retaining enough restraint not to publish it. If he had allowed such a damning document to circulate freely, he could have been punished with some justification for causing schism between the Orders, and not for the 'suspected novelties' for which, as we shall see, a fourteenth-century chronicler says he was imprisoned.

[1] A further small point may possibly support the theory that Bacon wrote from Oxford. Nolan, in his edition of the 'Oxford' Grammar, remarks that when Bacon had to choose an example of a four-figure number, chose 1224, which is the date of the founding of the Franciscan convent at Oxford. The choice might be a likely one if he were living there at the time. Nolan and Hirsch, *The Greek Grammar* . . . (1902), pp. lxxii, 25.

[2] Brewer finds this fourteenth-century paper MS. the best of those available for the *Opus Tertium* which is included, together with a part of the *Opus Majus* and the *Compendium* fragment (p. xli). He gives a facsimile of the MS. in the frontispiece to his edition. The MS. is much corrected, and might have been made by an intelligent and interested scribe from Bacon's own copy after his death.

[3] Charles, pp. 51–53; Bridges, *Life and Works* . . . pp. 29–32.

This imprisonment has been much disputed. The only authority for it comes from the *Chronicle of the Twenty-four Generals*, a work written in 1370, but containing earlier matter. Inaccuracies in this chronicle have been pointed out, especially by David Fleming,[1] apart from the passage about Roger Bacon; and since it calls Bacon a 'doctor of sacred theology' which we have tried to show was impossible, this very passage is suspect. However, if the chronicler was in error, a reason must be found for his very specific statement. On the advice of many brothers, he tells us, the General, Brother Jerome, condemned and reproved the doctrine of Roger Bacon, the Englishman, doctor of sacred theology, as containing 'suspected novelties' on account of which the same Roger was condemned to prison. Jerome also wrote to the lord Pope Nicholas III that through his authority the perilous doctrine should be altogether suppressed.[2]

In order to come to some decision and examine the probabilities fully, it is necessary to go once again into some detail on the current conditions in the Franciscan Order, since the punishment, if any, was inflicted by the General of the Franciscans. The chief question at issue is: Was there any imprisonment at all? If there was an imprisonment, then we must ask why, and for how long?

The Abbé Feret, while not altogether denying the fact of an imprisonment, insists that it must have been mild and of short duration,[3] Vanderwalle takes substantially the same view.[4] Thorndike points out the unlikelihood of any imprisonment for scientific novelties, and quotes with approval an opinion questioning the veracity of the *Chronicle*.[5] Charles does not doubt the fact of the imprisonment, and, in keeping with his general thesis, attributes it to suspicion of Bacon's scientific novelties and his general attacks on the society of his time, and blames also the tyrannical character of Jerome of Ascoli, the Franciscan General.[6] Mandonnet, in his customary manner, put forward an ingenious hypothesis that Bacon wrote a work hitherto attributed to Albertus Magnus which defended astrology. And since astrology had been recently condemned, amongst other erroneous doctrines, by the Bishop of Paris, Bacon drew upon himself the unfavourable attention of the authorities.[7] This attractive hypothesis, which would explain so many things if it

[1] D. Fleming, 'Ruggero Bacone e la scolastica' (1914), p. 542.
[2] *Chronicle of the Twenty-four Generals*, p. 360.
[3] P. Feret, 'Les Imprisonnements de Roger Bacon' (1891), pp. 119–42.
[4] Vanderwalle, *Roger Bacon dans l'histoire . . .* (1929), pp. 149–55.
[5] Thorndike, *History of Magic . . .* (1923), II, 628–29, 675–77.
[6] Charles, pp. 37–39, 51–53.
[7] Mandonnet, 'Roger Bacon et le Speculum . . . (1910), pp. 313–35.

were true, captivated amongst others Little, who had evidently not examined very closely the basis of Mandonnet's conjectures, and was not familiar with his virtuosity in overlooking inconvenient facts.[1] Bridges attributed the imprisonment to repercussions resulting from the publication of the *Compendium studii philosophiae*.[2]

Feret and Vanderwalle find it difficult to reconcile an imprisonment of any severity with the production of the *De retardatione accidentium senectutis*, which, according to them, was addressed to Pope Nicholas III in 1281, and with the opening lines of the *Compendium studii theologiae* which seem to show that Bacon had been engaged on the work for some time prior to 1292, and make no mention of any troubles suffered by the author. We have tried to show earlier that the *De retardatione* was an early work,[3] and that there is no reason to suppose it was composed for Nicholas, since the only evidence in favour of this idea is that Nicholas was 'noble on both sides'. In view of this, it is surprising that Vanderwalle, in his otherwise extremely critical work, should have said that Charles 'demonstrated' the fact that it was sent to him.[4] Charles, in fact, adduces no other evidence beyond the fact that Bacon, in the beginning of the work, states that he has been held up by lack of resources and popular rumour, and has not been able to 'faire des expériences qui eussent été faciles à tout autre'. This passage does not even occur in the edition of the *De retardatione* by Little and Withington, though Charles says he consulted MS. Bodl. Canonic. Misc. 334, which was collated for their edition.[5] Even if the passage was in the MS., all that Charles says does not amount to much as proof, in comparison with the undoubted fact that Bacon in his *Opus Majus* refers to the *De retardatione* as already written, and deals with the contents at some length.[6] It is, however, possible that another edition of the work was sent to Pope Nicholas III, but the suggestion is gratuitous, as there is nothing to support it beyond an apparent cross-reference to the *Opus Majus* in the *De retardatione*, and the fact that we know from internal evidence that there were at least two editions of this work, one addressed to a secular prince, and one to a pope. As for the cross-reference,[7] the offending words are omitted in three MSS. of the *De retardatione*, and in any case look suspiciously like a gloss. Internal evidence, so far as can be ascertained, supports the theory of an early rather than a late date.

[1] Little, *Essays* . . . (1914), pp. 23–27.
[2] Bridges, *The Life and Works* . . . (1914), pp. 29–32.
[3] *Supra*, p. 24.
[4] Vanderwalle, *Roger Bacon dans l'histoire* . . . p. 154.
[5] Charles, pp. 48–49.
[6] *Opus Majus*, II, 209 ff.
[7] Steele, Fasc. IX, 54.

Professor Thorndike questions the motive for the imprisonment given in the *Chronicle*. He discounts the suggestion that the suspected novelties could have been of a scientific nature, and makes it clear that the Franciscans did not object to science as such, as evidenced by the career of John Peckham, author of the *Perspectiva communis*. He remarks that the wording of the *Chronicle* suggests 'some details of doctrine, whereas had Bacon been charged with magic we may be pretty sure that so sensational a feature would not have passed unnoticed'.[1] Elsewhere he shows that Bacon's views on astrology were shared by Albertus Magnus, and he was more of an opponent of magic than any of his distinguished contemporaries.[2]

Charles, in attributing Bacon's imprisonment partly to his outspokenness,[3] is probably on the right track, though research in his time had not yet shown the prevalence of many of Bacon's ideas, including his scientific ones. He also lacked information on Jerome of Ascoli, whom he makes the villain of the piece.[4] A short account of this man, together with an estimate of his character by one who certainly had no cause to love him, may serve the purpose of clarifying his position as head of the Franciscan Order at the time of Bacon's imprisonment, and lay the foundation for the hypothesis which will be presented later that Bacon was the victim of a 'political' sentence.

In 1274 Pope Gregory X called a council at Lyons to discuss the troubles in Christendom, including the quarrels between the Orders and the seculars, to which representatives of both parties were invited. Before the Council got under way the Franciscan General, who was still St. Bonaventura, after seventeen years in his position, died, and was replaced by Jerome of Ascoli. This man had already had a considerable experience in performing various missions for the Church, and even during his generalate, which lasted till 1279, the Church, it appears, could not dispense with his services. He had to hurry back from a mission to the Greek emperor in order to take part in the later sessions of the Council of Lyons,[5] and in 1276 he was again sent by Pope Innocent V to Greece, though he did not complete the journey. He tried to resign his position as head of the Franciscan

[1] Thorndike, *History of Magic* . . . II, 628–29.
[2] *Ibid.*, II, 675–77.
[3] 'Le moine d'Oxford a payé de son repos et de sa liberté le privilège d'avoir devancé son temps, d'en avoir aperçu, exagéré, si on veut, les vices et les faiblesses, d'avoir fait, une guerre ouverte aux hommes et aux choses . . . et d'avoir froissé toutes les idées et tous les amour-propres de son temps.' Charles, p. 53.
[4] 'Jerome d'Ascoli, caractère tyrannique et porté à la rigueur encore que par la politique.' Charles, p. 37.
[5] Huber, *A Documented History* . . . pp. 167–68.

Order because he had no time to fulfil his duties properly, but was not permitted to do so. He was sent in 1277 on another papal mission to France, and even when he was appointed Cardinal in 1279 he could not get his resignation accepted until the next General Chapter.[1] He seems to have been genuinely worried that he could not perform his duties to the Order, and no doubt the Order suffered from his absence. But there is no impression here of a hard-hearted tyrant.

Angelo of Clareno, a Spiritual who was condemned to prison by Jerome for his adherence to Joachitic ideas, calls him 'moderate enough, slow to anger and to inflict injuries, though lax and lukewarm in his support of good men'. And he illustrates Jerome's character by telling us of the impression made upon him by the character of Peter John Olivi, and by his sanctity. The friars tried to persuade Jerome, after he had become Pope as Nicholas IV, to take punitive action against Peter, who was the intellectual leader of the Spirituals, but he refused to take any such action against a man of Peter's saintliness. And when Jerome did condemn a book of Peter's that went too far in adoration of the Virgin Mary, Peter at once submitted, and Jerome said afterwards that he had condemned the book, not 'ad injuriam', but 'ad cautelam'.[2]

It was Jerome's misfortune that during the period of his generalate he should have been forced to deal with a serious schism in his Order to which he had no time to attend. The punishment meted out to Angelo and others who actually rebelled against the Order, and caused what seems to have been a political disturbance in the March of Ancona, and who later tried to secede from the Order, was severe. The dissident friars, who had believed that a decision of the Council of Lyons, which allowed the brothers to dispose of movable goods without the intervention of papal procurators, meant the end of poverty for their Order,[3] were kept in chains and deprived of the sacraments even on their deathbed. They were called schismatics and heretics; no one was to speak to them, not even the jailers who brought them food. Angelo describes, evidently as an eyewitness, the appalling conditions under which the sentences were carried out,

[1] Huber, *A Documented History* . . . pp. 169–70.

[2] Angelo gives a full account of the history of the persecuted Spirituals, which, though exaggerated, cannot be impugned for its general veracity. The account has been edited by F. Ehrle in *Archiv* . . . Vol. II. Of Jerome, Angelo says: 'Vir mansuetus et satis modestus et tardus ad iram et injurias inferendas, licet esset remissus et tepidus in promotione bonorum'. *Archiv* . . . II, 288. The following are Jerome's words when he was asked to condemn Olivi: 'Avertat Deus a corde et mente nostra, tanto viro, qui excedat penes omnes homines nobis notos in devotione et reverentia et amore honoris Christi et matris eius injuriam aliquam vel molestiam . . . inferre'. *Archiv* . . . II, 288.

[3] Huber, *A Documented History* . . . p. 168, n. 8.

and mentions the case of one friar, who had not been previously involved, who dared to call the sentences displeasing to God. This man was treated so inhumanly that he died after a few months in prison, and his corpse was thrown into a ditch and refused burial.[1]

It is impossible to say how far Jerome himself was responsible for these sentences. But one thing is certain. He had little sympathy for the left-wing group of his Order, and he was probably, as a busy man engaged in the diplomatic affairs of the Church, extremely irritated that he should be forced to give them so much attention. Indeed, he never carried out his mission of 1276 to Greece because of the trouble in the March of Ancona. Another incident related by Angelo shows the degree of his irritation that his attention was continually being diverted to what he considered trivial matters. Jerome was one day disagreeably surprised by a visit from Peter John Olivi. Seriously annoyed (non modicum iratus), he sent for the Provincial Minister, and said to him: 'Didn't I instruct you to give orders that no brothers should presume to come here unless I called them? Why did you give Peter John permission, without my knowledge?' To which the Provincial Minister replied that Olivi had neither asked for, nor received permission. Whereupon Jerome publicly reprimanded Peter for his infraction of the rule.[2] These facts will be taken into consideration when we come to consider the case of Roger Bacon, who, according to the *Chronicle*, was dealt with by Jerome himself, who also took the trouble to send a letter to the Pope explaining his decision.

With regard to the thesis of Mandonnet that Bacon in 1277 wrote the *Speculum Astronomiae*, which was a defence of astrology against those who had attacked it and been responsible for the mention of a number of astrological errors among 219 doctrines condemned by the University of Paris, two serious inconveniences are at once apparent. First of all, Thorndike has shown absolutely conclusively that there is no good reason for attributing the *Speculum* to anyone but Albertus Magnus, to whom the bulk of the MSS. attribute it. The views are those of Albert and not of Bacon.[3] And Vanderwalle has shown, equally conclusively, that the *Speculum* is in no sense to be regarded as a reply to the particular astrological errors condemned, and, indeed, is almost certainly to be attributed to a much earlier period in Albert's career.[4] Almost as important is the second

[1] *Archiv* . . . II, 304. [2] *Ibid.*, II, 291.
[3] Thorndike, *History of Magic* . . . II, 692–713.
[4] Vanderwalle, *Roger Bacon dans l'histoire* . . . pp. 178–96.

consideration. Even Siger of Brabant, against whose teachings the Parisian condemnation was primarily directed, received only a mild punishment of light imprisonment.[1] There is no reason to suppose that Bacon was at the University of Paris at the time, or even would consider himself affected by a local Parisian decree, while the similar condemnation at Oxford by Robert Kilwardby makes no mention of any doctrines condemned except certain Thomistic teachings and the 'Averroist' theses on the unity of the active intellect.[2] And Robert only calls the opinions dangerous and not heretical, and does not excommunicate, but only threatens, their holders. Moreover, Bacon was disciplined by his Order, and by the Minister-General himself, a quite different proceeding from what would have happened if he had offended against a blanket condemnation of errors by either the Bishop of Paris or the Archbishop of Canterbury.

From the above discussion it seems clear that students of Bacon have not yet agreed on the nature of the suspected novelties for which he was condemned. If they were not scientific novelties, could he be said to have introduced theological novelties of a kind to merit condemnation? I cannot find any such 'novelties', but discussed in an earlier chapter the evidence for his sympathy with Joachism, and have mentioned that his work of 1272 was a political tract likely to give offence, if it was ever published, both to the more conservative members of his Order, and to the Dominicans who were attacked, possibly, though not certainly in this work, by name. It breathes the same spirit as the prophetic literature of the time favoured by the Spirituals, and is quite unrestrained in its emotional fervour. Moreover, Bacon makes special reference to the fact that he had been called a heretic when he tried to prove that Antichrist was at hand. Furthermore, at the time of Bacon's supposed imprisonment the problem that most exercised the Franciscan authorities, and Jerome of Ascoli in his position as Minister-General in particular, was the problem of schism within the Order, and not any such minor affair as doctrinal divergencies on such matters as astrology or even magic. Finally, the *Chronicle* tells us that Bacon was condemned on the advice of many brothers (de multorum fratrum consilio). Whether he had published the *Compendium studii philosophiae* or not, wouldn't Bacon's views be well known to his fellow-friars, and wouldn't they be likely to have suffered from his tongue? Knowing that certain Spirituals had been

[1] 'Sous une forme d'ailleurs très débonnaire.' Van Steenberghen, *Siger de Brabant*... p. 3.
[2] *Chartularium*... I, 560 and note 3; De Wulf, *Histoire de la philosophie*... II, 262–63.

condemned, wouldn't it have been a good chance to get rid of Roger also?

Little, Vanderwalle and others have considered the possibility that Bacon's condemnation was connected with a meeting between Jerome of Ascoli and John of Vercelli, the Dominican General, which is recorded also in the *Chronicle of the Twenty-four Generals* but not elsewhere.[1] At this meeting the two generals decided to 'exhort their respective friars to cherish a spirit of friendship amongst themselves, after the example of St. Francis and St. Dominic',[2] or, more accurately, in the words of the *Chronicle* itself, it was decided that 'anyone offending, or who had offended, a brother of the other Order, should be punished by the Provincial Minister'. Although the 1277 meeting is only recorded in this chronicle, the presumption that it took place is supported by undoubted earlier efforts to effect an agreement between the two Orders, as attested especially by two letters between the generals published in Dominican records. And Clement IV in a bull of 1267 had tried to lessen competition between the Orders for members, one of the more serious causes of dissension.[3] In any case, in view of the attacks made upon both mendicant Orders by seculars and clerics, it was clearly to their interest to consolidate their forces as far as possible.

But if this meeting and resolution were indeed connected with Bacon's imprisonment, it is curious, as Vanderwalle has pointed out,[4] that the Chronicler does not make the connection. He records both pieces of information at a distance of only five pages. It is clear, then, that if Bacon were indeed condemned for promoting dissension, the Chronicler at least did not know of it. It is time then to discuss the authenticity of the *Chronicle* itself and see whether its evidence is to be relied on at all, or if, perhaps, the Chronicler himself was ignorant of the true facts of the case.

We do not know who the author was, but he is certain to have been a Franciscan. He cites no sources, and, as Vanderwalle has pointed out, since it does not have the character of an official document, he may be relying upon oral tradition within the Order.[5] Now if we consider how much is likely to be remembered after nearly a hundred years, and the authenticity of such information, I do not think we can dismiss the condemnation of the *doctrine* as likely

[1] *Chronicle of the Twenty-four Generals*, p. 365.
[2] Huber, *A Documented History* . . . p. 170.
[3] *Ibid.*, p. 170 and notes.
[4] Vanderwalle, *Roger Bacon dans l'histoire* . . . p. 152.
[5] *Ibid.*, pp. 151–53.

to be based on false information. A doctrine condemned in, say, 1278 will still be known as forbidden in 1370 unless the ban had been lifted. Though MSS. might be read and circulated, there are certainly no known incunabula of Bacon, and we can be sure that either his works were not so greatly in demand that it was worth a publisher's while to print them in the middle of the fifteenth century, or they were frowned upon by the Church and his Order. Quotations are made by eminent persons in the century following Bacon's death, but reading of his works may still not have been officially permitted, at least, not by the Franciscans.

But the condemnation of the person of Bacon to prison is quite a different matter. It could have become, within a hundred years, a tradition to account for the suppression or neglect of his doctrines. It was more common to condemn a book than a man in the thirteenth century, as we have seen in the case of Olivi, Joachim of Flora, and David of Dinant in the course of this study. On the other hand, when a man was condemned his books would certainly be condemned with him. But if his books were condemned, and not his person, we are left again with the problem that we were concerned with at the beginning. What was the matter with his books? Could it by any chance have been the other way round? Is it possible that his person was condemned, for personal offences, and his books followed as a matter of course; or even, as a pretext, something was found in his writings that would never have been condemned in itself?

If we examine this hypothesis to see if it will fit the story in the *Chronicle*, it seems to me that everything can be accounted for. I suggest that the real reasons for his condemnation were a combination of many—his general attitude towards authority, his independence, his numerous petty infractions of discipline as in his original appeals to the Pope for support, his attacks on respected members of the other Order, and upon authorities and practices in his own. Moreover, it is possible that his known sympathies with the Spirituals, his persuasive and scurrilous tongue, his inability to suffer quietly or recant any of his views, and above all, his belief in prophecies and his tirades on the subject of Antichrist, may have excited a genuine fear on the part of his superiors that at any moment he might break out with a writing that would be seriously damaging to their difficult and delicate task of preserving unity within the Order.

If these were the real reasons, why could he not be condemned for them, instead of for 'suspected novelties'? These were not good reasons for a public condemnation, to be announced to the Order, whatever they may have seemed to the friars who wanted him condemned. Moreover, whatever Bacon may have been before, he was not now a person of no importance, but the author of the *Opus Majus*, and a scientist of some repute. And he had friends in England, and possibly still a family of some social position. 'Suspected novelties' is such a convenient blanket term, like the modern 'deviationism', that it hardly sounds like a definite crime at all. It is the sort of thing, however, that a chronicler a hundred years later might have heard, and himself been given as the reason when he inquired within his Order.

Now if the English Provincial Minister, who was responsible for discipline within the province of England, had wanted to accede to the demands of his friars, and himself suspected Bacon of Joachism or, at the least, a desire to promote schism within the Order, he might well have sent him to the Minister-General to be dealt with personally, although, as we have seen, it was his own responsibility to deal with brothers who caused friction between the Orders. Jerome, with the schism within his Order on his mind, and particularly disliking neglect of his instructions about handling disciplinary matters locally, would not have been sympathetic to Bacon. And if the Provincial Minister, who happened to be John Peckham, or his vicar if he were away in Rome, as he was for part of his period as Minister, had wanted to clinch his case, he could easily have chosen something out of Bacon's writings as a pretext for the action he wanted his superior to take. If this was so, then the whole condemnation was what we should to-day call a 'political' one, without reference to the charges officially offered against the offender. And this would account for the last statement of the *Chronicler* that Jerome wrote to the Pope a special letter asking that 'through his authority the dangerous doctrine should be totally suppressed'. If there were no dangerous doctrine at all, or if Jerome had wished to condemn a harmless doctrine, he would probably, indeed, have written to the Pope asking him not to interfere with his decision, explaining that it had been taken on political grounds.

All that the Chronicler, or, indeed, the ordinary members of the Order, would be told, would be that Bacon and his doctrines had been condemned, and they were forbidden to read his books; and long after his death they would remain forbidden until some definite action were taken to restore them to favour. Generations of good Franciscans may have wondered what there was in the books that could have been responsible for their condemnation. But, if there is any truth in our hypothesis, they and scholars in modern times speculated in vain, for there were no offending doctrines; as there is nothing in the published writings of Radek or more recent apostates from the Soviet religion to explain their condemnation, which came as a result of their deeds and not their words. Under our hypothesis the truth will never be known what the suspected novelties were, and there is no further need for speculation.

Very little can be said on the probable length of the imprisonment. There is no reason to suppose it was particularly rigorous. In view of the absence of mention of any serious difficulties in the way of his writing, which he might have mentioned in his last work, the *Compendium studii theologiae*, and the fact that his mind, considering his age, was still active, it does not seem likely that Bacon suffered very much. On the other hand, if there is any truth in his imprisonment story, the first thing he will have been forbidden was writing.

While there are no writings from his pen that may be attributed to the 1280's, this might be sufficiently accounted for by the hypothesis that he was written out, and the state of his emotions was not conducive to good scientific work. And although his grammars are subsequent to the *Compendium of Philosophy*, these, of all the works of his career, require less enthusiasm and fervour than any. Bacon no longer hoped to be able to change the world by his activity, and when this hope was lost he probably aged rapidly. We have seen earlier that when a much younger man, he was so severely discouraged by the censorship and his 'exile' that he did not feel like writing at all. How much more now that he was older, even if his actual imprisonment amounted to no more than confinement in the same Parisian convent where he had spent so many of his years already. I think, however, that we cannot altogether account for this absence of work from his pen during these years by this hypothesis, for that he still desired to write is shown by the fact that he certainly did attempt another work as soon as he regained his liberty.

In 1289, Raymond de Gaufredi was elected General of the Franciscan Order, contrary to the wishes and expectations of Jerome of Ascoli, who had now become Pope Nicholas IV.[1] Raymond, whose sympathy with the Spirituals was to get him into trouble later, showed it at once after his election by visiting many provinces of the Order, and, according to Angelo of Clareno, he took special care to visit the March of Ancona, where the dissident Spirituals were confined. He examined the sentences passed against the prisoners, and

[1] Huber, *A Documented History* . . . p. 181.

said: 'Would that all of us and the whole Order were guilty of such a charge as this!' And at once he released them, and sent Angelo and his surviving companions as missionaries to Armenia, where, incidentally, they succeeded in converting the king.[1] Now a late tradition asserts that Raymond released Roger Bacon from prison, but as the account is in other respects garbled, it cannot be trusted.[2] Yet, if Roger had indeed been imprisoned as a suspected Spiritual—and this would be known to the General of his Order, if it was not to an ordinary friar—it would have been natural for Raymond to visit him and free him also. This would have been in the year 1290; and if Roger had returned to England immediately after his release he would have had two years' freedom to prepare and write his *Compendium of Theology*.

Though this work is that of a tired and elderly man, there are some points of interest in it for us. Mention has already been made of the biographical material, the recollections of his youth in the memory of an old man, and the points that stand out in his life—his teachers, the banning of Aristotle, the doctrines of Richard of Cornwall. But something else has happened to Roger, which can be explained as the result of the mellowing process of old age—though the outburst against Richard of Cornwall might seem to cast doubt on this—or of the acquisition of a store of prudence, a virtue which he extols for the first time since the days of his philosophical lectures.[3] I believe there is also to be detected a note of delicate irony. All these new virtues might have stemmed from his increasing years; but they may also be credited to a hardly learned discipline of his emotions, the result of his imprisonment.

He begins the book by saying quietly that he has been prevented from writing 'some useful things' on the subject of theology, 'as is known to many'. But, as a favour to his friends, he has made as much haste as he could (two years if our hypothesis of his liberation in 1290 is correct). He is aware of the 'great difficulty which cannot be overcome by reading and listening', and of the multitude of experiments that he ought to make; but, nevertheless, he will do his best.[4]

[1] Raymond, unlike Jerome, was in Angelo's eyes 'omnium bonorum amator'. *Archiv* . . . II, 305–6.

[2] A note on an alchemical MS. of Bacon's states that Raymond released Roger from prison because he taught him the work, having himself put him in prison because of it. The MS., however, dates from the fifteenth century, and while it supports the fact of Bacon's imprisonment, it cannot otherwise be trusted. Whoever committed him to prison, it certainly was not Raymond de Gaufredi. Little, *Essays* . . . pp. 27, 397, item 21.

[3] 'It is the first part of prudence to make an estimate of the person to whom you are talking.' I wonder if Roger ever thought of that before! *CST*, p. 71.

[4] *CST*, p. 26.

Then comes what I think is a delicate irony. 'Since the principal occupation of theologians is concerned with questions . . . and theological disputes are settled by means of authorities and arguments, I will conform, and make abundant use of other authorities and reasons, since "variety is the spice of life" as Seneca says (nihil est jocundum nisi quod reficit varietas, ut ait Seneca).'[1] And Roger proceeds to quote numerous commonplaces from pagan authorities!

'Since this is the way it is', he seems to say; 'since none of the powers that be is interested in anything but authorities in theological discussions, and no one is interested in my ideas, why, then I'll give you some pagan authorities. I'm quite willing to conform to your standards.' But the pagan authorities are quoted on behalf of an entirely innocuous proposition.

At once, as his custom was when in his prime, he plunges into the causes of error. But here, most significantly, there are only three. The fourth and worst, the error which in the *Opus Tertium* he had called 'the defence of one's own ignorance through speaking ill of those things which we do not know combined with showing off what we do',[2] is missing. And against the three errors which he still cites he only quotes harmless and reputable authorities, including Boethius, Jeremiah, Solomon, and St. John Chrysostom; following this up with some calm remarks on the way our childhood training predisposes us to accept authority and the sayings of our parents, although these may be false and vain and useless.[3] He deplores soberly the lack of interest in, and understanding of, Aristotle, and says, in the tone of an elderly and disillusioned scholar: 'Few therefore there were who were considered skilled in the aforesaid philosophy of Aristotle, yes, very few indeed, and almost none up to this year of 1292 . . . there were only three who could make true judgments on those few books which have been translated, as will be carefully proved from many points of view'.[4]

This ends the introduction, weary, disillusioned, and without Bacon's old fire, though there is nothing surprising in this, since he must have passed the age of seventy-five. But I was unable to see how Charles, who pointed out the missing fourth error, could say that Bacon had 'lost none of his hatred for authority and routine' until I noticed that several pertinent sentences were missing from his transcription, without any indication that anything had been omitted. He has simply chosen the passages where Bacon speaks of authority

[1] *CST*, p. 25.
[2] Brewer, *Op. Tert.*, p. 71.
[3] *CST*, p. 32.
[4] *Ibid.*, p. 34.

and run them together.[1] The full passage, though it would still contain the sentences quoted by Charles, reads as a far milder indictment, and has a quite different tone, as a whole, from similar attacks in his earlier works.

Bacon begins the main body of the work by speaking of the study of theology, and reiterates his old objection to the study of *Quaestiones* instead of the sacred text. He warms up for a few pages when he remembers Richard of Cornwall's lectures on the *Sentences*; but for the rest the holders of theories are not condemned by name. The arguments, for Bacon, are reasonable, and there is nothing specially new. 'Averroism' is suitably condemned, though the Commentator himself is not considered altogether wrong on many of his points. There follows a long scholastic disquisition in the prevailing manner, but nothing seriously controversial, and nothing that the most fervid friar or church censor could have objected to.

It says a lot for Bacon's will power that he was able to attempt such a work as a compendium of theology in his extreme old age. And his intellectual powers have by no means withered altogether, as he is still able to sustain an argument. His powers of memory, however, have nearly deserted him, as his wildness of quotation shows. But when we consider what Bacon thought of theology, and how from his earliest years he must have planned this culminating work of his life, the work possibly that would replace the *Summae* of his rivals, a *Summa salvationis per scientiam*, it must have seemed a pitiful enough effort. But he was old, and did not live to complete it.

As it has come down to us, the *Compendium of Theology* is not very long. Charles thought that it may have been longer originally than it appears in our MSS., and he mentioned a few other fragments that in his view could have belonged to it. But these, as far as we can tell from Charles's description, probably belonged to the *Communia naturalium*.[2] So, although the year is given in the book itself as 1292, it still is possible that the traditional date for his death is correct, June 11th, 1292.[3] There is certainly no reason to insist that he must have outlived the year 1292 in order to write the remainder of the fragment. So, in the absence of any serious evidence for any other

[1] Charles, pp. 412 ff. Crowley also adopts Charles' point of view. 'Imprisonment did not teach him moderation and his last work lacks none of his customary vigour.' *Roger Bacon* . . . p. 198.

[2] Charles, pp. 415–16; *CST*, 1–2.

[3] This information comes from the Warwickshire antiquarian Rous, who states also that he was buried at Oxford. Little, *Essays* . . . p. 28.

date, his death may be placed in 1292.[1] He died, therefore, while he was still at work, as such an indefatigable student and writer would have wished.

Since this study has been written as a biography, and opinions on the value of Bacon's contributions to science and thought have been offered during the course of the work, it does not seem necessary to conclude with an elaborate summing up of the value of these contributions, nor of the legends that have sprung up since his death. The writer has made no special research on this subject, which seems to have been adequately handled in the *Commemoration Essays* of 1914. My intention throughout has been to place Bacon in relation to the events and thought of his time rather than in the framework of all history, and to consider him as a person rather than as a phenomenon.

If there is much in this study that is hypothetical and much that is constructed out of rather slender evidence, it may at least serve to stimulate further thought and research, and perhaps prevent the constant repetition of facts that cannot be sustained by any evidence, but which were still as recently as 1938 the commonplaces of Baconian biography.

[1] Wadding gives his death as having occurred in 1284, but in view of the internal evidence for exactly 1292 as the year of writing the *Compendium studii theologiae* (*CST*, p. 34), and for more than forty years since 1250 (*CST*, p. 53), this date, unsupported, has little to recommend it. Wadding, *Annales Minorum*, V, 134.

THE END

APPENDIX A

THE LECTURES OF ROBERT GROSSETESTE TO THE FRANCISCANS, 1229–35

IN view of the enthusiasm with which some historians have accepted Little's views on the studies by the Oxford friars from 1229 to 1235 under Grosseteste,[1] it should be pointed out that the evidential support for the curriculum outlined by Little is very slight.

As pointed out in a note in the text,[2] this famous scientific school, such an innovation at that early date, would have been a matter of great interest to Thomas Eccleston. The study of mathematics, physics, and languages would have been an innovation without parallel in faculties of theology anywhere, and could not fail to have been known to a brother as interested in the progress and fame of his Order as Eccleston. Yet Eccleston only says that the brothers under the instruction of Grosseteste 'tam in quaestionibus quam predicationi congruis subtilibus moralitatibus profecerunt', that is, they studied theology and moral subjects.[3] The *Lanercost Chronicle*, which records the fact that Grosseteste taught the friars before becoming Bishop of Lincoln, does not give any information on the curriculum.[4]

Little does not seem to have been struck by this omission. After quoting Eccleston, he goes on to say: 'But we are able to recover the chief features of Grosseteste's teaching both from his own works and from the frequent allusion to it in Roger Bacon's writings'.[5]

Though the work of S. H. Thomson on Grosseteste seems to show that no scientific writings can be attributed to the years when he was teaching the friars, it is certainly established that Grosseteste did have a knowledge of science at the time, and *could* have lectured on it. This no one would deny. But the question is whether he did in fact lecture on it. And here all Little's evidence comes from Bacon. 'His

[1] Little, 'The Franciscan School . . .' (1926), pp. 807–22. Father Huber, for instance, devotes two full pages to recapitulating Little's findings, without saying they are conjectural (*A Documented History* . . . pp. 816–17); De Sessevalle accepts the statements, though he does not go into details (*Histoire générale* . . . I, 497). Little's predecessor, Felder, suggested the scientific learning, but did not go into detail; he had no more evidence at his disposal than Little (*Geschichte der Wissenschaftlichen* . . . pp. 263–67).

[2] *Supra*, p. 90, n. 2.

[3] Thomas de Eccleston, *De adventu* . . . pp. 60–61.

[4] *Chronicon de Lanercost*, p. 45.

[5] Little, 'The Franciscan School . . .' pp. 807–8.

(Bacon's) allusions are particularly interesting for our purpose because he frequently classes together Grosseteste and two of his successors, namely Thomas of Wales and Adam Marsh, and establishes the fact that a special tradition of learning was founded by Grosseteste, and prevailed through several generations of masters in the Franciscan School.'[1]

Little sums up the Franciscan curriculum of study under three heads: the study of the Bible, the study of languages, and the study of mathematics and physics. There can, of course, be no doubt of the first. But for the other two, Little's evidence is extremely thin. He admits that even Bacon himself said that Grosseteste did not know languages well enough to translate except towards the end of his life,[2] though he quotes also a letter of Grosseteste's[3] showing that 'he translated Greek as a relaxation during a few days' respite from his official labours' in the early years of his bishopric.[4]

Little then says: 'It is a fair inference that his mind was occupied by the subject while he was lecturing to the friars'; and he 'confirms' this inference by a quotation from Bacon: 'We have seen some of the earlier generation who laboured much at languages, such as the Lord Robert, the above-mentioned translator, and Thomas, the venerable Bishop of St. David's, now deceased, and Friar Adam Marsh'.[5]

Now this passage from Bacon only says that Thomas of Wales, who became lector to the Franciscans about 1240, studied languages, and his successor, Adam Marsh (lector 1247 to 1250), also studied them. Of the intervening three lectors between Grosseteste (retired 1235) and Thomas, we know nothing. But both Thomas and Adam, as we know, were in constant touch with Grosseteste during these years, and it is at least possible that they only became interested in languages when he brought his Greeks over to England during the years of his bishopric. Grosseteste probably began to learn the language during his time at Oxford, and felt the need for it. But since he did not yet know, even according to Bacon, more than the rudiments of it (Bacon's third degree of efficiency in translation), it does not seem at all probable that he should have introduced it into the Franciscan curriculum. He could not teach it himself, and he had not yet imported his Greeks. If he had teachers available in England, why should he have imported Greeks later? It is a very different

[1] Little, 'The Franciscan School . . .' p. 808.

[2] Brewer, *Op. Tert.*, p. 91.

[3] Grosseteste, *Epistolae* . . . p. 173.

[4] Little, 'The Franciscan School . . .' p. 809.

[5] *Opus Majus*, III, 88.

matter to teach Greek and insert Greek studies into a new curriculum, from learning to read it one's self in one's spare time.

Thomas of Wales may have introduced it in 1240 and been followed by Adam Marsh; but since this only rests upon the unsupported declaration by Bacon that they laboured much in the languages, the evidence is hardly enough to establish even a prima facie case.

For mathematics and physics the evidence is even more feeble. Little says: 'Here again the repeated conjunction of Adam Marsh's name with that of Robert Grosseteste in Roger Bacon's writings may be taken as evidence that Grosseteste expounded his views on these subjects to the friars'.[1]

There is no doubt that Bacon extolled the proficiency of both these men in mathematics, and, as pointed out in the body of this study, on at least one occasion Grosseteste used his knowledge of light to illustrate a theological point.[2] I have seriously questioned Adam's proficiency, and given a possible reason for Bacon's praises. However this may be, it is certain that Adam was not teaching at Oxford in Bacon's day until 1247; and though he may have studied mathematics in his earlier life, any proficiency he acquired was previous to his studies in theology. All that Bacon tells us, in a passage quoted by Little, is that Robert and Adam 'have known how to unfold the causes of all things, and to give a sufficient explanation of human and divine phenomena; and the assurance of this fact is to be found *in the writings* of these great men'.[3] (Italics mine.)

If they had indeed lectured, why didn't Bacon take the opportunity to mention it, instead of only referring to the writings? I suggest that the reason is that Bacon himself gained his knowledge of the work of at least Robert Grosseteste from his writings.

As for the so-called tradition carried on by the four intermediate masters, Bacon tells us nothing of any mathematical ability on the part of any of them. The only Englishman to whom he gives credit for mathematical knowledge besides Grosseteste and Adam is the unknown John of Bandoun.[4] Though Bacon, of course, is fond of exaggerating, would he have gone so far as to say that 'there are few who know this science' if there had been a flourishing Oxford tradition, stemming from the original work of Robert Grosseteste?

I think the most probable conclusion is not that Grosseteste set up any such curriculum for the friars, but that Grosseteste himself, of

[1] Little, 'The Franciscan School . . .' p. 810.
[2] Grosseteste, *Epistolae* . . . pp. 360–61.
[3] *Opus Majus*, I, 108, quoted by Little, 'The Franciscan School . . .' p. 810.
[4] Steele, Fasc. XVI, 118 (*Communia mathematica*).

whom Bacon had heard much and whose writings he had read, used mathematical and optical illustrations for his classes in theology; and Adam Marsh, having received an early training from Grosseteste, and being a close friend of the great bishop, followed his example. Bacon, though not attending Grosseteste's classes, was able, on his return to Oxford, to hear Adam Marsh lecture on theology, and was stimulated by him to use a similar method when dealing with theology in his own writings. And as Adam was a superlative teacher, capable of inspiring his pupils with enthusiasm,[1] Bacon acquired a love and respect for him that led to an exaggerated opinion of his mathematical and linguistic ability.

In the absence, therefore, of any further corroborative evidence for Little's idea that a school for scientific studies was established at Oxford during the years 1229 to 1235, it would seem that the suggestion should be relegated from the established fact of Father Huber to the status of an improbable but possible hypothesis.

[1] For Adam's influence as a teacher on Thomas Docking and Thomas of York, see Little, 'Thomas Docking and his Relations to Roger Bacon . . .' (1927), p. 301.

APPENDIX B

WHO WAS THE UNNAMED MASTER?

I

IN the *Opus Minus* and the *Opus Tertium* Bacon attacks two masters of the Parisian schools, one of whom is dead, and the other living. The errors of these men, he declares, are disastrous. But it is not, as in the case of Richard of Cornwall, a specific error that he condemns so much as their whole influence, and particularly the fact that they are cited as authorities.

This is a heinous sin for Bacon, not only because he objects to authorities as such, but because he refuses to recognize that the time has come to allow any Latin contemporary to be taken as an authority, however willing he may be to accept Aristotle, Avicenna, and Averroes. Indeed, he even goes so far as to say that Christ Himself was not accepted as an authority in His lifetime.

So then it is the whole influence that he is trying to undermine, rather than any particular doctrine. And if we are to determine convincingly who the second master is (the first, Alexander of Hales, Bacon names), we must not only see whether the known details of his life and work correspond to Bacon's statements, but also whether Bacon's own teachings would conflict with those of this master in such a way as to account for his remarkable spleen against him. In other words, if we accept Bacon's estimate of the man's influence, would this undermine his own work, and turn students from his own point of view to that of the master?

Opinion is still divided on who the master can have been. The majority has probably swung round to the point of view that it was Albertus Magnus. Little was apparently unable to make up his mind about it. In his edition of the *Opus Tertium* fragment in 1912 he believed it was Thomas Aquinas, in 1914 he conceded that it was probably Albert, while in 1928 he had again turned to Thomas Aquinas.[1] P. Crowley, in a recent Louvain doctoral dissertation on Bacon's psychology, which has not yet been published, was apparently of the opinion that it was not Albert, though the published

[1] Little, *Op. Tert.*, p. xxv; *Essays* . . . p. 8, note 9; 'Roger Bacon: Annual Lecture . . .' p. 280. In this last paper Little seems to be founding his decision on the differences between Bacon and Thomas on the nature of the soul. Albert's ideas on the soul, however, did not differ substantially from those of Thomas.

account of this dissertation does not give his reasons.[1] Miss Sharp, in her book on Franciscan philosophy at Oxford has not made up her mind, but allows him as either Albert or Thomas.[2] Brewer thought it was neither, but Richard of Cornwall, though he had not in his day sufficient material for an informed judgment.[3] Professor Thorndike offers by far the most substantial reasons against Albert, concluding that if he was indeed meant, then Bacon was both an incompetent and an unfair critic.[4] Bacon's criticism, he says, does not seem to apply to Albert at all closely. Not only was Albert only for a short time in Paris, but he does not seem to have been in sympathy with the conditions Bacon describes. These are serious charges, and the attempt will be made here to answer them in detail, and without showing Bacon to have made any errors of fact; though his biased criticism stems from his highly personal view of the nature of science and theology, and the relationship between them.

If neither Albert nor Thomas is the man, then someone else must be provided. Few can have attained the eminence on which Bacon is so specific. Though he may have disliked and disapproved of Richard of Cornwall, Richard was no such authority in the fields which Bacon specifies. Moreover, he was dead before 1267, and Bacon says that the master is still living. So Brewer's suggestion may be dismissed at once. St. Bonaventura, the General of the Franciscan Order at the time, was an authority in theology; but again his influence was by no means as pervasive as that of Albert or Thomas, and the details of the life of the master do not correspond in any way to those given by Bacon. It is intended to show in this appendix that only to Albert do these details apply. The relationship of Albert's work to Bacon's and the extent of his influence will be treated in the second section of the appendix. Though it is conceded that Albert was not in Paris for much of his life, his influence nevertheless pervaded the whole Parisian school, partly through his published work, and partly through the influence of his chief pupil, Thomas Aquinas.

The longest consecutive account of the master appears in the *Opus Minus*. First Alexander of Hales is attacked, and then the unnamed master. There is a relationship between these two, as will be shown. They are not arbitrarily selected because both were authorities, as

[1] *Revue Neo-scholastique de Philosophie* (November, 1939), pp. 647–48. With the publication of this dissertation it is now possible to state that Crowley makes no mention of the passages dealt with in this appendix, but only of the passage in the *Compendium studii philosophiae* (p. 426) where Bacon refers to the 'boys of the two Orders'. He does not think these can be Albert and Thomas (Crowley, *Roger Bacon* . . . p. 63). For this passage see *infra* pp. 218–19.

[2] Sharp, *Franciscan Philosophy* . . . p. 117.

[3] Brewer, *Op. Tert.*, p. xxiv, n. 6.

[4] Thorndike, *History of Magic* . . . II, 639–41.

might appear at first sight. On the contrary, both represented a certain approach to theology which Bacon detested. This subject will be resumed when the details have been examined and their correspondence to what is known of Albert has been established.

The master entered the Order of brothers as a young boy, Bacon tells us.[1] He never did read philosophy, nor hear it in the schools, nor was he *in studio solemni* before he became a theologian; nor could he be taught within the Order, as he himself was the first Master of Philosophy. And *he* it was who taught the others; what he knows he has from his own study.

Now recent researches into the early life of Albert show this to be precisely and exactly true. Mandonnet, as we have seen in this study, may not be reliable in many things, and he is inclined to gloss over too much opposing evidence. But his judgment that Albert was born in 1206 and entered the Dominican Order in 1223[2] is based on the very best contemporary evidence, and by no means only on what is cited in his early article in the *Dictionnaire de théologie catholique* referred to by Thorndike.[3] In particular the letters of Jordan of Saxony, Albert's own superior in the Order at the time, and one letter from Pope Honorius III at the time of his entry into the Order, cannot be gainsaid, any more than the chronicle of Etienne de Bourbon, which as clearly refers to Albert at this period.[4] The date is now almost universally accepted by authorities, and no one who has written in this field since the publication of Mandonnet's researches has any further doubt, unless it be to put the date of birth back one year to 1205.

Born then in 1206, Albert was taken to Bologna by his uncle in 1222 to study. The following year he went to Padua, where he joined the Dominican Order; late in the same year Jordan of Saxony sent him to Cologne to the Dominican convent in that city. He was still not yet eighteen, and his education, twice interrupted, cannot have been very profound; and outside the few months at Bologna it was not at a recognized university. Certainly he had not yet obtained any bachelor's or master's degree. At Cologne there was not yet a *studium generale* when Albert went there, because he himself founded one in 1248. Moreover, the Dominican house was new, and

[1] *Opus Minus*, p. 327.

[2] Mandonnet, 'La date de naissance . . .' (1931), pp. 233–56.

[3] Thorndike, *History of Magic* . . . (1923), II, 523.

[4] A. Garreau, *St. Albert le Grand* (1932), pp. 29–50. M. Aron, *Un Animateur de la jeunesse* . . . (1930); *Lettres du bienheureux Jourdain de Saxe* . . . (1924). M. Grabmann, *Der hl. Albert der. Grosse* (1932). It should be emphasized that none of these writers uses Bacon's remarks as evidence, so theirs may be justifiably used to support the truth of his.

without eminent teachers, of which the Order indeed had very few at that moment. One of Albert's great works for his Order in the later years of his career was the training of such masters.

Albert, therefore, can be said to have been self-educated. The best evidence for this, outside the negative evidence of lack of opportunity, is the extreme weakness in philosophy shown in his first work, *Tractatus de natura boni*, which was written while he was still in Germany. His earliest Parisian writings which can be dated with certainty in the 1240's, show a much fuller grasp, especially of Aristotle, though they also are not to be compared with his later works.[1]

Yet after a few years in Cologne he is appointed as lector in theology to his own convent. This position he retains for a few years until he is transferred in 1235 to Hildesheim, still a convent within the Dominican Order. Finally, in 1240 he is allowed to go to Paris to take his official grades and gain his real education in formal theology.[2] Yet even here he does not go to the Faculty of Arts—in any case the Dominicans did not study in this faculty—but is accepted at once as a Bachelor Sententiarius, presumably because of his reputation as a teacher, and because of the influence of the Dominican Order. Finally he is granted his doctorate in 1242, after only two years of official study at Paris, but with many years of hard self-education and reading and lecturing as his qualifications.

These facts are no longer in dispute, even though there is still much difference of opinion on the dates of the writing of his various scientific works. And it is certain that, after only these two years of formal study at Paris, and as soon as he attained his doctorate, he was appointed to the Dominican chair in theology at the university, taking over a position that had been held with no special glory by a Master Guéric of St. Quentin for nine years—a relatively long period frowned upon by the Order on principle, but accepted at this time because of the great shortage of qualified masters of theology.[3] In the whole thirteenth century only two German masters of theology are known by name, Thiérry of Freiberg and Albert.[4]

It is therefore clear that Albert never could have fulfilled the formal residence requirements for a degree in theology, and that it was only the influence of his Order that ensured his acceptance at an advanced standing at Paris, enabling him to take his doctoral degree in two

[1] These are the *Summa de creaturis*, and a commentary on the *Sentences*. R. de Vaux, 'La première entrée . . .' (1933), p. 237.

[2] Glorieux, *Répertoire* . . . p. 54; Garreau, *St. Albert* . . . p. 69.

[3] Garreau, *St. Albert* . . . p. 76.

[4] *Ibid.*, p. 89.

years. So, if he had not exactly 'taught before he had studied', as Bacon says, he had at least taught before he had obtained his formal grades in theology. 'What he knows', as Bacon says, 'he had from his own study.' On the other hand, Thomas Aquinas did study philosophy at Naples under Peter of Ireland, and though he may not have received as good a formal education as he might if he had gone to Paris at once, he could not be said to have 'taught before he studied'. And his education was entirely correct and formal until he followed Albert to Cologne rather than stay and finish at Paris. St. Bonaventura also had a correct formal education, as did almost all masters of this period. It was only Albert who went through this original type of education, as far as we know.

To continue with the words of Bacon:

> He is a most studious man, and has seen an infinite number of things, and been put to considerable expense; he was able to gather many useful things in the unbounded sea of authors.[1]

This is the only meed of praise allowed by Bacon to his enemy. There can be no question that Albert consulted many authors, and wrote much. So, of course, did many others of his contemporaries.

> But because he never had a foundation, since he was not instructed, nor did he exercise himself in listening, lecturing, or disputing; so he couldn't help being ignorant of the common sciences (philosophy).[2]

This, of course, is Bacon's prejudice, and his judgment based on the facts above. Albert at Cologne was doubtless a student for a few years, but without an accomplished master. Only from 1240 to 1242 was he a student at Paris, but already an advanced one, and with a reputation as a teacher of many years' standing. Because he was self-taught it doesn't follow that he knew no philosophy. But this is a criticism to be expected from the ex-professor Bacon, brought up on public disputations in the Faculty of Arts.

> Since he did not know languages, he couldn't know anything really valuable.

When Albert uses a Greek word, he generally gives a definition or an extraordinary etymology.[3] It is clear that he never did learn Greek or Hebrew, and no one has ever claimed that he did. He relied on the translations available.

> He does not know *perspectiva*.

Though later authorities have attributed some works in this field to Albert, Thorndike does not accept them, and has found no MSS.

[1] *Opus Minus*, p. 327.
[2] *Ibid.*, p. 327.
[3] Garreau, *St. Albert* . . . p. 32.

attributed to him on this subject.[1] None of the printed material would contradict this assertion.

> And, knowing nothing of this, he couldn't know anything worth while about philosophy, because this, together with *scientia experimentalis*, alchemy, and mathematics, is the most important requirement for this study.

And on those sciences, especially botany, on which Albert really did know something, Bacon is discreetly silent. If this passage implies that Albert did not know alchemy, then Bacon could have been ignorant of Albert's remarks about alchemy in his *Mineralium*, which show his interest in alchemy and the efforts he made to obtain information about it. But Thorndike does not admit any of the strictly alchemical works of Albert to be certainly genuine, and allows him only one 'probable'.[2] In his lifetime it is quite possible that Albert was not known as an alchemist, even if in fact he had made experiments in this field.

The remainder of the passage is concerned with the master's position as an authority. Since this is a general, and not a specific, charge, it will be taken up later.

Early in the *Opus Tertium* there is a reference to Albert, of the Order of Preachers, by name. Bacon tells the Pope that if he had asked Albert to produce such a work as he is himself writing, Albert would have taken ten years about it.[3] Later the unnamed master is once more attacked. This attack is made very carefully and systematically, and his deficiencies in each of the useful sciences are stated one by one—but only when applicable. When the master is not deficient, Bacon is silent.

He charges him in general with four sins: (*a*) vanitas puerilis infinita, (*b*) falsitas ineffabilis, (*c*) superfluitas voluminis, and (*d*) omission of those parts of philosophy 'which are of magnificent utility and immense beauty'.[4]

The first two are merely Bacon's customary value-judgments, and signify nothing but his disapproval. As to the third, no one would deny that both Albert and Thomas wrote many books. According to Bacon 'the whole power of these sciences (i.e. those dealt with by Albert) can be compressed into a useful tract, true, clear, and perfect, which would occupy only a twentieth part of these volumes'. Both Albert and Thomas wrote at least twenty volumes, and on subjects that Bacon could regard as scientific. Since Bacon thought of

[1] Thorndike, *History of Magic* . . . II, 529.
[2] *Ibid.*, II, 571.
[3] Brewer, *Op. Tert.*, p. 14.
[4] *Ibid.*, p. 30.

perspectiva and mathematics as the 'most beautiful and useful' of sciences, his fourth accusation may be considered as justified from his point of view.

He goes on to say:

> He never heard the parts of philosophy, nor did he learn from anyone, nor was he nourished in the University of Paris, nor anywhere where the study of philosophy flourishes.[1]

This is an obvious reference to Cologne, and not so easily applicable to Naples. Albert, of course, did not study philosophy at the University of Paris, but theology, and then only for a short time.

> Nor did he have a revelation because he did not live in such a way as to be able to receive one, but accumulating false, vain, and superfluous things, and leaving out useful and necessary things, which would not indicate a revelation; but of his own accord he presumed to treat of things he did not know. Not without cause have I spoken of this supposed authority, because not only does he fit in with my statement (ad propositum meum facit), but it is to be deplored that the study of philosophy is corrupted by him more than through all who have ever been among the Latins. For though others have been deficient, yet they have not set themselves up as authorities. But he writes his books *per modum authenticum*, and so the whole crazy crowd cites him at Paris, like Aristotle, Avicenna, Averroes, and other authors. And he has done great harm, not only to the study of philosophy, but of theology, as I show in the *Opus Minus* where I speak of the seven sins of the study of theology. Above all the third sin concerns him, and I discuss this openly on his account.[2] There I note two (authorities), but he is the chief. The other had a greater name, but he is dead.

From this passage it is clear that Bacon is speaking here in the *Opus Tertium* of the same master who was the target of his attacks in the *Opus Minus*. He then proceeds to take up those studies he does consider useful:

> The aforesaid authority knows nothing of the power of languages.[3]

Then he shows that geometry and *perspectiva* are necessary 'because all sciences are connected and nourish each other'. And he continues:

> But he who sets himself up as an authority, of whom I spoke earlier, knew nothing of the power of this science, as appears in his books, because he did not write a book on this science, and he would have done so if he had known it. Nor did he say anything about this science in his other books, and yet the use of this science is necessary for all the other sciences. And so he cannot know anything of the wisdom of philosophy.[4]

[1] Brewer, *Op. Tert.*, pp. 31.
[2] i.e. ignorance of those four sciences 'quae sunt in usu theologorum'. *Opus Minus*, p. 325.
[3] Brewer, *Op. Tert.*, p. 33.
[4] *Ibid.*, pp. 36–37.

Bacon then tells the Pope that he is sending him a special treatise on the subject.

> But he who has multiplied volumes does not know these *radices*, for he does not touch on them at all; and so it is certain that he is ignorant of natural things and everything which belongs to philosophy. And not only he, but the whole mob of philosophizers which goes astray through him. If you were to write to him, you would find him *impossibilem ad eas*.[1]

The last remark looks like a reference to Bacon's earlier thought that Albert could not have written such a work in ten years if the Pope had asked him.

Dealing with speculative alchemy and the generation of animals, his criticism is subtly different. Here Bacon says:

> But he who has composed so many and such great volumes *de naturalibus*, about whom I spoke earlier, does not know these fundamentals, and so his building cannot stand.[2]

This is perhaps the clearest and most convincing reference to Albert. Was there any one of his contemporaries who could possibly have been considered to have written 'so many and such great volumes *de naturalibus*'? Thomas Aquinas wrote commentaries on Aristotle, but these were minor parts of his work, and coming in connection with Bacon's remarks on the generation of animals I do not think he can have had Aquinas in mind. Vincent of Beauvais and Bartholomew of England wrote *de naturalibus*, but none of the other criticisms or specific statements can apply to them, nor could they in any way be regarded as authorities on *philosophy* and *theology* in their own lifetime.

Then, significantly, testifying to Bacon's accurate knowledge of Albert's work, in speaking of *scientia experimentalis* he omits all mention of the master, and only sings the praises of Peter de Maricourt as the perfect experimenter.[3] Would Bacon have failed to press the attack if he had not known that Albert was as experienced a practical scientist as himself? I cannot see Thomas Aquinas being let off so easily.

Finally, when dealing with the fourth cause of error, Bacon makes his parting shot:

> The fourth error is the worst, since a man defending his own ignorance, making a display of what he knows and reproving those things which are alien to it, makes himself an authority, though a feeble one . . . his madness spreads to his neighbours, as Seneca says . . . so this authority (iste auctor) spreads his opinions and taints the whole crowd.[4]

[1] Brewer, *Op. Tert.*, p. 37.
[2] *Ibid.*, p. 42.
[3] *Ibid.*, pp. 43–47.
[4] *Ibid.*, p. 70.

And he continues:

> To acquire wisdom all holy men have separated themselves from the world . . . and in this *he*, as in so many other things, is wrong, and never becomes perfect.[1]

Once more this seems to have a definite applicability to Albert, who never did retire from the world though he belonged to a mendicant Order. On the contrary, he lived the most active of lives, organizing chapters, founding *studia generalia*, preaching a crusade, publicly attacking a heretical opinion at Paris, and even for a while filling the office of Bishop of Ratisbon. He never retired from the world until old age compelled it.

In the *Compendium studii philosophiae* Bacon returns to the charge that Albert and Thomas, whom he mentions now by name, are ruining the study of theology. There is nothing new and specific in these charges, but the terms of the attack are very similar to those on the unnamed master in the *Opus Minus*:

> For forty years some people have risen in the University who have made themselves into masters and teachers of the study of philosophy when they have never learned anything worth while and either will not, or cannot, because of their status. . . . These are boys of the two Orders such as Albert and Thomas and others who in so many cases enter the Orders when they are twenty years or less . . . they are not proficient because they are not instructed by others in philosophy after they enter, because within their Order they have presumed to investigate philosophy without a teacher. So they become masters in philosophy before they were disciples, and so infinite error reigns.[2]

Professor Thorndike has questioned the integrity of this passage as it seems incongruous for Bacon to speak of a man who was almost certainly his senior as a boy.[3] Now it is certain that neither Albert nor Thomas was still a boy in 1272. But Bacon, in the writing of this work, is more full of fury than usual. It is, indeed, by far his most violent work. He speaks of the 'boys' on four occasions, and it is clear that what he had in mind was the common practice of allowing boys to enter the Orders. Albert and Thomas did enter their Order as boys, though they were no longer boys at the period Bacon was writing. He could quite easily have classed them all together as 'brothers who entered the Order as boys' rather than intending to refer to them as presently boys. In view of the general exaggeration and unrestrained nature of Bacon's attacks on everyone in this work, I think this is possible. Yet I too should prefer it if the offending words 'ut Albertus et Thomas et alii' could be dismissed as a gloss,

[1] Brewer, *Op. Tert.*, p. 71.
[2] *CSP*, pp. 425–26.
[3] Thorndike, *History of Magic* . . . II, 639.

since the identification of the unnamed master by no means depends on this passage.[1] Indeed, I think a gloss of this kind would strengthen the case I have been building, since the glosser will have added these words precisely because he knew that Albert, Thomas, and others had entered the Order as boys. Seeing these remarks it would be natural for him to add these well-known examples from his own knowledge.

The final attack comes from the *Communia naturalium*, and, as it occurs in the early pages of this work, it is probably written before any of the passages quoted above, and before the *Opus Majus*:

> Even Aristotle wrote some things which are superfluous for us. . . . But some moderns err, who exceed the quantity of a book of Aristotle, and give to *one* of their books a greater quantity of matter than Aristotle thought worth while giving in *all* his books. So, deservedly, they are convicted of great ignorance as they do not know how to stick to essentials, and not only accumulate most useless things, but multiply endless errors. And the root cause is that they have not studied the sciences of which they write, nor lectured upon them *in studio solemni*, nor even have they listened to them, because they were masters before they were disciples, so that they go astray through relying upon themselves and multiply errors among the public. The *libri naturales* and common works cannot be known without the other seven sciences, nor even without mathematics. But two renowned moderns, as they have not listened to the sciences on which they make statements, so they have neither read on them, nor exercised themselves in them, as appears from their writings. So it is clear that everywhere they are confounded by errors and vanities. Their error is multiplied in the natural and other common sciences, whose translations, which they use, are perverse, and nothing worth while could be said by them nor understood by others, through translations of this kind.[2]

This is perhaps the most moderate statement made against these masters, of whom there can be hardly any doubt in this passage. It is the only time that they are criticized directly because they have no access to the best text because of their ignorance of languages. But this is connected with the way in which Albert and Thomas use Aristotle, and the reason why it was not necessary for them to have the knowledge of languages that Bacon demanded. It is this essential difference between their view of science and theology and the more conservative one, in many respects, held by Bacon, that will now have to be considered. This will supply a motive for the personal attacks, and, in showing how the method of the 'moderns' was the one that prevailed, throw light upon their acceptance by the *vulgus philosophantium* as 'authorities'. In this Albert, and not Thomas, who merely followed him, was the pioneer, and so the fit target for Bacon's spleen.

[1] The *Compendium* is found in only one MS., and it is already a much corrected one.
[2] Steele, Fasc. II, 11.

II

Bacon is not too scrupulous in his attacks, but, as a rule, he is well informed. If we examine his criticism of the masters of his time, and particularly the unnamed one, we shall find that it is two-pronged. He objects to his baneful influence on theology, and he objects to his lack of understanding of what constitutes a true science. The two are connected, since for Bacon science must be useful for theology. But they can best be dealt with separately.

It is clear that Bacon had no idea of what the theologians were really trying to do. Being himself an anti-rationalist, he does not comprehend their problem, and, if he had understood it, he would not have sympathized with it. But his attack is not really informed with knowledge as if he had studied within the Faculty of Theology. He seems to have had a kind of intuitive knowledge of what was going on, and he doesn't like it. His approach to the Scriptures is aesthetic. He does not want to understand God, but rather to appreciate and marvel at His works. He is primarily a man of faith. He wants to believe, and he is fortunate enough to be able to do so. But his belief is not reserved only for the Scriptures. He wants to believe also in Aristotle, Avicenna, and the prophets; and his belief is rationalized by his continuous statements that they were inspired by God and the knowledge was revealed to them. The statements of the Bible are not only literally true; they are allegorically and spiritually true. The geography of the Bible is likewise not only geography, but geography with spiritual meanings; the relationships between the places, and even their names, have meaning.[1] He wants to add to the content of his religion, not question it. Peter Lombard and his followers merely argue painfully and laboriously over what is patently obvious to him. And they leave the inspired words of the Scriptures behind in the process. Bacon does not for a moment question the source and validity of the knowledge contained in the Scriptures; he merely wants to add to it, so that there may be a more profound understanding of them. It is important from his point of view to know of the different composition of the body of Adam before and after the Fall because this increases our knowledge.[2] But he does not think of questioning this knowledge itself, as the theologians were doing. Meditation on the text of the Bible had been carried on for hundreds of years, long before there was any pronounced intellectual movement which favoured the use of natural

[1] *Opus Majus*, I, 185 ff., esp. p. 186 on Jericho. [2] *Opus Minus*, pp. 370–71.

reason and granted it some rights. Bacon lived within this old tradition, and wanted to enlarge it. The activities of the Faculty of Theology at Paris, and even at Oxford in the persons of Fishacre and Kilwardby, must have appeared terribly dangerous, and likely to destroy the very foundations of his primitive faith. He appears ignorant of the philosophical questions involved; he himself begs most of the questions—not because he was necessarily incompetent in philosophy, but because he did not recognize the competency of philosophy in the sphere of religion.

It is a possible point of view, and in many ways it is Bacon's spirit that has triumphed since. Luther also wanted to return to the strict text of the Bible, and he regarded faith as primary, reason having few rights. Protestants in general have not tried to make their beliefs appear reasonable and in conformity with natural philosophy. One believes the Scriptures and can draw useful moral lessons from them; but one does not expect philosophy to confirm them. The modern secularist would claim that the whole content of theology rests upon an irrational faith, which may or may not be valid, but certainly cannot be proved, though, surprisingly, it may apparently be *dis*-proved, by natural reason.

The thirteenth century still believed that it could be proved; and its tremendous effort still remains one of the monuments of constructive thought. The theologians were trying nothing less than to complete what the Fathers of the Church had done in their day. Following St. Paul, in the early centuries after Christ the Fathers had built a systematic body of doctrine out of what was, after all, externally, only the life and death of a great prophet, and his words and deeds as recorded by his companions. It was an enormous intellectual feat; but it had only reached part of the way to its goal when the Roman civilization collapsed, the barbarians entered the empire, and progressive thought on this doctrine, and its reinterpretation and development, came to an end. The thought crystallized into dogma, tiny jewels of belief which were now preserved by the Church and handed down as something to be accepted, and no longer questioned or developed. And a new technique came into being, suited for the comparatively unsophisticated barbarian mind, the technique of meditation upon this dogma. It came into the hands of poets, makers of allegories, mystics, who elaborated the sacred words of the Scriptures—which was not too difficult, and revered and drew inspiration from the dogmas and sacraments which they could not understand, but accepted. They loved their faith, and their teachings, and their Scriptures, but they no longer tried to understand them. So theology as a 'science' died.

It did not revive until the Western mind had again reached the point where it could cope with the problems left unsolved by St. Augustine, and had both the desire and the technique to do so. The great problem was, as it has remained since, the problem of knowledge—what do we know and how? But it was coloured in the Middle Ages by the certainty that some, if not all, knowledge had been *revealed*, the content of this revelation had been enshrined in the Scriptures, and the Fathers who had interpreted them had received grace from God to enable them to do their work. If this was the only knowledge available, if the unaided human mind could not understand truth at all, then this problem was no problem at all. Original sin had prevented man from knowing anything, and he could only know through grace. This was St. Augustine's solution.

But it did not please everyone in the thirteenth century. What about the knowledge of Aristotle? This, for Bacon, was simple. He merely cut the knot by saying that Aristotle had been inspired or had worked from the inspiration of others, notably the Hebrew prophets. But it was no answer to a rationalist who was not interested in Aristotle personally, but in the whole problem raised by the fact that he obviously said things that were true to the rational mind. This was the reason that no one was so desperately interested as Bacon in having the exact words of Aristotle at his disposal; other people did not trouble to learn Greek for the purpose, and they accepted poor translations without murmur. It was good to have the best available text, but not vital. They used their own minds on the problems formulated by Aristotle.

In the Faculty of Arts, as the thirteenth century progressed, the delight in natural knowledge, in philosophy, increased. There was no such sense of responsibility to the revealed truth as there was in the Faculty of Theology. Here the problem was peculiarly grave. It could not be settled in the way that Gregory IX wanted by merely meditating upon the word, and keeping clear of philosophy.[1] The theologians had a heavy sense of responsibility. They were not authoritarians, as Bacon seems to have believed; they were wrestling with a problem so vast and so tremendous in its consequences that they were willing to give credence to anyone who could suggest a way in which the answer could be found. What was the relation between revealed and natural knowledge? They could not presume

[1] *Chartularium . . .*, pp. 114 ff.

to doubt the fact of revealed knowledge. But what happened when there appeared to be a contradiction between natural knowledge, as Aristotle and they themselves worked it out, and the revealed knowledge of the Scriptures and the dogmas of faith?

The book of *Sentences* served for a time. It was a first step in the direction that must be followed. Peter Lombard was a theologian, a teacher who attempted to give answers to persistent questions that arose from the study of revealed knowledge, to make it, in Bonaventura's words, 'intelligible to the human mind'. His solutions were no more definitive and final than those of his successors, but the form was accepted as a suitable one for all theological discussions. Bacon is quite right when he says that the theologians give more attention to the book of the *Sentences*[1] than to the scriptural text. Their problems were not textual ones, but persistent problems as to which knowledge is to be preferred, and whether the doctrines of the Scriptures are in accord with natural reason. What is the function of faith in the process of knowing?

In Peter's time, with only the logical work of Aristotle available, the problems were not yet deeply serious; so his solutions could be easily acceptable. But Aristotle's *Physics* and *Metaphysics* and his *De anima*, based as they were upon a naturalistic and common-sense view of the world, and thus making a natural appeal to all ordinary human minds, raised a number of specific questions that needed solution and which seemed to conflict with the data of revealed knowledge. And, persistently, as the questions were settled in detail, and a breathing space was gained, the great central problem came out into the daylight, striking at the whole system of revealed knowledge: UTRUM THEOLOGIA SIT SCIENTIA—the mind questioning itself, asking if its findings are valid, or if some other knowledge that requires faith for its acceptance is alone true. *Scientia* is knowledge by natural reason; it has, taught Aristotle, its own methods of inquiry and its own subject matter. Can theology, the substance of revealed knowledge, be subjected to these methods? May one ask anything of theology except that it be believable? Must it be intelligible, too? Or can we even, as some philosophers would do, actually *add* to our knowledge of God through the findings of reason?

Early in the century, William of Auxerre, one of the theologians chosen by Pope Gregory IX to expurgate Aristotle, says that it is impossible to transfer our knowledge of nature to the knowledge of God, because they are different in kind. Natural reason may support

[1] *Opus Minus*, pp. 328–29; *CST*, p. 34.

faith, confirm it among the faithful, defend it against heretics, and even lead simple people towards the faith. Then William raises the important question whether philosophy is 'like' theology; and to this he has a remarkable answer. The *principia* of theology are the articles of faith. Philosophy, then, *is* like theology. Both have *principia* (the *archai* of Aristotle), from which further knowledge may be deduced. In the one case they are self-evident principles, the principles of natural reason; and in the other they are the data of the Scriptures. The whole riches of Scripture can be used for deduction.[1] St. Thomas, as we shall see, follows this suggestion. But William does not answer the main problem.

Alexander of Hales starts out forthrightly with the fourfold question: 'Inquirentes de doctrina theologiae':

(*a*) Utrum sit scientia.
(*b*) Utrum distinguatur ab aliis scientiis.
(*c*) De quo sit ista scientia.
(*d*) De modo traditionis huius scientiae.[2]

But, though he thus shows his awareness of the problem, and is willing to discuss it, Alexander's solution is not satisfying, for he avoids the main point by a distinction which does not solve it. *Scientia*, he says, is the knowledge of all things which have been caused; while the name of wisdom (*sapientia*) must be given to the cause of causes. Theology, therefore, is wisdom and not a science; it has a different purpose, leading to salvation, and a different method. It is *sui gratia*, and it transcends all other sciences. The method of dealing with theology is 'praeceptivus, exemplificativus, exhortativus, revelativus, orativus, quia ii modi competunt affectui pietatis'. That is to say, the study of theology is more or less what Bacon approved of, the method of exegesis; and rational arguments drawn from natural knowledge are not used to support the faith. So Bacon is right when he says that Alexander's education had not been sufficiently Aristotelian for him to feel the force of Aristotelian natural knowledge; but quite wrong in thinking that Alexander himself was primarily responsible for the use of questions instead of the text. He used both, as all theologians had done since Peter Lombard. But he was undoubtedly one of those who gave an additional impetus to questions that dealt with the problem of whether theology was a

[1] William of Auxerre, *Summa aurea, Prologue* and book IV (*De baptismo*), condensed and quoted by M-D. Chénu, *La Théologie comme science au XIII siècle*, pp. 34–36, 61.

[2] Alexander of Hales, *Summa theologica*, Introduction, Qu. 1 ff.; Chénu, *La Théologie* . . . pp. 38–42.

science. His successors went further than he, though in his day he was an authority. If his *Summa* was neglected, as it may well have been, it was because his collection of solutions, his *magistrales sententiae*, dealt inadequately with the most pressing problem.

Eudes de Rigaud, one of Alexander's successors in the Franciscan chair of theology at Paris, who later became Archbishop of Rouen, takes up where he left off, posing at the beginning of his work the same questions. If theology has no *principia*, then it is no science. But it *has principia*, says Eudes. In its own way it has principles, axioms, and conclusions; but these are only to be perceived after the mind of a human being has been illuminated by faith. No extrinsic aid is needed to perceive the principles and axioms of science; but this does not mean that the science of theology is in any way dependent on natural knowledge. In addition to the principles (which in scholastic terminology Eudes calls *suppositiones*, and in theology are the articles of faith) there are also *dignitates*, a kind of innate knowledge about God which is visible to all men in the light of faith—namely that God is good, powerful, just and to be loved. Such knowledge, says Eudes, is 'scripta in corde nostro sicut et cognitio principiorum'. It may therefore be confidently used for deduction and conclusions.[1]

There the problem rests until St. Thomas offers a fuller solution along the same lines. But Bonaventura, in one of his early philosophical works, before the practical problems of the world required his full attention, gives a hint as to the lines along which progress in the problem would be made. The book of the *Sentences*, he says, tries to make matters of faith intelligible to the human mind. There are things which are to be taken on faith only, and this constitutes what he calls a 'subalternate' field of knowledge. Within this field one may *believe* anything; but to see whether these data of faith can be understood by the natural reason another method must be employed. The purpose of *quaestiones*, from Peter Lombard onwards, is to make things 'believable because they can be understood' (credibile ut intelligibile), and not believable as a pure act of faith. The book of the Lombard is connected with Scripture by subalternation, as optics is connected with geometry. But they have different rules and procedures.[2] No one has any 'authority' in this subalternate field, since all are struggling towards the truth—towards trying to make

[1] B. Pergamo, 'De quaestionibus ineditis Fr. Odonis Rigaldi . . .' (1936), pp. 3–54, 308–64, esp. pp. 20–24; Chénu, *La Théologie* . . . pp. 42–43, 62–66.

[2] Bonaventura, *Comm. in Sent.*, esp. Qu. II, ed. 4; Chénu, *La Théologie* . . . pp. 54–59.

the Scriptures and articles of faith intelligible. We have now gone a long way indeed from Gregory IX and his instructions to the Faculty of Theology not to try to make faith intelligible, because it is a nobler thing and greater merit to believe something which cannot be proved.

Now Albert the Great takes little part in the solution of this problem. He is aware of it, and remarks that arguments on the basis of natural reason are the suitable instrument for proving the truth and for making error clear. This, he adds, was the method adopted by Peter Lombard in the book of *Sentences*. But theology is certainly not a science yet with Albert, but rather *sapientia*, as for Alexander.[1] No doubt this insufficiency on the problem that agitated all theologians was due to Albert's absence of technical training in theology before he began to lecture on it. But his work approached the problem from the other end, and it was on this work that his reputation and authority rested.

Albert prepared the ground for St. Thomas because of his immense work in the Aristotelian sciences. Instead of making scripture intelligible, as the theologians wished to do, he made Aristotle and all natural knowledge conform to the data of revelation, and tried to show that there was no discrepancy. His work, therefore, was not only of interest to students of theology where it solved part of their problem, but to students of arts also; and those who were unacquainted with the technical problems of theology but were aware of the specific difficulties raised by Aristotle, such as the question of the eternity of the world, the unicity of the soul, etc., could also have their doubts laid to rest. St. Thomas, who studied with Albert, was sufficiently interested in what he was doing to follow him to Cologne instead of finishing at Paris with other theologians—a really remarkable decision when the most important centre of theological studies was undoubtedly the University of Paris, as Glorieux' list of Parisian masters conclusively shows, with its tremendous roster of names, including almost every churchman of repute in theology throughout the century. Thomas had both the theological training to be aware of the epistemological problem, and the Aristotelian training to be aware of the persistent and insatiate demands of natural reason. So with his own extraordinary gifts as a philosopher and theologian, he was able to produce his synthesis which was to satisfy both philosophers and theologians for centuries.

[1] Albertus Magnus, *Opera* . . . XXV, 19–20 (*Comm. in Sent.* lib. I, dist. i, art. 5); Chénu, *La Théologie* . . . pp. 43, 72, 109.

Albert states succinctly in his introduction to the *Physics* of Aristotle just what he proposes to do. He intends to make Aristotle *intelligible* to the Latins. This he will not do by merely commenting on Aristotle and using him, as other masters had before his time, but by re-thinking the entire subject-matter which Aristotle had handled.

In his introduction to his commentary on the *Physics*, which is addressed to members of his Order, a practice Bacon never followed —no doubt because he was never *persona grata* with the Franciscans— Albert says:

> It will be our method in this work to follow the order and opinion of Aristotle and to say in explanation and proof whatever will be necessary; but also to deal with what the text does not mention. For this reason we shall make *digressions*, declaring those underlying matters of doubt and supplying whatever has been inadequately stated by some people and obscure in the opinions of the philosopher. ... By proceeding in this manner we shall achieve the same number of books as Aristotle, and they will have the same names. We shall also add in some places those parts of his books, and whole books, which are missing or were left out, or Aristotle did not make—or if he did make them they have not come down to us. . . .
>
> Philosophy is not caused in us by our work, as moral science is caused; but it is caused by the work of nature in us. . . . It is agreed that the human intellect creates a science by reflecting on the material of sense; and so it is easier for a teaching to begin with what we can accept from sense and imagination and intellect than with what we can accept from intellect and imagination (without sense), or, least of all, with what we can accept from the intellect alone. And so by treating of the parts of philosophy we shall first, with God's help, complete the natural sciences, then we shall speak of all mathematics, and we shall finish our purpose with divine science.[1]

Now this passage alone would at once put Albert outside the class of Bacon, but sufficiently close to constitute severe competition for him. Albert believes in a universal science, as everyone did in his time; but the connection between the sciences depends, as modern logicians would have it, on the greater or lesser degree of abstraction (mathematics not depending on sense, but on imagination and intellect; and theology on intellect). Bacon is aware of this connection and recognizes that all the sciences depend on metaphysics. But when he says that they 'mutuis fovent se auxiliis'[2] he is thinking of their interdependence, and the impossibility of learning about any single part in isolation. Moreover, his belief that all science had once been known and revealed, and that it is to be used for the purpose of filling in theological details, is quite alien to Albert's method. Albert says that knowledge is to be reached through the sense world. It is

[1] Albertus Magnus, *Opera* . . . III, 1–2, 4 (*Comm. in. Phys.* lib. I, tr. i, cap. 1).
[2] Brewer, *Op. Tert.*, p. 18.

its own field of inquiry, autonomous and separate. It relies on no divine books.[1] Aristotle is a starting-point for science, as the book of *Sentences* was for theology. The books of Aristotle represented the best knowledge available to the Greeks, as Avicenna and Averroes represented the best knowledge of the Arabs. All the way through his scientific works Albert adds pieces to Aristotle from his own observations, explaining here and giving instances there. His book on 'minerals' is really a new piece of work, supplementary to Aristotle. He calls himself *physicus*, a student of nature.

Albert's primary assumption is that there can be no conflict between natural science and theology because *both* are true. But we can make mistakes about nature. He will make mistakes, Aristotle made mistakes, Plato made mistakes. One of the most remarkable things about Albert is his sympathy for both the Platonists and Aristotelians, as legitimate seekers after knowledge, though they chose different paths. And in this he shows himself a far truer man of science and a 'liberal' in the best sense of that much maligned word than Roger Bacon, the authoritarian and fundamentalist, though Bacon had a greater feeling for technology and was far more imaginative. Though the analogy should not be carried too far, one feels that Albert was more of a professional, while Bacon was the gifted and imaginative amateur. We hear nothing from Albert on the beauty and utility of his specialty. He is occupied in one task only:

> It is our intention in natural science to satisfy to the best of our ability those brothers of our Order who have been asking for many years that we should compose a book on the *Physics* from which they can come to a full understanding of natural science and be able to have a competent understanding of the books of Aristotle . . . our intention is to make all the said parts intelligible to the Latins.[2]

Elsewhere he has told us:

> Some ignorant men want to attack the use of philosophy, especially among the Preachers, like brute animals blaspheming things of which they know nothing.[3]

There is no doubt that the huge corpus of scientific writings that came from the pen of Albert brought him great renown, even in his

[1] It is clear that Albert has, if not Bacon, then others of Bacon's persuasion in mind when he writes: 'Dicet autem fortasse aliquis nos Aristotelem non intellexisse; et ideo non consentire verbis eius: vel quod forte ex certa scientia contradicamus ei quantum ad hominem, et non quantum ad rei veritatem. Et ad illum dicimus quod qui credit Aristotelem fuisse deum, ille debet credere quod nunquam erravit. Si autem credit ipsum fuisse hominem tunc procul dubio errare potuit sic et nos.' Albertus Magnus, *Opera* . . . III, 553 (*Comm. in. Phys.*, lib. VIII, tr. i, cap. 14).

[2] Albertus Magnus, *Opera* . . . III, 1–2 (*Comm. in. Phys.*, lib. I, tr. i, cap. 1).

[3] *Ibid.*, XIV, 910 (*Comm. in. Epistolas B. Dionysii*, Epist. VII, no. 2).

own lifetime. He may not have been a specially competent theologian, and it is certain that he did not directly contribute as much to this science as the specialists in theology. But he was at least a Master of Theology (even if by the back door) and he had for a few years held the important Dominican chair at the University of Paris. And throughout his long life he lectured on theology, if not at Paris; and he founded the Faculty of Theology at Cologne. In 1266 he even suggested to the General of his Order that he should return to teach at Paris at the time of the quarrels between the Faculties of Theology and Arts, during the ascendancy of Siger of Brabant. St. Thomas was bearing the brunt alone, and Albert believed he could help him. But he was not permitted to go, and taught theology intermittently at Strasbourg instead.[1] It is thus entirely proper for critics to point out that Albert was rarely in Paris, and was not there in 1267 when Bacon wrote; and there were others more competent than he to whom Bacon could have referred.

But Bacon is well aware of the new trend in the study of theology, and the use made by St. Thomas of work which has certainly stemmed from Albert. Thomas was not yet as great an authority as he became later, although much revered by his own Order; the greatest authority was the man who had already done the preliminary work for his pupil, who had established the trend, and was now of an almost legendary reputation 'while he still lived'. 'Sicut Aristoteles, Avicenna et Averroes allegantur in scholis, sic et ipse—et adhuc vivit et habuit in vita sua auctoritatem quod nunquam homo habuit in doctrina.'[2]

This reputation rested on Albert's Aristotelian and scientific work, and the use Thomas made of it. But Albert was the one who held the renown in the thirteenth century, and Thomas partly gained his at this time from the glory reflected by his master. Already in 1256, when Pope Alexander IV needed someone to defend Aristotelianism against the doctrines of Averroes, which was gaining currency in the schools, he called upon Albert, asking him for a scientific solution. It seems probable that there was an actual conference in Rome to discuss the method of attack, and the person most competent to deliver it. And who should this be but the man who had conciliated Aristotle and the Bible?[3]

[1] Garreau, *St. Albert* . . . pp. 151–61.

[2] Brewer, *Op. Tert.*, p. 30.

[3] 'Contra hunc errorem jam pridem disputavi, cum essem in curia.' See Van Steenberghen, *Siger de Brabant* . . . p. 471 and note 4.

In 1270 Gilles de Lessines wrote to Albert to ask for his comments on the first group of propositions studied at the Faculty of Arts, which were soon to be condemned by Stephen Tempier.[1] In his public announcement of Albert's decisions on these questions (*De quindecim problematibus*), Gilles says: 'Haec est positio multorum magnorum, et precise domini Alberti'. Another contemporary calls him 'illum famosum'. One of his favourite disciples, Ulrich of Strasbourg, himself a scholar of note and the author of a *Summa*, calls him 'nostri temporis stupor et miraculum'.[2]

What Albert had done was to realize, as no one else before him, that the time had come to establish the legitimate realms of knowledge, the realm of natural science, and the realm of faith. He had shown that the work of Aristotle, the Greeks, and the Arabs, was valid in its own realm; but it was not infallible. Yet such of their knowledge as was true did not and could not conflict with the data of revelation. Albert showed the way by which Aristotle's work could be carried on and advanced by the Latins through the use of personal observation, with the addition of new findings in every realm of natural knowledge. He recognized and stated explicitly that the study of nature was legitimate and it had its own methods valid for its study. While Aristotle had no title whatever to speak in the realm of faith and theology, and Augustine in this field was a far better one, Aristotle, in spite of his mistakes, was still the greatest master of natural science.[3]

Bacon's objections to the science of Albert are more quickly dealt with. As shown in the text of this study, Bacon believed in a universal science which must be complete. This science had been fully revealed to the patriarchs and prophets in early times, and in part to Aristotle. The Arabs had rediscovered some more, especially in the field of optics. The Latin world, in Bacon's view, had a special chance to recover science, because to the Latins had been revealed the truths of Christianity; and through God's grace a Latin Christian, if he lived a suitable life, might be vouchsafed the opportunity of completing it once more. Bacon probably hoped he was such a man. When he found he could not do it by himself he proposed a corps of scientists, each working on different branches of science; but none could be

[1] Garreau, *St. Albert* . . . p. 159; De Wulf, *Histoire* . . . II, 130. Cf. Van Steenberghen, *Siger de Brabant* . . . p. 719, 'l'ancien maître parisien, qui était demeuré la principale autorité dans l'ordre en matière philosophique'.

[2] These tributes are drawn from De Wulf, *Histoire* . . . II, 144–45.

[3] For the influence and position occupied by Albert in the intellectual world of his time, the pages of Van Steenberghen, *Siger de Brabant* . . . pp. 475–79 may be the best short account.

left out if it were to be perfected. There could be no subdivision and analysis of one part of science; no science in itself was autonomous.

This grandiose conception was utterly alien to Albert, even though he made contributions to many sciences. The relation between the sciences for him was by subalternation, a dependence of one science on another, as optics on geometry, the lower dependent upon the one higher in the scale (degrees of abstraction). But Bacon wanted more than this. He wanted a whole self-contained and beautiful building (his own analogy). Moreover, Albert had omitted optics, and was deficient in mathematics, and knew no languages but Latin and the vernacular. Yet the world followed Albert; he was an authority and Bacon was not. Bacon had a few poor students as his special care and a limited public. Albert preached to his Order and to the whole world of educated men.

If Albert had been a nobody, an ignorant man, Bacon would have had nothing against him. But he claimed to be a scientist, and he was an authority.

> He who composed so many and such large volumes about natural things . . . is ignorant of these fundamentals, and so his building cannot stand.[1]

For the want of a few parts he allowed his whole to collapse. Who but Albert had tried to do this?

[1] Brewer, *Op. Tert.*, p. 42.

APPENDIX C

TWO PRINTED WORKS ATTRIBUTED TO BACON

AMONGST the works of Bacon published by Steele and Delorme there is a tract called the *De sensu et sensato*, which appears in no bibliography of which I am aware, and which is not definitely ascribed to him in the MS. BM. Add. 8786, in which it appears. Steele edited and printed it,[1] giving the following reasons for his acceptance of the tract as genuine. A certain Thomas, probably brother Thomas, *capellanus* of Robert, Duke of Calabria, who was King of Sicily from 1306 to 1343, in his work *De lapide philosophico* mentions a writing which he calls 'Rogerius de sensu'. There is no other work by any Roger, as far as is known, to whom this could refer. The other texts in the MS. are genuine works of Bacon, with the exception of the *Perspectiva communis* of John Peckham. For the rest Steele says: 'Internal evidence of style and matter amply confirm the attribution', but he gives no concrete details.[2]

After a careful study of the material in the printed text I am in agreement that the work is by Bacon, and it suggests a number of interesting paths of investigation for anyone who may be in a position to examine the multitudes of unpublished MSS. in European libraries, and may come upon works of this kind, dating from the first half of the thirteenth century, and which cannot be ascribed to anyone else.

Although Bacon's style in his later period is extremely distinctive and easily recognizable, this does not apply in the same degree to his Parisian work, where he is following a regular form of discussion. So I should hesitate to ascribe any work definitely to him on the basis of style or even content, since this content was also to some degree determined by the custom of the time. The style of this commentary is certainly very similar to that of Bacon's Parisian work, but I should not care to go the whole way with Steele, and say that 'internal evidence of style and matter amply confirm the attribution' to him.

I think, however, that there are two passages in the commentary which point directly to Bacon as the author. These refer to a book *De generatione* which does not seem to be the *De generatione et corruptione* of Aristotle (nor, of course, the *De generatione animalium*, which,

[1] Steele, Fasc. XIV, 1–134.

[2] *Ibid.*, Fasc. XIV, v.

for the medievals, was part of the eighteen books on animals). Steele lists these two passages in the index under Aristotle's *De generatione*, though without having been able to find the particular passage referred to. This, in my view, was simply because they were not there, but on the contrary were in Bacon's *De generatione*, to which he refers in several places in his series of *Quaestiones*.[1]

On page 27 of the *De sensu* Bacon is talking about light, and how it is transmitted; and in the whole long paragraph there is no reference to Aristotle. He is dealing with the subject from his own 'excogitations'. The passage runs:

> Sive exspiret spiritualiter a corpore lucido sive generetur in medio quod non habet hic determinari, set in libro *de generatione* ubi habet determinari de multiplicatione virtutis in universali ab omni agenti naturali, oportet ponere quod. . . .

The other passage is even more clear:

> Illud quod multiplicatur in medio a corpore luminoso vel colorato vel odorabili est expressa similitudo totius corporis, tam a parte materie quam a parte forme, ut prius tactum est et in libro *de generatione* probatum.[2]

There is no such exact proof in Aristotle's *De generatione*, though Bacon, in a commentary on it, might well have found it necessary to make one. This is very similar to another reference to this same *De generatione* in his *Quaestiones* on the *Physics*.[3]

The method of dealing with the subject is the same in this commentary as in the *Quaestiones*, but the form is different. It is extremely literal, following closely the text of Aristotle's *De sensu*, though it is much expanded from Aristotle's short work. Bacon makes much use not only of Aristotle's other works, but of Avicenna, Averroes, and Al Hazen, with a few quotations also from Avicenna's first book on medicine, and from Isaac. It is not a separate tract on the subject of sense-perception, but a real commentary on Aristotle, as is seen by his use of the terms 'in hoc textu', and 'in littera', as in the *Quaestiones*. On the other hand it is utterly different from Albert's structurally loose but more generally informed work on the same subject.[4] As usual at this period of his life, Bacon is trying to reconcile his authorities with each other and extract the truth from them, rather than use his own experience. There are no references to experience in the whole work, although he is dealing with light and colour which later become so important to him. But this is to be expected, if it belongs, as I believe it does, to the Parisian period. And we have already seen how Bacon deals with light in the *Quaestiones* in the same abstract

[1] For instances see Steele, Fasc. XIII, xxx.
[2] Steele, Fasc. XIV, 118.
[3] *Ibid.*, Fasc. XIII, 422.
[4] Albertus Magnus, *Opera* . . . IX, 1–93.

manner, after the fashion of the scholastics.[1] It is interesting also to note that, though the work is in the form of a commentary, when Bacon comes across a very difficult point which is discussed at considerable length, as in the question of the relationship between light and colour, he falls again into the question technique: 'Queritur an sufficienter dabit colori natura visibilis. . . . Quod sic videtur . . . set contra, etc.'[2]

The range of reading, with the exception of the hitherto unquoted parts of Avicenna, and Isaac, is exactly the same as in the later series of *Quaestiones*, though on this subject far more is taken from Al Hazen than was necessary in the *Physics*. Until, therefore, it can be shown that there was another master who dealt with these subjects, who used the same books and the same techniques, and had the same interests, as Bacon, I think that the work should be attributed to him, even without taking into consideration the two references to a *De generatione* which seem to belong to the writer and not to Aristotle.

If we are to decide whether it belongs to Bacon's Parisian period or later, Steele has pointed out that it must come before the first draft of the *Communia naturalium* and the *Perspectiva*, as evidenced by the greater range of quotation in the two latter works. While this is, of course, important, far more significant, in my view, is the handling of the subject matter. None of the problems which became recognized as such as soon as Bacon began to take a specialized interest in optics is dealt with here. Bacon has evidently not penetrated yet beyond the formal arguments used by the schoolmen. In later life he makes the same distinctions, but uses geometry and makes diagrams. In the *Perspectiva* (part V of the *Opus Majus*) Bacon uses all his medical knowledge to discuss how the eye is physiologically made up, how we perceive, how we make judgments; but above all he considers why the eye sees in the way it does, and how the rays reach it, why we concentrate our vision on a certain point, what kind of rays are given out from the object and the path they travel, etc.

There is no sign that Bacon has as yet become in the least interested in such problems. The 'multiplication of species' is referred to because his authorities refer to it, but that is all. It is inconceivable that he should have felt the weight of all these problems and possessed the information that he had later and still kept quiet about it, even if his official subject was only the short book of Aristotle. Indeed, in his later days he would not have confined himself to Aristotle, and contented himself with a commentary on the work of the Master.

[1] Steele, Fasc. XIII, 206. [2] *Ibid.*, Fasc. XIV, 45.

It was not Bacon's practice, as it was Albert's, to use Aristotle as a jumping-off point, and build his own views around it in the form of a commentary. Even in the *Communia naturalium*, where he uses the formal scholastic method, Bacon always deals with, or at least shows himself aware of, the problems he was concerned with at the time.

The only reason against an early date seems to be the fact that no other commentaries are known for this time. This point has been dealt with in the main body of this study,[1] and does not require to be examined again here.

I have also considered the fragment published in *Isis* (1937) by S. H. Thomson, under the title of *An Unnoticed Treatise on Time and Motion*, and attributed by the editor to Bacon.[2] On internal evidence I think the Baconian authorship can be accepted. But the fragment is definitely not a commentary, though it is difficult to say from such a brief fragment exactly what it is. There can be no doubt that it belongs to a later period of Bacon's work than his Parisian days. It is concerned with the subjects dealt with in the same manner in the *Communia naturalium*. Noticeable is the use made now of the 'mathematical' method, never used in Bacon's Parisian period, and the use of the letters a, b, and c to indicate different periods of time, and divisions of motion. Also noticeable are the general firmness of the argument and the effectiveness of the exposition.

The treatise could be either a piece in itself, or a fragment of a larger work. As no such larger work is known into which it would fit, and as it can be regarded as in some respects complete in itself, I should tentatively place it as a few pages specially written for someone who had asked Bacon for a discussion ('ad instantiam amicorum') on the problem of time and motion, and the relation between them.

The fragment was found in a MS. that contained also some of the scientific work of Grosseteste, and Thomson places the script itself as not later than 1275. The best theory that would account for these few facts would be that it was written in the ten years prior to 1275, during which Bacon was thinking about the problems dealt with in the fragment, and that he wrote it for a friend who was interested in these things and already possessed works of Grosseteste. The owner of the MS. may have been the very friend for whom Bacon composed the treatise; or he may have been a scientific inquirer who knew of the works of both Grosseteste and Bacon, and included this pertinent piece in his MS.

[1] *Supra*, pp. 59–60.

[2] S. H. Thomson, ed., 'An Unnoticed Treatise . . .' (1937), pp. 219–24.

BIBLIOGRAPHIES

A. Works of Roger Bacon used in this study.
B. Critical bibliography of biographies of Roger Bacon; these are given in chronological order since Charles (1861).
C. Other works.

A

Brewer, J. S., ed., Opera Fr. Baconis hactenus inedita, London, 1859, 'Rolls Series'.
Compendium studii philosophiae, 393–519.
Epistola fratris Rogeri Baconis de secretis operibus artis et naturae, et de nullitate magiae 523–51.
Opus Minus, 313–89.
Opus Tertium, 1–310.

Bridges, J. H., ed., *The 'Opus Majus' of Roger Bacon*, Vols. I and II, Oxford, 1897. Vol. III, containing revised text of first three parts and corrections, emendations, and additional notes, London, 1900.

Burke, R. B., *The 'Opus Majus' of Roger Bacon* (translation), Philadelphia, 1928.

Gasquet, F. A., 'An Unpublished Fragment of a Work by Roger Bacon', *English Historical Review*, XII (1897), 494–517.

Little, A. G., ed., Part of the *Opus Tertium* of Roger Bacon, Aberdeen, 1912.

Nolan, E., and S. A. Hirsch, *The Greek Grammar of Roger Bacon, and a Fragment of his Hebrew Grammar*, Cambridge, 1902.

Rashdall, H., *Fratris Rogeri Baconis Compendium studii theologiae*, Aberdeen, 1911.

Steele, R., *Opera hactenus inedita Fr. Rogeri Baconis*, Oxford, 1905(?)–41. All works edited by Steele, unless otherwise indicated.
Fasc. I. Metaphysica Fratris Rogeri (De viciis contractis in studio theologiae,) N.D. (1905?).
Fasc. II. Liber primus communium naturalium, parts 1 and 2, N.D. (1905?).
Fasc. III. Liber primus communium naturalium, parts 3 and 4, 1911.
Fasc. IV. Liber secundus communium naturalium (De celestibus), 1913.
Fasc. V. Secretum secretorum cum glossis et notulis Fratris Rogeri, 1920.
Fasc. VI. Compotus Fratris Rogeri, 1926.
Fasc. VII. Quaestiones supra undecimum prime philosophie Aristotelis, 1926.
Fasc. VIII. Quaestiones supra libros quatuor Physicorum Aristotelis, ed. F. Delorme, 1928.
Fasc. IX. De retardatione accidentium senectutis cum aliis opusculis de rebus medicinalibus, edd. A. G. Little and E. Withington, 1928.
Fasc. X. Quaestiones altere supra libros prime philosophie, 1930, pp. 1–336.
Fasc. XI. Quaestiones supra quatuor libros prime philosophie, 1932, pp. 1–170.
——. Quaestiones supra librum de plantis, pp. 173–252.
Fasc. XII. Quaestiones supra librum de causis, 1935, pp. 1–158.
Fasc. XIII. Quaestiones altere supra libros octo Physicorum Aristotelis, ed. F. Delorme, 1935.

Fasc. XIV. Liber de sensu et sensato, 1937, pp. 1–134.
——. Summa de sophismatibus et destruccionibus, pp. 135–208.
Fasc. XV. Summa grammatica, 1941, pp. 1–190.
——. Sumulae dialectices, pp. 193–359.
Fasc. XVI. Communia mathematica Fratris Rogeri, parts 1 and 2, 1940.

Thomson, S. H., 'An Unnoticed Treatise by Roger Bacon, on Time and Motion', *Isis*, XXVII (1937), 219–24.

B

Charles, E., *Roger Bacon, sa vie, ses ouvrages, et ses doctrines*, Paris, 1861 (cited as Charles).

This invaluable pioneer work can only be used now with extreme caution, since Charles did not have the benefit of an unrestricted use of the MS. which contained the Parisian lectures, and was too much attached to his conception of Bacon as a 'martyr of science', persecuted by his Order. Much of his book is special pleading, and there are instances of quotations out of context which he has used to bolster his arguments. His influence on Baconian studies has been enormous; but reliance upon his research and his conclusions would now be dangerous if one desires to have a proper understanding of Bacon and his time. Few of his judgments have fully stood the test of a century's research.

Anonymous, 'The Life and Writings of Roger Bacon', *Westminster Review*, 1864, pp. 1–30 (cited as *Westminster Review* (1864)).

A remarkably good article for its time, especially interesting for its estimate of the psychology of Roger Bacon, a subject rather neglected since his day. Based primarily on the work of Charles and Brewer, it nevertheless tries to avoid the excessive hero-worship of these predecessors, and makes a good attempt of relating Bacon's work to the history of his age—although the lack of specific knowledge of this history in 1864 was a serious handicap.

Neil, S., *Epoch Men*, Edinburgh, 1865, pp. 89–122.

A technical facility for writing and a fertile imagination fortified by ignorance were insufficient qualifications for writing a chapter on Roger Bacon and experimental science. May be safely disregarded.

Jourdain, C., 'Discussions de quelques points de la biographie de Roger Bacon', *Excursions historiques et philosophiques à travers le moyen âge*, Paris, 1888, pp. 129–45.

A serious, well-argued discussion of several points of importance in Roger Bacon's biography that had been neglected by Brewer, Charles, and earlier writers. Most of his findings were accepted by all later students of Bacon, and are no longer in dispute.

Feret, P., 'Les Imprisonnements de Roger Bacon', *Revue des questions historiques*, L (1891), 119–42.

Feret, pursuing more thoroughly some of Jourdain's suggestions, effectively disposed of the evidence for a first imprisonment. He was not, in my view, so successful in his criticisms of the second, and in any event overstated his case. But it was a necessary work, and has been accepted in the main by later biographers. Especially interesting for its systematic account of the gradual accretion of the legend of Bacon as martyr.

Witzel, T., Art. 'Roger Bacon' in *Catholic Encyclopaedia* (1910).

The kind of article to be expected from this publication. Based on good secondary sources, but piously anxious to redeem the Church and the Franciscans from any suspicion of having persecuted their illustrious member. Its danger is the authority wielded by the official nature of the publication. Too many later biographers have suffered from Witzel's hasty acceptance of a hypothesis of Schlund of which even Schlund himself was doubtful.

Delorme, G., Art. 'Roger Bacon' in *Dictionnaire de Théologie Catholique* (1910).

A sympathetic account, skirting most of the difficulties and problems, but clearly based on a reading of the most important of Roger Bacon's works. A few surprising statements, but for the most part clear and unexceptionable, and a very fair introduction to the subject in a short space.

Bridges, J. H., *The Life and Work of Roger Bacon*, London, 1914.

As editor of the *Opus Majus* (1897), Bridges did a great deal of valuable work on Bacon's science, which he wrote up in his introduction and notes. Bridges, a noted positivist, had a considerable knowledge of nineteenth-century science and was in sympathy with Bacon's outlook, as he perceived it; but his knowledge of medieval history, culture, and science was very imperfect, and he was still too much influenced by Charles in his estimate of Bacon as a rebel against authority. But his analysis of Bacon's more important work is still very useful, though it is probably best read in conjunction with the text and notes of the *Opus Majus*.

Little, A. G., 'Roger Bacon's Life and Works', *Essays . . . on the Occasion of the Commemoration of the Seventh Centenary of his Birth*, Oxford, 1914, 1–32 (cited as Little, *Essays . . .*).

A well-documented estimate of the facts that are really known about Bacon, and a useful basis for all subsequent studies; but not attempting in this short space to do more than supply an outline. Suffers from partial ignorance of the cultural, and serious ignorance of the scientific, environment of the thirteenth century, which leads to an overestimate of the uniqueness of Bacon, and the acceptance of several doubtful hypotheses from others such as Mandonnet, whose knowledge in this field was equally limited.

Thorndike, L., 'The True Roger Bacon', *American Historical Review*, XXI (1916), 237–57, 468–80. See *ibid.*, *History of Magic . . .* 1923, below.

Steele, R., 'Roger Bacon and the State of Science in the Thirteenth Century', *Studies in the History and Method of Science*, ed. C. Singer, Oxford, 1921, II, 121–50.

Suffers from complete lack of documentation; but it is the best early attempt to show the continuity of Bacon's thought, and to place the Parisian lectures—of which Steele was the chief editor—in the framework of Bacon's life. Some of his conclusions are over-hasty and built on very slender and doubtful foundations. If Steele had ever revised this article in the light of the greater knowledge he acquired later, he might have done an outstanding job. Still well worth reading, especially in conjunction with Thorndike.

Thorndike, L., *History of Magic and Experimental Science*, New York, 1923, II, 616–713.

An adaptation and extension of two earlier articles (*see* 1916, above). Invaluable for the information on thirteenth-century science which was hitherto not available, and for criticisms of other historians who had overestimated the uniqueness of Bacon. Probably Thorndike goes too far in the direction of 'debunking' him, but the procedure was necessary in view of the prejudices of his predecessors. The biographical material is brief, and the Parisian period omitted as irrelevant to his subject; but his judgments are always based on careful thinking and thorough documentation. No student of Bacon can neglect it.

Vanderwalle, C. B., *Roger Bacon dans l'histoire de la philologie*, Paris, 1929. (Reprinted from three articles published in *France Franciscaine*, 1928.) Two separate paginations are given in this reprint. The pagination adopted in the footnote references is the one given in parentheses in the top corner of each page.

In the Paris edition pp. 77–210 constitute a series of appendixes on the life of Roger Bacon and certain disputed questions. This is an extremely valuable study, perhaps the best in recent years, fully documented and carefully thought out. It is not, however, an ordered consecutive biography, since it is clear the author's research was too specialized to permit this. In several places where he could have doubted with profit he accepts uncritically material which had been convincingly discredited before his time; which is a great pity, since when he does doubt and criticize he always throws much needed light in dark corners.

Sarton, G., *Introduction to the History of Science*, Baltimore, 1931, II, 952–67.

Not very much on Bacon's life, this account is nevertheless useful as a most careful and systematic record of Bacon's work, with a bibliography on each phase of this work. The incidental comments are most enlightening, and show a thorough acquaintance with Bacon; and Sarton's knowledge of much of medieval science and his thorough understanding of modern science enable him to gain an accurate perspective, missing in almost all works of his predecessors.

Lutz, E., 'Roger Bacon's Contribution to Knowledge', *Franciscan Studies*, St. Bonaventura, N.Y., 1936, 1–76.

Inferior, derivative work, based almost exclusively on secondary materials, written apparently with the intention of rehabilitating Bacon as a good friar and Christian. Has little knowledge of even the best authorities on his subject; does not seem to know who has, and who has not, done original research in it, including members of his own Order, such as Vanderwalle, who is not mentioned. Accepts even the supposed ciphers of Bacon, apparently unaware of the unanswerable criticism of these ciphers given by Manly, 'Roger Bacon and the Voynich Manuscript', *Speculum*, VI (1931), pp. 345–91.

Woodruff, F. W., *Roger Bacon, a Biography*, London, 1938.

Intended to 'satisfy the curiosity of the general reader without confusing his mind with too many digressions into contemporary history', based upon a very few secondary sources and the 1928 translation of the *Opus Majus* (Burke), this little book is readable, and interesting as an introduction to the subject. Since the author has not troubled either himself or the reader with the real problems of

Bacon's biography and his relation to his time, there are too many serious mistakes for it to be in any way satisfactory to a student. The best thing in the book is the telling use of quotation from the *Opus Majus*; its chief danger is that it states doubtful hypotheses and errors as definite facts. Even the popular biographer should not lay claim to such omniscience, in spite of the laudable aim of 'not confusing the reader'.

Sharp, D. E., Art. 'Roger Bacon' in *Encyclopaedia Britannica* (edit. 1947).

Very short, but to the point, and embodying most of the best results of recent English research, though a consultation of Vanderwalle's monograph might have supplemented the information. (Replaces the out-of-date article of Adamson in earlier editions.)

C

Abbreviations—

AFH — Archivum Franciscanum Historicum (Quaracchi).
AHDLMA — Archives d'Histoire Doctrinale et Littéraire du Moyen Age (Paris).
RNS — Revue Néo-scholastique de Philosophie (Louvain).
RTAM — Recherches de Théologie Ancienne et Médiévale (Louvain).

Adam Marsh, Epistolae. *See* Monumenta Franciscana, Vol. I.

Albertus Magnus, Opera omnia, ed. A. Borgnet, Paris, 1890–92.

Alexander of Hales, *Franciscan Studies*, XXVI (1945), special number devoted to.

Amid, M., Essai sur la psychologie d'Avicenne, Geneva, 1940.

Anonymous. *See* under titles of books.

Aron, M., Un Animateur de la jeunesse au XIII siècle, Paris and Bruges, 1930.

——, Lettres du bienheureux Jourdain de Saxe à Diane d'Andolo, Paris, 1924.

Baeumker, C., 'Roger Bacons Naturphilosophie', *Franziskanische Studien*, Munster, III (1916), 1–40, 109–39.

Bierbaum, H., 'Bettelorden und Weltgeistlichkeit an der Universität Paris in der Mitte des XIII Jahrhunderts', *Franziskanische Studien*, Munster, VII (1920).

Birkenmajer, A., 'Avicennas Vorrede zum "Liber Sufficientiae" und Roger Bacon', *RNS*, XXXVI (1934), 308–20.

——, 'Le Rôle joué par les médecins et les naturalistes dans la réception d'Aristote au XII et XIII siècles', *La Pologne au VIme congrès international des sciences historiques*, Oslo, 1928 (reprinted Warsaw, 1930).

Bonaventura, St., Opera omnia, Quaracchi, 1882–1902.

Bouyges, M., 'Roger Bacon, a-t-il lu les livres arabes?', *AHDLMA*, V (1930), 311–15.

Callus, D. A., 'Introduction of Aristotelian Learning into Oxford in the Thirteenth Century', *Proceedings of the British Academy*, London, XXIX (1943), 229–81.

——, 'Two Early Masters on the Problem of the Plurality of Forms', *RNS*, XLII (1939), 411–45.

Carton, R., L'Expérience physique chez Roger Bacon, 'Etudes de philosophie mediévale', Vol. II, Paris, 1924.

——, L'Expérience mystique de l'illumination intérieure chez Roger Bacon, 'Etudes de philosophie mediévale', Vol. III, Paris, 1924.

Carton, R., La Synthèse doctrinale de Roger Bacon, 'Etudes de philosophie medievale', Vol. V, Paris, 1924.

Chartularium Universitatis Parisiensis, ed. H. Denifle and A. Chatelain, Paris, 1889, Vol. I.

Chénu, M. D., La Théologie comme science au XIII siècle, 2nd edit., N.P., 1943.

Chronicle of the Twenty-four Generals, *Analecta Franciscana*, III (1897).

Chronicon de Lanercost, ed. J. Stevenson, Edinburgh, 1839.

Crowley, T., Roger Bacon: the Problem of the Soul in his Philosophical Commentaries, Louvain and Dublin, 1950.

Davy, M. M., Les Sermons universitaires parisiens de 1230–31, 'Etudes de philosophie mediévale', Vol. XV, Paris, 1931.

Denifle, H., and A. Chatelain, *See* Chartularium.

Denifle, H., and F. Ehrle, Archiv für Litteratur und Kirchengeschichte des Mittelalters, 6 vols., Berlin, 1885–92.

Dickson, C., 'La Vie du Cardinal Robert de Courson', *AHDLMA*, VIII (1934), 56–142.

Duhem, P., Le Système du monde de Platon à Copernic, Paris, 1916, III, 260–67, 411–42; V, 375–411.

Eccleston. *See* Thomas de Eccleston.

Ehrle, F. *See* Denifle and Ehrle.

Felder, H., Geschichte der wissenschaftlichen Studien im Franziskanerorden, Freiburg, 1904.

Fleming, D., 'Ruggero Bacone e la scolastica', *Rivista di Filosofia Neoscolastica* Florence, VI (1914), 529–71.

Franceschini, E., 'Aristotele nel medioevo latino', *Atti del IX Congresso Nazionale di Filosofia*, Padua, 20–23, September, 1934.

Garreau, A., Saint Albert le Grand, Paris, 1932.

Gilson, E., 'Les Sources grecoarabes de l'augustinisme avicennisant', *AHDLMA*, IV (1929–30), 1–158.

Glorieux, P., 'Contra Geraldinos. L'enchaînement des polemiques', *RTAM*, VII (1935), 129–55.

——, 'Les Polemiques "contra Geraldinos",' *RTAM*, VI (1934), 5–41.

——, Répertoire des maîtres de théologie de Paris au XIII siècle, 'Etudes de philosophie mediévale', Vols. XVII and XVIII, Paris, 1933–34.

Grabmann, M., 'Les Commentaires de St. Thomas sur Aristote', *Annales de l'Institut Supérieur de Philosophie*, Louvain, III (1914), 229–81.

——, I Divieti ecclesiastici contro Aristotele sotto Innocenzo III e Gregorio IX, 'Miscellanea historiae pontificiae', Rome, 1941.

——, Der Hl. Albert der Grosse, Munich, 1932.

Grosseteste, R., Epistolae, ed. H. R. Luard, London, 1861, 'Rolls Series'.

——, Die Philosophischen Werke des Robert Grosseteste, Bischofs von Lincoln, ed. L. Baur, *Beiträge zur Geschichte der Philosophie des Mittelalters*, Munster, IX (1912).

Haskins, C. H., Studies in the History of Medieval Science, Cambridge (Mass.), 1924.

Hauréau, B., Histoire de la philosophie scolastique, Paris, 1872–80, Vol. II.

Hoffmans, H., 'L'Expérience chez Roger Bacon', *RNS*, XXVII (1926), 170–90.

——, 'La Genèse des sensations d'après Roger Bacon', *RNS*, XV (1908), 474–98.

——, 'L'Intuition mystique et la science', *RNS*, XVI (1909), 370–97.

Hoffmans, H., 'La Sensibilité et les modes de la connaissance d'après Roger Bacon', *RNS*, XVI (1909), 32–46.

——, 'La Synthèse doctrinale de Roger Bacon', *Archiv für Geschichte der Philosophie*, XIV (1907), 196–224.

——, 'Une Théorie intuitioniste de la connaissance du XIII siècle, *RNS*, XIII (1906), 371–91.

Hover, H., Roger Bacons Hylomorphismus als Grundlage seiner philosophischen Anschauungen, Limburg, 1912.

Huber, R. M., A Documented History of the Franciscan Order, Milwaukee and Washington, 1944. Vol. I.

Hutton, E., The Franciscans in England, Boston, 1926.

Joachim of Flora, Tractatus super quatuor evangelia, ed. E. Buonaiuti, Rome, 1930.

John of Garland, De triumphis ecclesiae, ed. T. Wright, London, 1856.

Lacombe, G., Aristoteles latinus, Rome, 1939. (Vol. I only published.)

Lanercost Chronicle. *See* Chronicon de Lanercost.

Lea, H. C., A History of the Inquisition of the Middle Ages, New York, 1887, Vols. I and III.

Liber Exemplorum, ed. A. G. Little, Aberdeen, 1905.

Little, A. G., Franciscan Papers, Lists, and Documents, Manchester, 1943.

——, 'The Franciscan School at Oxford in the Thirteenth Century', *AFH*, XIX (1926), 803–74.

——, The Grey Friars in Oxford, Oxford, 1892.

Little, A. G., 'Roger Bacon. Annual lecture on a Master Mind', *Proceedings of the British Academy*, London, XIV (1928), 265–96.

——, ed., Roger Bacon, Essays . . . on the Occasion of the Commemoration of the Seventh Centenary of his Birth, Oxford, 1914.

——, 'Thomas Docking and his Relations to Roger Bacon', *Essays in History Presented to Reginald Lane Poole*, Oxford, 1927, 301–31.

——, and A. Pelster, Oxford Theology and Theologians, Oxford, 1934.

Lottin, O., 'L'Identité de l'âme et ses facultés pendant le premier moitié du XIII siècle,' *RNS*, XXXVI (1934), 191–210.

——, 'Note sur les premiers ouvrages théologiques d'Albert le Grand', *RTAM*, IV (1932), 73–82.

——, 'La Pluralité des formes substantielles avant St. Thomas', *RNS*, XXXIV (1932), 449–67.

——, 'Psychologie et morale à la faculté des arts de Paris aux approches de 1250', *RNS*, XLII (1939), 182–212.

——, 'Quelques *Quaestiones* des maîtres parisiens aux environs de 1225–35', *RTAM*, V (1933), 79–95.

Mandonnet, P., 'La Date de naissance d'Albert le Grand', *Revue Thomiste*, XXXVI (1931), 233–56.

——, 'Roger Bacon et la composition des trois opus', *RNS*, XX (1913), 52–68, 164–80.

——, 'Roger Bacon et le Speculum Astronomiae', *RNS*, XVII (1910), 313–35.

——, Siger de Brabant et l'averroisme latin au XIII siècle, 2nd edit., Louvain, 1911.

Martin, R. M., 'La Question de l'unité de la forme substantielle', *RNS*, XXII (1920), 107–12.

Matthew Paris, Chronica majora, ed. H. R. Luard, 7 vols., London, 1872–83. 'Rolls Series'.

Monumenta Franciscana, ed. J. S. Brewer, London, 1858, Vol. I. 'Rolls Series'.

Paton, L. A., Les Prophécies de Merlin, 2 vols., New York, 1927.

Pelster, F., 'Zür Datierung einiger Schriften Alberts des Grossen', *Zeitschrift für katholischen Theologie*, XLVII (1923), 475–82.

——, 'Um die Datierung Alberts des Grossen Aristoteles-paraphrase', *Philosophisches Jahrbuch*, XLVIII (1935), 143–61.

——, 'Roger Bacons Compendium studii theologiae und der Sentenskommentar des Richardus Rufus', *Scholastik*, IV (1929), 410–16.

—— *See also* Pelster and Little.

Pelzer, A., 'Une Source inconnue de Roger Bacon, Alfred de Sarashel', *AFH*, XII, (1919), 45–67.

Pergamo, B., 'De quaestionibus ineditis Fr. Odonis Rigaldi', *AFH*, XXIX (1936), 3–54, 308–64.

Picavet, F., Essais sur l'histoire génerale et comparée des théologies et des philosophies mediévales, Paris, 1913.

Rashdall, H., The Universities of Europe in the Middle Ages, edd. F. M. Powicke and A. B. Emden, 3 vols., Oxford, 1936.

Russell, J. C., 'The Preferments and Adjutores of Robert Grosseteste', *Harvard Theological Review*, XXVI, 1933, 161–72.

Salimbene, Fra, 'Cronica fratris Salimbene de Adam ordinis Minorum', ed. O. Holder-Egger, *Monumenta Germaniae Historica*; *Scriptores*, Hanover, 1905–13, Vol. XXXII.

Sarton, G., Introduction to the History of Science, Baltimore, 1931, Vol. II.

Schlund, E., 'Peter Peregrinus von Maricourt, sein Leben und seine Schriften', *AFH*, IV (1911), 436–55, 633–43; 1912, 22–40.

Sessevalle, F. de, Histoire générale de l'ordre franciscain, 2 vols., Paris, 1935.

Sharp, D. E., Franciscan Philosophy at Oxford in the Thirteenth Century, Oxford, 1930.

——, 'The Philosophy of Richard Fishacre', *New Scholasticism*, VII (1935), 281–97.

Singer, D. W., 'The Alchemical Writings of Roger Bacon', *Speculum*, VII (1932), 80–86.

Statuta Antiqua Universitatis Oxoniensis, ed. S. Gibson, Oxford, 1931.

Steele, R., 'Roger Bacon and the State of Science in the Thirteenth Century', *Studies in the History and Method of Science*, ed. C. Singer, Oxford, 1921, Vol. II, 121–50.

Steenberghen, F. van, Siger de Brabant d'après ses œuvres inédites, 'Les Philosophes belges', Vols. XII–XIII, Louvain, 1931–42.

Taylor, H. O., The Medieval Mind, 4th edit., London, 1923.

Théry, G., 'Autour du décret de 1210,' *Bibliothèque Thomiste*, Vols. V and VI (1925–26).

Thomas de Eccleston, De adventu fratrum minorum in Angliam, ed. A. G. Little, Paris, 1909.

Thomson, S. H., The Writings of Robert Grosseteste, Cambridge, 1940.

Thorndike, L., History of Magic and Experimental Science, 6 vols., New York, 1923–41, Vols. I and II.

——, 'Roger Bacon and Experimental Method in the Middle Ages', *Philosophical Review*, XXIII (1914), 271–98.

——, The Sphere of Sacrobosco and its Commentators, Chicago, 1949.

Thorndike, L., 'The True Roger Bacon', *American Historical Review*, XXI (1916), 237–57, 468–80.

——, Latin Treatises on Comets from 1238 to 1268 A.D., Chicago, 1950.

Ueberweg, F., Grundriss der Geschichte der Philosophie, Part II, ed. B. Geyer, Berlin, 1928.

Vanderwalle, C. B., Roger Bacon dans l'histoire de la philologie, Paris, 1929 (reprinted from *France Franciscaine*, 1928).

Vaux, R. de, 'Notes et textes sur l'avicennisme latin aux confins des XII–XIII siècles,' *Bibliothèque Thomiste*, Vol. XX (1934).

——, 'La Premiere Entrée d'Averroès chez les latins', *Revue des sciences philosophiques et théologiques*, XXII (1933), 193–245.

Wadding, L., Annales minorum, Rome, 1733.

Webb, C. C. J., 'Roger Bacon on Alphonse of Poitiers', *Essays in History Presented to Reginald Lane Poole*, Oxford, 1927, 290–300.

William of Auvergne, Opera omnia, 2 vols., Orleans, 1674.

Wingate, S. D., The Medieval Latin Versions of the Aristotelian Scientific Corpus with Special Reference to the Biological Works, London, 1931.

Wulf, M. de, Histoire de la philosophie mediévale, 6th edit., Paris and Louvain, 1936, Vol. II.

INDEX